MENTAL
TOUGHNESS:
THE GAME CHANGER

*How to Create Elite Players, Teams,
and Athletic Programs*

**A Guide for Coaches, Administrators,
Players, Parents, and Business Leaders**

COACH BOB KRIZANCIC

with

CATHY LOMBARDO

NEWMAN SPRINGS PUBLISHING
320 Broad Street
Red Bank, NJ 07701

First originally published by Newman Springs Publishing 2022

ISBN 978-1-63692-253-9 (Paperback)
ISBN 978-1-63692-254-6 (Hardcover)
ISBN 978-1-63692-255-3 (Digital)

Printed in the United States of America

To my sons Cole and Conner,
all former and current players,
coaches and assistant coaches,
and countless others whose
dedication, hard work, and mental toughness
made my vision a reality.

CONTENTS

SUCCESS STORIES: POSITIVE OUTCOMES FOR ATHLETIC TEAMS, BUSINESSES, AND YOUTH

The powerful concepts emphasized in this book are highly relevant to the sport of basketball, yet transcend the realm of athletics and positively impact business enterprises and the development of successful young people and adults.

The comments below attest to the positive results realized by implementing Coach Bob Krizancic's strategic approach to actualizing potential, establishing quality relationships, effectively working as a team, and developing mental toughness.

Success in Athletics
witnessed by
Basketball Official Donald P. Lewis, Jr., DDS

I am honored to have been asked to contribute to Coach Krizancic's book from an official's viewpoint. Over the past twenty-five years of officiating high school basketball, I have had the opportunity to be assigned to the Mentor High School Boys Basketball games over two dozen times and therefore feel that I can offer an "on-court" observation of Bob Krizancic's basketball program.

I have found through the years that basketball teams, assistant coaches, and players take on the personality of their head coach, and there is no better example of this than Coach "K."

Coach Krizancic is a tough, no-nonsense individual, and his teams play the same way. When asked to put my thoughts into this book, the words to describe Coach "K" and his team were not hard to find.

Each time I saw on my schedule the Mentor Cardinals Boys Basketball game, I knew that I was going to officiate a tough and physical contest. What I also found through the years of officiating these games was a common thread instilled in each of his players year in and year out.

Coach K's teams were always well-prepared, disciplined, and mentally tough. Time and time again, I would watch his teams wear down the opponent by expressing these attributes that Coach K lives by himself.

I always knew that not only were the players going to be well-prepared, disciplined, and mentally tough, but there was no doubt in my mind where this was coming from. I had to look no further than the coach pacing the sideline, holding his perpetual cup of water and chewing on some hard candy, while all the time coaching the players and trying to coach the officials.

Teams guided by Coach Krizancic were also fearless. I observed firsthand on a number of occasions how Coach K would implore his players not to be afraid of the moment or the situation at hand. He taught them it was not a failure to try but a failure not to try. At the core of his teams was trust. The players trusted Coach K, and he instilled trust in them.

Next, his players were some of the most courteous young men that I have ever had the pleasure of officiating. No matter what was going on during the game, each player always would say "Thank you, sir" when receiving the ball from an official.

In the first number of games that I officiated involving the Mentor Boys Basketball team, I made note of this as a show of respect. During one game, I asked a player, "Who taught you to interact with the officials that way?" He didn't hesitate to say that Coach K demanded that of his players, and it became second nature. Discipline and respect were demanded by Coach K because that's the way he runs his program.

And finally, what impressed me the most was the love and care that Coach K gave to each and every player on the team. It didn't matter if you were on the first team or the last player on the bench—he cared. When the "bench would be cleared," Coach K continued to coach those players as if they were the starting five and the game was overtime.

For the many years that Bob Krizancic has been my respected friend, I can say it was always a pleasure to officiate his games. He has a special way of even addressing the officials, not always in agreement but always with respect. With that being said, I also knew that for the two hours during the game, we were not friends as we both had a job to do. We didn't always agree, but then again, I was always right!

Bob Krizancic is a special person and a special coach. I have been telling him to write a book for a number of years, and finally he listened! Enjoy the book.

Donald P. Lewis Jr., DDS
Oral and Maxillofacial Surgeon
Basketball official, Ohio High School Athletic Association

*****

Success in Business
experienced by
Business Leaders Deborah A. Foley and David Hollis

I was at a trouble spot in my position as the organization's top leader after achieving widely recognized success over many years. I had a new generation of young 20- and 30- something professionals who didn't appreciate my leadership style. And I was edging towards the belief that I never thought I'd have: I thought "This new generation is self-centered and entitled babies, or I'm just getting too old.

Things just weren't working.

Trying to forge a better working environment and understanding, I held a one-day off-campus retreat that was designed to break the current tensions, build better relationships, and motivate everyone to move forward with new energy.

Coach Bob Krizancic was invited to speak because he consistently achieves winning seasons while working with teens and young adults. I also knew that his players went to the wall for him and every year, against all odds, they delivered championship seasons. I'm sure my staff thought, *You invited a basketball coach? What? And why?*

Talking basketball was not Coach Krizancic's central theme. He rather talked about individual and collective responsibility. He laser-focused on attitude and commitment that is developed on and off the court. Coach helped us check our own values. Attitude isn't contained within certain hours of the day, he said. It's learning, growing, and developing each hour of the day, every day, year after year. Improving and making ourselves the best we can be is hard and consistent work. As a work team, we also have an obligation to improve one another. We take responsibility.

Coach shared that during the first year, a player usually hates him and balks at the drive required. By the second year, players have an acceptance, but not love. But by the time players graduate and throughout their lives, Coach Krizancic is a lifelong mentor and counselor. Growing skills and working hard don't happen overnight.

When the conversation ended, I could visibly feel the change. I felt gratitude for a renewed belief and energy. Most of all, Coach Krizancic made us understand that shaping the best attitude is our own responsibility, individually and collectively.

No, Coach Krizancic didn't talk basketball. Rather, he gave us insight on how we guide the destiny for success at *any age*.

I was not too old to learn.

Deborah A. Foley
United Way of Lake County President, retired; Columbus
Public Schools Executive Director, former

I had the opportunity over several years to watch Bob Krizancic coach before getting to know him. His teams were always disciplined, hardworking, respectful, and successful. I witnessed Coach always calmly pacing the sidelines instructing, encouraging, and guiding his teams to league titles and deep runs in the Ohio High School Athletic Association state tournament.

Fortunately, Coach gave me the opportunity to observe his practices and also discuss with him his philosophies on teamwork, accountability, and motivation. He then agreed to address my company and applied the successful principles he employed in motivating his staff and the young men he coached to my employees.

His message of the importance of commitment and hard work was something that resonated with my staff; however, the impact of his message of the importance of team members (and employees) looking out for, caring, pushing, and coming together for a common purpose was profound.

Whether you are trying to communicate to your child life lessons they can learn playing sports or employees the rewards of coming together as a group, invest the time to listen to Bob's insights and experiences. You will not be disappointed.

David Hollis
President, Rx-21 Pharmacy

*****

Success in Life
recognized by
Pastor Kurt Landerholm

At six feet two, everyone thought I was a basketball player. While I had some height, I lacked athletic ability. That did not take away from my love of the game at the intramural level, pickup games, and most importantly, as a spectator. I was a strong fan of my high school team and continued a special appreciation for the prep level as I moved on to college and adulthood. There is something about high school basketball that is exciting in its raw form. Taking away all the layers of big-time recruits and high salaries at the next levels, high school basketball is more naïve and purer. Having lived in several communities in Ohio, I found my way to the gym for Friday-night games whenever possible.

For the past five years, I have been invited to be available to lead Coach Krizancic's Mentor varsity team in pregame prayer. I have witnessed his dedicated interaction with his players.

Coaches are oftentimes thought of as X's and O's people. While that is to some degree correct, when one like Coach Krizancic comes along and you get to know him, his coaching goes much deeper, penetrating to the heart and soul of each player. Concerned for the whole person, Coach K nurtures the motivation and drive in each unique player and personality, and then welds them together into the synergy of a team. In the end, "wins and losses" on the court fade while giving way to young men with lessons for success in life.

Pastor Kurt Landerholm
Retired Pastor, Mentor United Methodist Church

ACKNOWLEDGMENTS

Never in my wildest dreams did I ever think that I would be writing an acknowledgement for *my* book. It is surreal, but basketball has afforded me so many unbelievable opportunities: coaching in Europe, Hawaii, New Zealand, and Australia in summers, coaching in the World Basketball League (which was a May–August summer professional league 1988–1992), speaking at the Nike Championship Clinics, and getting to build lifelong relationships with numerous players and coaches. For these opportunities, I am forever grateful.

Thanks has to go to my family—my parents Mick and Fran, sisters Michele and Susan, and their families. They are all so successful because they believe in themselves and everything comes from the heart.

My sons, Cole and Conner, are my life. I could not be more proud of the men they have become. They both were a huge part of my coaching career, going to state basketball finals with Cole and winning the state basketball championship with Conner. Cole was first team All-Ohio in basketball and is currently a player on the Burning River Buckets of the American Basketball Association (ABA). Conner was Football Player of the Year in Division I in the state of Ohio and first team All-Ohio as a football quarterback. Both also received athletic scholarships to college for their respective sports. Also we were able to have that great father-son-coach relationship, which is not always easy.

Without a doubt, this book could not have been written without the hard work and dedication of my players and my staff. They are like family, and I am forever grateful.

Special thanks to Dr. (Doc) Don Lewis for performing a detailed edit of this book. His critical eye, mastery of the English language, knowledge of the sport of basketball, and personal experience as an author of professional reference books has been invaluable.

Finally, I would love to name all the individuals who were so influential and helpful to my career, but I am also fearful of leaving out someone accidentally. One of my favorite sayings is: "Show me your friends and I'll show you your future." And I have the most unbelievable core of friends and family! Thank you all.

FOREWORD

When I came to Mentor Schools twelve years ago, I was well aware of Coach Krizancic's success as a basketball coach. I knew he had guided his alma mater, Girard High School, to a state championship in 1993. I also knew Mentor was lucky to have him because the program was becoming increasingly competitive under his direction. But for the first time as an administrator in Mentor Schools, I would finally have a chance to look firsthand for some of the secrets to his success.

I had been a varsity assistant basketball coach for Gilmour Academy, a smaller private school in the region, during the early nineties. I was fortunate to be on a great staff with an athletic team that earned state runner-up in Ohio in 1992. I quickly learned there were fundamental differences in the great coaches I saw. Some ran spectacular offenses. Many constructed suffocating defensive schemes. Others excelled with a fast-paced, fast-break game that exhausted opponents. So many different styles could win. But for the programs that had a tradition of excelling—and Mentor had become one of them—what were the essential elements that helped them stand out year after year? I was working to figure that out.

Another extremely specific thing I learned early on was not to judge a team by how they looked or performed in warm-ups. As another legendary Mentor coach said about our student-athletes, "We don't look very impressive getting off the bus." For one of the largest high schools in Ohio, there are surprisingly few players with exceptional height or jaw-dropping athleticism. During warm-ups, one could easily assume Mentor had its JV team on the floor.

Over the past twelve years, I have had several chances every season to watch the Cardinals play. Most often, I have seen them on a big stage, in intense playoff competition, including their 2013 run to Mentor's first boys' basketball championship. The opponents are some of Ohio's best, including Lebron James in the early 2000s, and nationally ranked teams from around the country that we have faced in holiday tournaments.

Despite some natural deficits in size, speed, or ability, Mentor's players always compete with extreme intensity. They always know their assignments, and they perform without fear of failure. Coach K would not settle for anything less. Initially, I wondered how they can maintain this level of excellence so consistently. Over time, I saw that he was drilling this focus into them at every opportunity. The training builds over time through summer workouts, motivational speakers, laser-focused practices, and reinforcing the idea that the system works, and everyone has to trust each other. This is critically important when there is adversity, which every team faces.

The best weapon Coach K has instilled in his players is mental toughness. The championship teams, and the teams that exceed expectations, all have exhibited mental toughness. It is learning to survive the grueling training when the body wants to quit. It is trusting one another when the game is on the line. It is running the schemes enough times, with great attention to detail, to employ the nuances that will maximize chances of success. Mental toughness also includes reflecting on the mistakes that may have cost the team a win and applying what is learned to the next situation or the ability to bounce back from adversity, like a major injury.

Interestingly, the 2019-2020 season may have presented some of the greatest challenges yet for Coach K and his players to remain mentally tough. On March 11, 2020, Mentor fought hard to secure a 76–72 double-overtime win over league rival Medina, who arguably had more size, speed, and raw athletic ability. It was the second time in three games against Medina this season that the Cardinals won with mental toughness down the stretch.

Just about a month before, I witnessed the greatest basketball comeback I had seen when we stormed back from seven down with about forty seconds left to win on a thirty-foot shot at the buzzer. Junior guard Luke Chicone put the team on his back to secure both wins, but several players stepped up to make big plays down the stretch to make both wins possible. It might have been a defensive stop or a pick or a rebound or a single-foul shot. Every one of these "little" contributions had to take place to secure these epic wins. And after both games, there was jubilation, as the feelings of accomplishment were significant. I believe mental toughness made the difference in both games.

The team was one step away from returning to the State Championship Final 4 when COVID-19 interrupted the season on March 12. As Mentor was getting ready to face Shaker Hts., another league rival whom they had beaten twice earlier in the season, the Ohio High School Athletic Association announced the indefinite suspension of the tournament, which eventually turned into a permanent cancellation of the season. Coach described how difficult it was to watch his players break down from the news. They had overcome so much to be just one step from the Final 4. And I truly believe this was one of those special teams that would have found a way to get past superior size, speed, and talent to capture the state championship.

COVID-19 has challenged our entire nation and world in multiple ways, as its invisible presence has taken so many lives. In comparison, a canceled basketball season seems like a minor inconvenience; however, when a team invests so much and shares a common vision over time in such an emotional way, it is a significant loss. Grieving this loss was the ultimate test of mental toughness for a basketball team, yet again, Coach K took this opportunity to challenge his players to rise above adversity. It was going to be an especially hard message to deliver to seniors, as this particular dream of winning states would never see appropriate closure.

I also think this underscores how important sports are for young people. It goes way beyond the game because the greatest takeaways are sacrificing yourself for a greater good, focusing on a common goal, and building mental toughness to overcome adversity—something we all have to face at times. I applaud Coach for reaching our student-athletes in such profound ways over the years. While it does not always look pretty or feel easy, it is effective, powerful, and long-lasting. The book will undoubtedly share many glimpses of the impact that has been made on generations of young men who have played basketball for the Cardinals.

William Porter, MEd
Superintendent, Mentor Exempted Village Schools

AUTHOR BOB KRIZANCIC'S LIFETIME COACHING RECORD

The **Ohio High School Basketball Coach Association** (OHSBCA) recognized Coach Bob Krizancic as the **2020 and 2021 Coach of the Year**. The National Federation of High School Coaches named him the 2019-2020 Coach of the Year for the Mideast Region of the nation.

Years as head coach	42	(13 Girard, Ohio Div. II; 29 Mentor, Ohio Div. I)
Winning Seasons	38	
Total Wins	699	(6th Winningest Coach in Ohio History)
State Champs	2	(1993 Girard, 2013 Mentor)

Only one of four coaches in Ohio to win state titles at two different high schools.

Top 10 State Ranking	19	
State Final Four	4	(1993, 2010, 2013, 2021)
Regional Champs	5	Co-regional Champs 2020-2021 due to COVID-19
Regional Runner-Up	4	
District Champs	20	
District Runner-Up	6	
Sectional Champs	36	Sectional Co-Champs 2021-2022
Hall of Fame Inductee	6	

Coach of the Year Awards

- Local, NE Ohio, Media, etc.   75 plus
- AP/Sportswriters of America, State of Ohio (2008, 2010, 2019, 2021)

Nike Championship Clinic Speaker in Omaha, St. Louis, Cleveland, Pittsburgh, Biloxi, Minneapolis and Myrtle Beach.

Professional Coaching   World Basketball League, two years
Summer Coaching   Europe, Australia, New Zealand, Hawaii
                         (7 years)

In the 2020 MaxPreps' "Top Ten Most Dominant High School Boys Basketball Programs of the Last Ten Years," published on April 16, 2020, the Mentor Boys Basketball Program ranked seventh out of 827 schools and second in public school programs out of 700 in the state of Ohio.

The 2020-2021 Season under Coach Krizancic resulted in the First Undefeated Regular Season in the history of the Mentor High School Boys Basketball Program and their final record of 25-1 is the best in school history. The Associated Press ranked Mentor the state champions in their final rankings for the 2021 season due to their undefeated record.

MaxPreps Top 10 Most Dominant High School Boys Basketball Programs of the Last Ten Years in Ohio

Top 10 high school hoops programs over the last decade in the Buckeye State.

Thursday, April 16, 2020 1:15 PM
By Jordan Divens/ MaxPreps.com

1. (Tie) Archbishop Moeller (Cincinnati) (282)*
2. (Tie) St. Vincent-St. Mary (Akron) (282)*
3. St. Edward (Lakewood) (238)*
4. La Salle (Cincinnati) (184)*
5. Villa Angela-St. Joseph (Cleveland) (150)*
6. Wayne (Huber Heights) (131)*
7. (Tie) Mentor (122)*
8. (Tie) Pickerington Central (Pickerington) (122)*
9. Trotwood-Madison (Trotwood) (114)*
10. St. John's Jesuit (Toledo) (112)*

*Numbers in the parentheses refer to the total number of wins in the last ten year period in Ohio.

Source:https://www.maxpreps.com/news/TdsEbatX8Eaina89enF-Og/top-10-most-dominant-high-school-boys-basketball-programs-of-the-last-10-years-in-ohio.htm.

Special note: These rankings are from the 2011-2020 seasons—a period of ten years. In 2010, the year before the noted decade and in 2021, the year after the noted decade, the Mentor Cardinals went to the state tournament. These accomplishments were not included in the decade rankings.

INTRODUCTION

The overriding purpose of this book is to present the elements that must come together to create an elite winning athletic program. It is a process of becoming mentally tough—of actualizing the full potential of all student-athletes associated with your program through dedicated efforts of coaches, parents, support staff, school, community, and the players themselves during the off-season as well as during the season itself. Although this book primarily discusses a basketball season or career, the greatest benefit of achieving mental toughness is that it will put you in a position to succeed in life.

When it comes to sports, to be "elite" means to be the best or most powerful. Elite student-athletes exude mental toughness. They have developed the ability to resist, manage, and overcome doubts, worries, concerns, and circumstances standing in the way of their success.

Elite teams are fearless, and they are mentally and physically at the top of their game. They relish competition, are exciting to watch, and they produce more wins against arguably more talented teams.

Creating an elite basketball program is about so much more than winning games. It includes mental toughness: effort, determination, discipline, dominance, and commitment.

I know what it takes to get this accomplished. I know how it can be done. My first head-coaching job was at Girard High School (Girard, Ohio), which was coming off twenty-seven out of thirty losing seasons. My next head-coaching position was at Mentor High School (Mentor, Ohio), whose history was two district wins and a record of 22–62 in the four years prior to my accepting the position. At both programs, I stated at the initial press conference that I was here to win a state title. Few, if any, believed me. To be perfectly honest, though I don't want to sound arrogant, I never doubted for one second that we would win a state title at either school. It is about setting your goals, staying the course, and doing what it takes to get there.

Everyone was taking bets on how long I would last. Girard hadn't won a district title in thirty years. It took me thirteen years to get Girard to the state title and to this day Girard is the only boys high school athletic program in Trumbull County to have won a state title. Twenty years later, we had the same success at Mentor High School. Mentor won the state title. There is no doubt in my mind that each success was achieved through mental toughness.

I also realize you are not born with mental toughness. It is important to know that mental toughness can be developed. Mental toughness is about ingraining in each student-athlete an attitude of hard work, hustle, and fearlessness while playing against the best competition. Mental toughness creates individuals and teams that never fear competing against anyone, both on and off the court.

Anyone can develop a habit, or an attitude, of mental toughness. It demands purposeful living and an unrelenting passion to succeed. Success requires an individual to have intensely focused energy. To focus this energy on achieving a goal, you must pay attention to detail, be self-confident, determined, and work tirelessly to change your weaknesses into strengths.

Your ability to set goals, make plans, and act on them determines the course of your life. I am not telling you what to do; I am telling you what I did and what worked. I am not telling you that it will be easy, but I am convinced that it will be well worth the effort. The layout of the following chapters is what I did at Girard and Mentor High Schools during preseason, season, postseason, summer season—every season. Identify your goals, and this book will help you realize your potential.

You too can achieve success through mental toughness.

FROM VISION
TO REALITY

THINK BIG, DREAM BIG, BELIEVE BIG
DREAMS COME TRUE—MIRACLES HAPPEN
BELIEVE IN IT!

Years of dedication to perfecting
his approach to the game took
Bob Krizancic from determined
young ball player to award-winning
high school basketball coach.

WKBN.com

Coach Krizancic has served as head coach of two high school boys' basketball teams—Girard High School and Mentor High School—for a total of forty-two years to date. He is one of four high school coaches in the state of Ohio to win state titles at different schools and received six Hall of Fame Awards as well. He currently has 699 career wins and the 6th most in Ohio high school history. In the past three seasons, the Mentor High school record is 68-10. Coach Krizancic is a pioneer in his field. He implemented the first drug testing program while head coach at Girard High School in 1985. Coach Krizancic has coached teams in New Zealand, Australia, Hawaii, and Europe, and is currently one of only a select few high school coaches to be included on the panel of speakers at Nike's annual Championship Basketball Clinics. He has also been a featured speaker numerous times at business events in Ohio.

Coach Krizancic is passionate about basketball and constantly strives to improve himself, his student-athletes, and his program. He has found inspiration and guidance in the words of others who have shared their experiences of struggle and growth. He advises his readers, "Listen, you will read a lot of quotes in here, but that's my life. You will see a lot of things in here repeated, but if you see something repeated in multiple places, it is important. This book is organized and created to give encouragement and valuable information to all who read it."

SECTION 1

HOW TO BE AN ELITE COACH

To be as good as it can be, a team has to buy into what you as the coach are doing. They have to feel you're a part of them and they're a part of you.

—Bobby Knight
Legendary NCAA Basketball Coach

A coach has many responsibilities. You must invest time in many areas and be committed to succeeding in your role as coach. The whole program depends on *you*. You must believe in yourself and your vision with an unwavering faith. Also, to keep focused, I recommend that you **live in the present, build for the future, and don't look back.**

CHAPTER 1

Start with a Vision and Stay True to It

Raise your expectations above what you think is possible.

I believe as you evolve as a player and young coach, you develop a philosophy, a style, or an approach to the game of basketball. This clarifies the identity that you want your team and program to have. This is your vision. My vision began when I was a sophomore playing for Youngstown State University during a game against the University of San Francisco. We played over Christmas break as they made an eastern swing. The University of San Francisco scored really quick. When there were nineteen minutes and fifty seconds left on the collegiate clock, I had the basketball as the point guard, and in my face was an opponent who was as quick and tough as I have ever faced defensively. As they rotated two point guards, it made for what was probably the most miserable basketball game I have played in my life. Their constant pressure made me work so hard with every possession that after that game, I decided then and there if I ever had the opportunity to coach, I would find a way to make our opponent as miserable as those two guards made my life. I decided the way to accomplish this was to play full court with the toughness, intensity, and style we have today—our run-and-press identity and philosophy. While modifications were necessary along the way, the original vision has always been my central focus.

I realized that to be worthy of elite status, you need to have a unique identity, something that makes you stand out from the rest.

Mentor High School has that unique identity: shooting the three, running the floor, and pressing hard. We demand our big men develop a complete set of skills, especially guard skills. Two examples of this are Adam May, at six feet eight, who played at Holy Cross University, and Micah Potter, six feet ten, who played at The Ohio State University and the University of Wisconsin and is now with the NBA. Both could shoot the three and handle the basketball as bigger players. Therefore both were an important part of the offense on their respective college teams because they had guard skills as big men. Maintaining this unique identity from season to season takes consistent effort and planning on the part of the whole organization, starting with the head coach.

If you want to make it to the mountaintop, you have to plan for the journey. You have to think big. You have to set the bar high for yourself and your program. You have to outwork and outrun your competition. One way is to prepare your schedule with a high degree of competition. If at all possible, compete on the national level. Play in tournament games and prepare the whole season for the tournament in March. You'll need to play in quality games and tournaments, invest time, and amass wins. Never play not to lose; always play to win.

Not everyone is born with mental toughness, however you need mental toughness to make it to the mountaintop. A key component of my vision is the strong belief that mental toughness can be taught and is not innate. Mental toughness **can** be developed.

Never assume that a young person cannot attain mental toughness. Developing mental toughness requires effort on both your part as a coach and on the part of the student-athlete. Whether it happens or not is up to you and the student-athlete.

Staying true to your vision is also of utmost importance. When you have the passion and the work ethic, you can become successful in your own right. Once you become successful, you will now have options—other jobs and of moving up. Be very careful. Make sure any move you make is consistent with your vision, and it is what you believe is the right thing. At one point, after three years of being successful at Girard, I was offered a pharmaceutical job paying four times what I was making as a high school basketball coach. It took me only ten seconds to say I absolutely knew where I wanted to be, and what I wanted to do in life, that I wanted to compete and get in that arena on a Friday night. My newfound success on the court at Girard and my success in building relationships really emboldened my interest, my belief, my culture, and my philosophy.

I also passed up numerous basketball jobs while at Girard and at Mentor High Schools. I wrestled with those decisions. I wasn't sure if it was the right move because of the programs themselves, and also the meaningful relationships I had developed. Without a doubt, those were the right decisions.

For your vision or goal of becoming mentally tougher to become a reality, it has been my experience that the more people that share this vision, the greater is the chance of achieving this goal. So, getting the people that are close to your student-athlete, such as parents, grandparents, or possibly a sibling, and securing their commitment to your vision so they adopt it as their own is extremely important. You can do this through email, text, or other communication outlining the steps you are planning to take to achieve this goal. You can get everyone in this inner circle committed to and engaged in the process. Pursuing the goal of achieving mental toughness has been very rewarding for me because when everyone buys into your vision as a head coach and leader it is a win-win for everyone involved. They share the frustrations and the achievements along the way, and as a result they too become mentally tougher.

To personally achieve mental toughness I believe that you must "[k]now your goal so clearly, precisely, and passionately that it is your constant companion" (Lisa Zawistowski—success coach, author, and entrepreneur). Have your goals set, and make sure when you set a goal, you commit to a deadline. At first your goals will be general and then they will become more specific. Stick to your goals. Put your goals up in your office or at home where they are a constant reminder of your journey. Read them often. Advise your players to make sure their goals are highly visible on a daily basis.

One of my goals is to have my players be in the best shape of any team in the state of Ohio. Another one of my goals is based on my belief to practice what you preach and always be a great role model. In keeping with this I work out two to three times a day, never missing a cardio, ab, or P90x workout, because if I am going to preach it, I better live it. Therefore, in keeping with the goal of having my players in the best shape, if I am in great shape and look healthy, it will be a lot easier to motivate my players.

Do not be afraid to implement an idea if it might mean an improvement to your program that brings it more into alignment with your vision. I wanted to implement a drug-testing program in 1985 at Girard High School. I had a vision, an idea, that I wanted my players to undergo drug and alcohol testing. I wanted to give my players an easy out if they were confronted with a situation in which drugs or alcohol were present. We became the first high school athletic team in the state of Ohio to test for alcohol and drugs. We tested for the 1985–1986 season, and then the next year, the state developed their own program, and that program superseded ours. For more information, please refer to chapter 8.

Remember, you are in coaching for the journey. There are little things you can do to make yourself and your program better. Everyone is always preparing to take the next step in life: a better coaching job, a bigger school, college, or better job opportunities. My point is that you will have detours or the option to take some different roads. Be very, very careful you do not lose sight of your vision, and you know what you love, and you know what is in your heart.

You must expect great things of yourself before you can do them.

—Michael Jordan
Hall of Fame NBA player

Aim high. My vision as head coach has always been to get my team to the state tournament every season!

CHAPTER 2

Assemble Your Staff

A coach must assemble a staff of trustworthy people who believe in their philosophy and program.

A coach must exercise due diligence in building their coaching team and surround themselves with quality people. Hire your staff based on work ethic and loyalty. A strong work ethic is extremely important as it can compensate for limited experience. It is also a good idea to hire ex-players as they know your program and are committed to it. This was the case when we won the state boys basketball title with my staff at Girard in 1993 and the staff at Mentor in 2013 where we had a number of ex-players in the role of assistant coaches.

If an assistant coach is new to your program, a great work ethic and intense passion for the game ensure they will be motivated to learn your system. You can review their resume, playing career, and do some research as part of the hiring process to assist you in making a wise decision. To avoid any appearance of impropriety between a coach and student-athlete, I strongly advocate that in hiring assistant coaches you set parameters for their interaction with all student-athletes immediately upon hire. I advise that assistant coaches are never in the gym alone with a student-athlete. They must be sensitive to the need to exercise caution to be on the safe side to protect themselves, the program, school, and school administration.

Stress to young coaches that, for your program to be successful, team cohesiveness is of utmost importance. Explain that your program's goal is to create an accepting environment through communication, establishing expectations, and being a role model for all athletes. Impress upon them that you strive to create an inclusive and supportive environment. Make sure there are go-to people on your staff to assist any student-athlete or anyone else associated with your program who does not feel good about something.

I have a staff of assistant coaches divided into varsity, junior varsity, and freshman. My assistants include a varsity defensive coordinator, a varsity offensive coordinator, and a JV coach who has the authority to move freshmen up and down from the freshmen team to the JV team. There are two freshmen coaches as well.

Don't be afraid to delegate responsibilities to your staff. It will make them feel important. They will become more proficient at their duties if you do. These staff members are involved in important roles such as coaching their team and individual players in offensive and defensive skills. They are also involved in coaching summer leagues and shootouts, four-man segments, and assisting in scouting. During varsity games, the entire staff is on the bench with designated assignments such as keeping a shot chart (especially three-point shots), minutes played by each player, and press breakers that the other teams are using. Then at halftime or when I ask for it, I get directives and stats on the other team. Given limitations imposed regarding how many quarters a player can play, the JV and freshmen coaches must keep track of quarters played by each player throughout the day and the year. This year we added a new assistant position, an analytics coach, which has helped immensely.

Developing a cohesive staff that supports one another is essential. This can be done by sponsoring social events at your home. I have postgame get-togethers with my staff at my home as well as social events like game nights. Game night is when I invite staff and their significant others (if applicable) and we play board games, card games, a game called Catch-Phrase, or other games, and the one criteria is that we do not discuss basketball at these get-togethers. This enables my staff and their families to get to know one another and develop a support system within their ranks. Young coaches will need reinforcement from you often regarding the actions, responsibilities, and mannerisms of a coach. Never "assume" they know.

Once a staff is assembled, it is imperative the coach communicates all year long. Be open to the staff's input and ideas and delegate responsibility to them to establish their trust. Your staff will relish opportunities to do something on their own. As the person in charge of the entire program, you can use their help, input, and perspective.

Numerous times one of my assistants would come to me with what they thought was a problem or deficiency in the program. It took me a while as head coach but now I tell them "If you are going to come to me with a problem or deficiency in the program, then you had better have a solution or partial solution along with the problem." When you take this position with your assistants as a head coach, you will be pushing your assistants out of their comfort zone and promoting their professional growth.

My varsity assistants always tell me, "I am going to throw things at you or bounce things off you, and you can use them as you want." I encourage their input and have found this to be a valuable way in which to interact with my staff.

Furthermore as a head coach, you must live in the present and build for the future. If a member of your staff leaves, appreciate the time you spent together but realize that change is inevitable. Express your best wishes and let them know you value your professional relationship with them, and the avenues of communication will always remain open. Never look back! There is ample time to get new staff members. Don't worry about experience if they have a great work ethic and you are convinced they will be trustworthy and loyal.

If I were a young coach today, I'd be extremely
careful in selecting my assistants.

—John Wooden
Hall of Fame NCAACoach

**Choose your assistants wisely. They are essential
to the success of your program.**

CHAPTER 3

Establish a Strong Varsity Booster Program

One of the best support groups that a coach and program can have is the presence of a strong booster program.

Booster clubs can come in various forms. When I was head coach at Girard High School, there were a number of booster organizations. Friends of the program and members of the safety forces formed one called the Players Club. The mothers formed another called the Mothers Club, and we also had a Booster Club for all sports. The local community was highly supportive of our program.

A strong booster program is absolutely a necessity in this day and age. It is imperative for you to have a great relationship with the officers and entire booster program. You want the booster club to be your ally. Not only does it serve as a vehicle for communicating your program to parents, the school community, and the general community but it also can help you when needs arise preseason and season.

As a head coach, your goal should be to run a class program. Class athletes dress and act appropriately. This includes quality equipment, such as shoes and uniforms.

You can approach the booster organization to secure such items as travel uniforms or new gym bags. While this may not seem important, in actuality it is a big factor in the success of your program and teams. How your players look affects how they feel about themselves. Self-confidence is essential to success both on and off the court. First impressions matter, and having quality uniforms and equipment is an expense that needs to be addressed.

In addition, the quality of your equipment can affect the quality of your play. Advances in the construction and material of sports equipment and apparel have influenced the sport. Uniform improvements have also enhanced players' comfort. Proper footwear is important in the game of basketball as players' feet take a beating on the court. Through the booster club's fund-raising events, our players are each allotted $100 to use to pay for shoes. All shoes are not formed the same and players' feet are different. I let my players choose from two or more styles of shoe to get a shoe that fits them best. They are, of course, limited to our team's colors.

The booster club will be an ally in other areas, such as fund-raising for tournament play. However, you can run into problems if you do not establish parameters in this regard. It is wise to put these parameters into writing. As an example, a situation may occur where a donor of a large sum of money expects their child to receive more playing time. Playing time cannot be bought, and this is the major point you have to set in stone immediately. It must be addressed every year since the people and donors involved in the booster program will change.

Just as in Girard, I found the Mentor community to be highly supportive. Mentor's booster program is known as the Mentor Cardinal Cage Club. It is a nonprofit 501(C)(3) organization established to provide support to the Mentor High School boys basketball program. The Mentor Cardinal Cage Club maintains a social media presence. This includes Twitter, Facebook, and a web site on which it posts season schedules, pictures and videos of games, activities engaged in by the student-athletes, and a Cage Club event schedule. It also prepares and prints press guides and media guides, as well as team posters that are distributed for display at area businesses and are given to booster-club supporters each season.

In addition, the club and the coach work together to prepare handouts for the last few games of the season. The handouts contain the names of donors, team's rankings locally, statewide, and nationally and the schedule of the upcoming tournament games. This is done in preparation for the postseason tournaments and gives recognition to significant financial contributors in the booster program.

The Cardinal Cage Club functions through its officers that currently include a president, vice president, secretary, treasurer, membership officer, and sports information director/media officer. It meets monthly at the high school to organize events such as annual fund-raisers (the sale of T-shirts, a fifty-fifty raffle, a night at the races, and a golf outing) as well as to organize an end-of-the-season banquet and summer picnic.

Communicate with the officers of the booster club. Show your appreciation for the organization. Keep in constant contact regarding meals, team travel, fund-raisers, and what they are doing for your program. While you want to regularly interact with your booster club, I advise against watching game films with booster groups or parents. If you do watch films with individuals for a specific reason, that is one thing. However, coaches have run into problems watching films with the booster club as a group.

The position of the booster club's sports information director is a very important one for the team and you as a coach. The sports information director will update your website with your team's and individual player's stats. They will also send press and media guides to previous players, donors, the media, the press, and colleges. This position can be filled by an interested individual and must be someone who you, as a coach, can trust. This individual is a valuable asset to get your players' names and statistics out to colleges for exposure and scholarships. An assistant coach can be the liaison between the head coach, the team, and the sports information director. To ensure that our booster program is of the highest quality, I inform the newly elected officers, at their first group meeting when we articulate our goals, that our goal is to be the best booster organization in the state of Ohio.

Be present at all fund-raisers and make sure that you meet everyone, if possible. Socialize so that they know you and the kind of person you are. Educate them on your vision, your ideals, your faith and what you believe in; little things can make a big difference. By being involved, you can let people become familiar with you. You are the parent figure to your players, and you are where the buck stops.

People want to know who you are and what you are about so that they feel comfortable supporting you.

The booster club plays an important role in facilitating team bonding. We have a team dinner the night before every weekend game. This is set up by our boosters. It is at a local restaurant or a parent's home. Many of our local restauranteurs will cater the dinner at our parents' home.

To ensure the longevity of your booster program, encourage your former players to get involved with the booster group and be supportive of events such as the golf outing. A players' alumni night at one of your home games with pizza afterward can get them back and give them a sense of togetherness and camaraderie. Your booster club can help arrange this. We have our alumni night at a home alumni game held during the Christmas break when most alumni are home from college or out-of-town alumni are visiting their parents.

Parents who are involved in the booster club invest a lot of time. These involved parents also find that they have a lot in common with one another. In my career as a coach in starting and developing strong booster clubs, I have found by-products of a strong booster club are many great relationships and friendships developed among parents involved. These relationships last far longer than their children's high school basketball careers.

Your goal as head coach is to form a booster organization strong enough to provide the help you need in your climb to the mountaintop. You are the face of the booster organization, and your coaching presence and leadership are the biggest factors in the strength and success of your booster club. The most important factors are a strong basketball program and a quality product on the floor. It is much easier to generate support for your booster program when you and your program are elite or approaching elite status.

The achievements of an organization are the results of the combined effort of each individual.

—Vince Lombardi
Hall of Fame NFL Coach

**A booster organization can arrange for team posters
to distribute to team sponsors and supporters.**

CHAPTER 4

Essential Relationships

**Quality relationships with people involved
in your program will ensure its success.**

Relationships are essential for a coach. The people who are involved in your program are a source of valuable information and support. Asking for their input will help you to assess your program and make necessary changes to ensure that it is, indeed, elite. This includes custodians, school staff, and ticket takers, as well as booster organizations.

As was discussed in a previous chapter, a coach must assemble a staff of trustworthy people who believe in their philosophy and their program. Make sure your emphasis is family first. Everyone you add to your staff will have a passion for the game, but you must always reinforce that family comes first. Developing a cohesive staff allows for the development of an internal support system. To develop a cohesive staff, encourage socializing outside of the basketball arena.

The relationship of the coach to their student-athletes is special. A strong player-coach bond is formed because of their intense interaction. The coach is a parent figure whether they like it or not. A coach wields a lot of influence when it comes to a player establishing their self-image. I have always said that my players don't care how much I know until they know how much I care. At our team banquet after the 2020-2021 season, one of my players, Steven Key, presented me with a framed picture of him and me hugging. The caption under the picture read: "Steven You Matter." As a coach, it was unbelievably gratifying to know that our coach-player bond and great communication was such a huge influence on this young man.

A positive attitude is essential for the player and keeps them open to growing athletically. For the coach-player relationship, positivity is important so that any growth in the sport is not negatively affected by corrections that need to be given. My rule of thumb is when you have yelled at a player (which you must do to push them to higher levels of play and to make a point), within twenty to thirty minutes you must tell them you are still 100% behind them.

Emotions are everything. The student-athlete must learn how to handle disappointment. They must understand your relationship with them. You are still behind them even when they make mistakes or fail in their attempts to improve their skills.

For fifteen- to eighteen-year-olds, emphasizing the positive is essential. I tell them what an exceptional young person they are. I explain to them they do 95 percent of the things correctly but have to improve on the 5 percent they do incorrectly. Players need to understand we are working to become elite players and an elite team. As a team, we are critiqued, and we must get better at our deficiencies. Everyone has shortcomings because if we didn't, we would always be undefeated. Each year our goal is to be one of the four teams to make it to the state basketball tournament finals. And we will.

It is also important that your players develop a strong relationship with one another and feel a commitment to one another. You can assist them in achieving a strong team identity. I recently realized how truly important this is to successful coaching. I am totally sold on developing strong relationships. When we won the state championships in 1993 and 2013, I let the players design their own rings. In 1993, etched on the inside in script, was the word "Together." I think this spirit played a huge part in why we won the state championship. It had been a Hoosier-type year. These players were so close; they actually loved one another. In 2013, the inside of the rings said "Brotherhood." In both of those two state championship cases, the bond between my players was exceptional. I think that this relationship gave us an edge in close games because my players knew what one another was going to do and how hard they were going to play for one another. They each had a deep trust and commitment to the team's success that transcended their individual goals.

Again, in the 2018–2019 season, the importance of the camaraderie between the members of the team was apparent. Our season record was 23-3 and in the district final game, we played Brush High School, a team that was very athletic. They had a great year and were favored to win. We won 77-73, and sixteen players had dressed for that game. That night, we had a team curfew, and all sixteen players stayed overnight together at team captain Luke Floriea's house. I thought their team unity was impressive and a main reason why we won 23 out of 26 in that season. Sixteen players—not going their own way, not going with their friends—but sixteen players staying together that night. It was amazing! And the same scenario played out in the 2020 and 2021 championships where players stayed at our captain's house the night of the district championship. I believe this type of player bonding contributed to our successful season.

You must effectively communicate with parents of your student-athletes and everyone involved in your program to establish quality relationships with them. We use a system, One Call Now, which can be found at https://www.onsolve.com/platform-products/critical-communications/one-call-now/. One Call Now provides schools, businesses, churches, and organizations across the country a way to improve and simplify their group's communications sending voice, text, and email messages to thousands of members simultaneously. This enables a coach to send information out to the team members and parents to advise them of schedules and changes to the schedule. Communication can also include inviting parents to observe practices so that they can see what you are doing has a valuable purpose. Alternatives to the One Call Now system are available.

While this is up to you, entertain the idea of visiting players and their parents in their homes during the season. The vast majority of information parents procure is from their child and you don't know how accurate that is. A conversation with all of them will make your program totally open and transparent. When visiting players at their homes you may consider taking an assistant along. You want parents to know that your purpose is to make their child successful in life and your team is a family!

Next a coach's relationship with their captains is based on communication and trust. The team captains must exhibit a strong work ethic and exude confidence as they will impact your team in so many ways. I became aware of this while playing college ball and coaching in the World Basketball League.

Nurture relationships with community leaders so they will respect your program and serve as mentors to your student-athletes. Coaches should be involved in the community and seek out character-building opportunities for their players. Presentations by successful members of the community such as businesspeople, judges, law enforcement officers, and spiritual leaders can impress upon the student-athletes the need to make good decisions and prepare them for the future. Community leaders should also advise them of the perils of social media.

You as a coach may seek out community employers and talk about jobs for your players so they can work around their basketball schedule. I have a number of proprietors and owners of small businesses who now employ many of our players, and they work around summer basketball workouts and camps, our spring and fall workouts, and even the season schedule. At the beginning of every month, we distribute a monthly schedule for players to give to their employers for scheduling purposes and also to their families so that they can schedule family events.

As noted in the previous chapter, your relationship with booster organizations must also be valued and cultivated. They can be an important bridge between you and parents and can also provide financial support. As the head coach, I meet with our booster group regularly to keep them aware of our team's record and any needs our team may have that can be addressed through their fundraisers. Our booster group is also a major factor in creating and maintaining our program's relationships within the local community and business sector. Relationships can also be boosted by this group's fundraising events, team dinners, end-of-the-season banquet, and a summer picnic.

Maintain positive relationships with the media. Public relations are an enormous factor in a coach's success. Interaction with the media such as print, broadcast media, and social platforms, should always be positive. Always back your players. Take a chance, be available, don't stay in a cocoon and back your program. Positive interaction with the media is essential to the success of your program.

Always maintain a good relationship with the Athletic Department at your school. Our game schedules and team rosters distributed at the games are created and published by our Athletic Department. They are also responsible for safety at games and for ticket sales. The athletic director serves as a valuable contact with the community and your state athletic association.

It is essential for you and your team members to attend the games of other sports teams in your school. Attend as many as you can to show your support. This way those teams are going to be more apt to support your team during the basketball season. It is great public relations for you to do that. It is also a great way to reinforce the strong relationship you have with your multiple sport players and also the other coaches in the school system. If you have time, you can also attend plays, art exhibits, concerts, and other school-related events. Your appearance at these events will generate positive support for your program.

It's not about any one person. You've got to get over yourself and realize that it takes a group to get this thing done.

—Gregg Popovich
NBA Coach

NH

Essential relationships provide the kind of network of support you will need as head coach to turn your vision into a reality. Our program is always a family.

Everyone must sacrifice the "Me" for the "We."

CHAPTER 5

Take Control and Assume Responsibility

You set the tone for your program and your team.

As a coach, you must exercise control over your attitude and emotions. You must believe in yourself and your ability to be an elite coach. It is easy to coach when you win. It is the elite individual that doesn't waver in their belief when they don't win.

As a head coach, you take on all responsibility for your program. Any problems that arise will be yours. Take ownership and let everyone in your program know and accept that you are in charge. Most coaches don't get fired for lack of strategic knowledge but, rather, for leadership deficiencies. As a leader you must make decisions for the best of the team.

Establishing parameters and drawing a line are essential responsibilities of a head coach. Without clear lines your vision becomes blurred and, when it is out of focus, it is out of reach. Willingness to deviate from your vision and the pursuit of your goal to be the best program in the state opens you to giving in when confronted with challenges. Never lose sight of your goal or the quality which you are striving to achieve. Never yield control to anyone.

Control and responsibility can include dealing with a situation when someone makes a significant donation through the booster program. They may expect their child to gain playing time because of that donation. To prevent coaches from running into a problem you must reiterate to parent and booster groups that money/support does not buy playing time.

In taking control and assuming responsibility, you must maintain a positive attitude. As a coach, your glass has to always stay half full. Perception is reality and your attitude will determine the attitude of the team. My first head-coaching job was at Girard High School where they were reeling after a long string of losing seasons. After winning the state title at Girard, I took the position as head boys basketball coach at Mentor High School and twenty years later we won the state boys basketball title. At both schools, at my initial press conference, I set the highest goal for both programs and teams—winning the state title. I firmly believe by taking control and assuming responsibility the tone was set for these teams to be successful.

Understand that you will face obstacles and frustrations. It is inevitable. When faced with obstacles, never give up. Difficult roads and difficult decisions can lead to great destinations. Your toughness and decisiveness will determine your success.

In fact, obstacles are required for you, your players, and team to achieve mental toughness. Address obstacles as opportunities for you and your staff and players to create a strategy for success. Teach them that any obstacle can be reduced to its components. Each step in the process provides an opportunity to successfully move beyond the obstacle. This builds self-confidence in dealing with setbacks in the future.

To bring your vision into reality, people must know you beyond your connection to basketball. The best way to influence people to support you is to allow them to believe in the person you are and in your vision.

Regarding your players, a coach has control over their development as athletes, students, and young adults. You must encourage development by taking action. Set the bar high for your players and don't lower the bar for anyone. Your goal should be as high as possible, such as winning the state title. This goal may be hard to reach, and it may be difficult to get others to support this goal, but with a strong work ethic and commitment, this goal is attainable. Remember, you as the head coach are a role model and your players and your staff will always follow your lead. Players also need to take control and assume responsibility if these goals are be met. There is a fine line between thinking about your goals and believing in your goals.

It is the nature of man to rise to greatness
if greatness is expected of him.

—John Steinbeck.
Nobel and Pulitzer Prize winning novelist

Stay strong after losses and bad practices. Players will learn so much more about you during tough times than good times. They must see things are never as bad as they seem, and they will get through it. I stress to players to always know I have faith in them. This is part of taking control and assuming responsibility.

The quality of the program depends on you. By making practices tough, we find out if a player has the mental toughness to be successful. It is better to find this out in practice rather than in a game.

When I came to the Girard and Mentor High School programs, I realized that I could not achieve the quality of results I desired with the programs as they were. I immediately made changes. In the case of Mentor, no fouls were called in open gyms. I put the players in the toughest summer league I could find. It was going to be uncomfortable, but that is what I needed to do to change the mentality of the program. It needed an overhaul. You, as the head coach, must take control and lay down the rules for open gym. Tough play, but no cheap fouls.

Rules create habits to allow your student-athletes and organization to reach elite status. Be patient. Allow yourself to be patient as your players establish new good habits which take a minimum of twenty-one days to establish. As a coach, you are responsible for facilitating this process. Establishing new habits requires consistency. Filming is a very important tool to use in teaching your student-athletes new habits.

Take responsibility as you are forming the character of your players on and off the court. Never label a student-athlete with a title such as "big man" or "guard"; it impedes the full development of the player's potential. Be a model of mental toughness as you are developing a young person to be successful in life. As a coach, you may not like it, but you are a parent figure. Set a curfew the night before the game and the night of the game. Get your captains' input. All year round, reinforce that attitude trumps talent and there can be no mental mistakes. You are working to be successful in the tournament where your season will be measured.

Because you are in control of the physical aspects of your student-athletes, you must familiarize yourself with medical conditions such as concussions, heart issues, and basic illnesses. You must establish a working relationship with the athletic trainers and other medical care providers so as to know how to work with and direct an injured player. I talk constantly with strength and conditioning personnel and get their views and philosophy on endurance, rest, and rehabilitation.

A coach is also responsible for the safety of all the staff, players, managers, student trainers, and even cheerleaders. While cheerleaders are not under your direct control, they are exposed to situations which you do control. The locker room is another area that the coach controls that can be a source of illegal and undesirable activities such as hazing and bullying. Rules on the bus also help to maintain order, and a rule such as total silence on the way to the games enables the team to concentrate on the upcoming game.

As head coach, you must be the overwhelming leader. That being said, you cannot ignore your responsibility to your superiors who can also be held accountable for what happens in your program. To be transparent and keep them in the loop, it is best to copy all your superiors on what you are doing in your program as more is better in this regard.

If your program is going to be as strong as you want it to be, at times you will have to take the blame and responsibility for 100 percent of things happening in your program. When you do that, it diffuses the problems and stress in the program. Even though it was most likely not your fault, periodically take the blame for any problems that go on—it will be positive for your program. This serves to preserve the cohesiveness among the players and staff and the bonds that make your program strong. In taking this action, you reassert your leadership and strength as head coach.

One of the areas in which you, as coach, will have little control is the floor of the basketball court during the game. If adverse actions occur during a game situation, you will not be immediately present to take control or assume responsibility. Therefore, I explain to my captains that they are an extension of me acting the part of a coach on the floor during games. I tell the captains that sometimes it is easier for them to take responsibility for something they didn't do during the game in order to diffuse any possible issue so that it will end right there and then the game will go on. This really helps younger players when a captain takes responsibility. In spite of this directive to my captains, during every postgame interview, I make it explicitly clear that everything that goes on both on and off the court is my absolute responsibility as head coach.

Through years of experience, I have found that being totally responsible for absolutely everything in my program has been one of the best actions I have taken. It ends pettiness, blame shifting, and finger pointing within the ranks.

A good coach can change a game; a great coach can change a life.

—John Wooden
Hall of Fame NCAA Coach

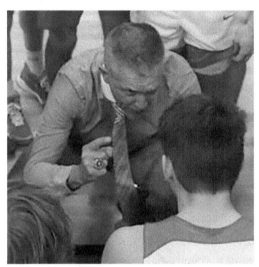

NH

Developing mental toughness in your players requires consistent effort on your part as a coach and on the part of the student-athlete.

CHAPTER 6

Address Problems Early

Never let fear stop you from making a decision.

Making difficult decisions early can benefit you greatly as the season progresses. Confident people aren't always right, but they never fear being wrong. Take chances. Take ownership.

Decisions have to be made. An experienced veteran coach once told me to never be afraid to make good, strong decisions. Sometimes it is necessary to delay making the decision. Therefore, indecisiveness is not always negative. Every coach and every player are indecisive at times. However, never let fear stop you from making a decision. As President Franklin D. Roosevelt said, "The only thing to fear is fear itself." Addressing problems early and finding a remedy is absolutely essential for your program and your career. The most important thing is to set a timeline to make those decisions and to go through the process of what you have to do to make the right decision. The longer you put it off, sometimes the worse it gets. For every decision you must make, create a timeline. This is similar to goal setting.

When it comes to members of the team, you have control over the athletic, academic, ethical, moral, and social aspects of a player so that the end result is a person who is an elite achiever. As a coach, you must find people who want to be motivated and then put your time into them. As a coach it is really difficult to motivate an individual who does not want to be driven. For the benefit of the team, you must determine which student-athletes are committed to putting in the time and effort to develop their skills. It is about quality time, not time in the gym. Make sure every one of your players and staff understand the difference between time and quality time. Constantly demonstrate quality time in shooting, one-on-one, and conditioning.

Once you have assessed the players' commitment to quality results, immediately get rid of players who are not committed to the goals and mentality of your program. Letting a problem fester or go unresolved can magnify or compound the problem. Releasing players is a tough decision, but it must not be postponed. You must make decisions for the best of the team. If you keep players who don't show effort, it will hurt the program. It can spread to other players, and that is why you must make the decision early. You can film practices and scrimmages. You can call in the parents and the player and watch the film together. The films will show the effort or lack of it. Numerous successful coaches have often said "Films don't lie."

In my very first year as head coach at Girard High School, twelve seniors came out for the team. We started preseason and had a good week of practice. The previous few years the players were not pushed; and they were not in great shape. This was a major problem. Out of the twelve seniors, I retained the two who worked the hardest. I took a lot of criticism, and there were repercussions in the community. I knew I made the decision for all the right reasons. In the third game of the season my very first year, I had to make another difficult decision regarding a junior player who was All-League the year before. I had a meeting in which I informed him he was off the team. Due to his lack of effort, I thought it was best he was released from the team. We only won one game that year. We played mostly sophomores and few juniors, and I think releasing that player set the tone for the whole program. Discipline was a big factor in why we eventually won a state title at Girard and at Mentor.

The young man that I released as a junior came back as a senior and had a phenomenal year. To this day, he and I have a great relationship. I have seen some of the seniors that I released that first year out in public, and after seeing what the program at Girard became and the program that I have established in Mentor, they agreed with me that the cut was justified because they had not worked as hard as they could have.

When we do release a player, I call the young man in, and I tell him the reason for the cut. Then we discuss what direction in life he is going, and I impress upon him whatever he is going to pursue in his life, he must give it 100 percent. I do believe even in a situation where you release someone for whatever reason, you can still have a positive impact in that young person's life.

When we release players, we don't just designate one day as "cut day." The evaluation involved in releasing a player at the varsity level should be a process of one to a few weeks with constant feedback on the student-athlete's chance to make the team. Since conditioning is the highlight of the month of October, evaluation at this time will determine who is dedicated and who wants to work.

I believe in keeping as many good, dedicated players as possible. You never know who will mature and develop later on. There have been a few years where a player who has not made the team has been kept on in the position of team manager. We made an agreement that if they worked really hard during their year as manager (performed drills and learned the system) and committed to off-season programs, then their chance of making the team the following year would be extremely good. In every one of those instances, that young man made the team the following year.

Finally, if you must address an issue with concerned parents, discuss the situation with them immediately. Do not put it off. To avoid a he-said—he-said situation from developing, from my experience I would recommend you never talk to a parent alone. Have an assistant with you whenever possible.

You are not going to please everybody. However, if you make your decisions for the right reasons, you can be confident in making them.

*Be willing to make decisions. That's the most
important quality in a good leader.*

—General George S. Patton
Decorated General, US Army

CHAPTER 7

The Importance of Communication

**The success and quality of your program
depend on effective communication.**

Communication is a skill, and to be successful, coaches must be effective communicators. Be open and transparent at all times with your staff and players. You should avoid hidden agendas.

The success and quality of your program also depend on effective communication. If your program is not as successful as you would like, see if your staff and players believe in your system. Ask your assistants and captains for input. You may initially be shocked at what you learn, but ultimately you will adapt and be more effective as a coach. You will improve your program.

You must communicate after games. Your attitude toward losses should be positive because every loss must be a good loss as you learn from it. Call the coaching staff together to review the game. Then gather the captains with the coaches to discuss how to correct any deficiencies. Finally, address the whole team. Remember that the game of basketball is both mental and physical. Your words make a difference. After the last game of the season, in the locker room, talk about the great things the seniors did. Wish them the best and tell them you and the coaches want to remain part of their lives and you will always be there for them. Talk briefly about the goals for the upcoming season and what the team is expected to do to reach those goals. Tell the players you will be meeting with parents and players individually and will be in contact.

In communicating, don't be afraid to use social media, such as Twitter. Tweeting can be geared toward specific players or the whole team. You can use social media to send quotes and motivational as well as educational material to your players. Never ever put anything negative in print and be very hesitant about responding to social media. You don't want comments to be given a different spin or restated out of context. I use Twitter because I am limited in my tech skills at present (I intend to get better).

Find the best and most effective way to communicate with team members and parents. In private, everyone should get your honest feedback. Be open and transparent about the player's actions both on and off the court. Review their quality of play as well as how they conduct themselves in public such as their appearance, and their actions. When making public comments, your players should get your 100 percent support. Our players are high profile and they represent the program in public. We impress upon our players that if you want to be elite then things are different in your life and much more is expected of you.

As noted in previous chapters, from my experience I recommend that when communicating with a parent or player always have an assistant coach or administrator with you in the meeting.

You may believe your players are not listening to what you say. I have found the use of quotes predominately by successful individuals to be highly effective in getting my message across to my players because the message is focused but not personal. My experience has been they absorb more than you know. Here are some comments from my former players to the news media during a past season:

> He is always pushing us out of our comfort zone to make us better, and he doesn't accept average. He wants us to be elite.
>
> —Kyle McIntosh

> He emphasizes how important defense is and how important mental toughness really is.
>
> —Andrew Valeri

He knows how to turn weaknesses into strengths.

—Conner Krizancic

He always pushes us, no matter if it's on or off the court, and always puts us against bigger and stronger opponents so that we become an elite basketball team.

—Paul Sateika

Coach always pushes us to be better students and athletes. He wants his players to be elite and play great defense.

—Joey Zaugg

Sometimes your message will be more effective coming from within the team. Consider using one or two strong leaders as your messengers. Usually your captains will be the vocal ones and most effective in getting your message across. It may be the same message, but when it is delivered by a different messenger who has earned the respect of their teammates, it will have a greater impact. Use your discretion when utilizing your captains as your messengers.

Communicating regarding the leadership ability of your captains is important. The captains set the tone for your team. Therefore, you need to critique your captains to ensure that they are worthy of this trust. As the head coach, make sure your captains totally understand that although it is important their voice be heard within the team, you are taking 100% of the responsibility for everything they are saying. This will relieve the stress on everyone.

Communicating with parents must start from day one. Have your first meeting in the spring with parents and eighth graders who are interested in joining your high school program. Communicate from the beginning with information about your program requirements and invite them to practices. Providing a physical copy of the schedule as well as online communication is effective. For example, we use a one-call system which is accessed through an 877 number and currently costs $120 per year to advise parents and student-athletes of the schedule and changes to it. Your booster program can help pay for and establish the service. When a head coach makes a call regarding a change in practice or other information to all on the one-call system, it will be received within one to two hours. The one-call program can communicate with large groups and usually we register one parent and the player. When it comes to communicating, Twitter and the one-call system are gold mines for coaches. It should be noted that the JV coach and the Freshman coach can use *One Call Now* to communicate with their respective teams.

In regard to social media, proper use must be addressed with your staff and players both preseason and during the season. Players and coaching staff alike must understand the proper use and pitfalls of social media. You want the social media to be your ally. In communicating through other forms of the media, always be humble and complimentary to your opponent. Instruct your players to give credit to their teammates and opposition.

Remember communication involves both actions and words. How you, your staff, and team members conduct themselves when in public matters. First impressions matter. You never get a second chance to make a first impression. As a coach you should advise your staff and team members that they are part of an elite program which they reflect by being self-confident, mentally tough, and displaying a strong work ethic both on and off the court.

Finally, make sure your message is comprehended accurately. I must impress upon you the importance of repetition to make sure that your message is comprehended. Regarding communication you cannot say anything that is important to the success of your program and team too often.

In this regard, I have to share with you a situation that occurred during my first year as head coach. After practice on a Friday in November, I said that tomorrow practice is 10 to 12. On Saturday morning, everyone was at practice at 10:00 AM except my best player. At 11:45 AM, that player walked into the gym. I looked at him and said "Where have you been?" He looked at me dumbfounded and responded, "Coach, you said practice was at 10 to 12." Apparently to him this meant 11:50 AM! So, from year one, I understood that I needed to spell out the exact time of practice and how to do it so it would leave no chance for misinterpretation: 10 o'clock to 12 o'clock.

As a result of this experience, I have also found it to be fool proof to choose two players at the end of any team meeting to repeat the message or my directive to ensure that the players have understood the message correctly, and that there is no miscommunication and no room for excuses. This is especially true regarding practice times. I also instruct my captains to write the time of practice on the board in the locker room. I found that when the players hear it and then see it written, there is less chance for miscommunication. Clarity is essential.

Effective teamwork begins and ends with communication.

—Mike Krzyzewski
Hall of Fame NCAA Coach

GBC

I am always talking during a game, but I totally realize that 99 percent of what happens in games is what happens in practice. My comments are for reassurance and confidence.

CHAPTER 8

Personal and Professional Growth

**How many opportunities have you missed
because you were not aware of the possibilities
that would occur if you applied a small amount
of effort beyond what you normally do?**

Embrace change and be cognizant of new developments. Early in my coaching career I accomplished this by attending clinics. I believe it would be extremely advantageous for you as the head coach and leader of your program to address new rule changes each and every year. In the majority of years, they are minor but as you well know, every few years you will have a major change to incorporate into your program. The sooner your players adjust to the rule changes, the better they will be.

Don't be afraid to implement new ideas or concepts. When the three-point shot was introduced into high school basketball in the 1987–1988 season, we embraced it immediately. The three-point shot created a lot of excitement in the high school game. We have so embraced the three-point shot that during my coaching tenure at Mentor High School, we have the first- and second-most three-point shots made in a season in the history of Ohio High School boys basketball.

Personal and professional growth creates understanding on how to use changes effectively. For instance, this is the first season we used an analytics coach and it worked out really well. These game statistics were extremely helpful in our understanding of our weaknesses and strengths at half time and at the end of the game.

You may institute a new way of approaching an issue that will benefit the entire sport. In 1985, with the approval of the Girard Board of Education, we were the first school and sport to conduct a drug test in the state of Ohio. With the support of two school board members, one of whom was affiliated with a financial institution, we were able to secure funds from four banks to randomly drug-test four times during the basketball season. The testing was optional, but every one of our player's parents signed the waiver form permitting a drug and alcohol test on their student-athlete. We tested team members for two years. Then the Ohio High School Athletic Association issued their own drug and alcohol policy. We conducted the test for the total good of our basketball program, and not as punishment or an invasion of an individual's privacy. We were not afraid to be the first to address this controversial subject. The program gave student-athletes parameters when any social activities exposed them to a potential violation of their basketball contract. The basketball contract contained provisions which were a combination of rules and regulations agreed upon by both our players and coaches. Even as this book is written, the legalities of sports contracts is an ever changing dynamic.

There are many clinics that are offered to coaches for personal and professional growth such as was sponsored by Nike and other groups. You may learn from the experiences of others. Listen to their successes and failures. Take with you relevant concepts that you can institute in your program. Keep what works; discard what doesn't. The only way to improve is to leave your comfort zone. Remember the definition of insanity is doing the same thing over and over and expecting different results. I learned that the hard way.

Personal and professional growth requires seeking out successful programs. I personally adopted concepts from other successful coaches and incorporated them into my program. Among these are Jim Valvano's fast break (NC State), Tom Davis's diamond press (Boston College), George Raveling's approach to special situations

(Washington State), and Bob Huggins's offense (University of Akron and University of Cincinnati).

Don't be afraid to acknowledge areas where you yourself may have to improve or change to be effective. As a coach, you have to be tough, which is important. Being tough was not in my personality at the beginning of my coaching career. I had been a player for years, and then I became a head coach at age twenty-five. Coaching was totally different than playing so I knew my personality had to change. I had to gain respect as a young head coach, and my players had to respect me. Early in my coaching career, I was tough. Our practices lasted for three hours, our camp was seven hours, and our practices in the gym were closed to non-team members. I wouldn't even let my father in to the practices, which caused some family issues. Over time, I learned to tell my players, "I am your biggest critic and your biggest supporter. You are here because you do 95 percent of things correct, but there are 5 percent of deficiencies that we have to address."

Today, I am a very demanding coach, and I constantly tell my players we are trying to change their deficiencies into strengths. When I have been hard on them during practice, within a half hour or so after practice, I place my hand on their shoulder and reassure them that they are an important part of the team; they matter. By doing that, you reinforce that bond between you and your player. When you do that, your players will respect you, and will understand. I always tell my players to this day, "Do not be concerned when I yell at you. If I don't yell at you, then you should be really concerned." My personal and professional growth was what I learned as a coach over time. I learned you can be strict and tough, but you need to make sure your players know that your goal is to develop them to their full potential. I constantly tell my players that I have a major respect for those who turn their deficiencies into strengths. That is the key to their success.

Leadership and learning are indispensable to each other.

—John F. Kennedy
35th President of the United States

Assist at elite camps, such as I did for LeBron's Nike Camp in San Diego. Such activities will make your program's elite quality apparent to those outside your program.

CHAPTER 9

The Issue of Trust

Trust is essential if an organization is to function well.

Establishing trust with administrators, athletic directors, parents, and players requires transparency and honesty. When a person is trusted, it means that others have confidence in them and in their honesty and integrity. Other people believe the person they trust will do the things they say. Being open and transparent as noted in the earlier chapters are the foundations for establishing trust. To establish trust, you must exhibit trustworthy behavior. Let the parents and community know what you are doing. Open practice to parents so they can see what goes on in practice. Follow through on what you say to reinforce others' trust.

Building rapport as early as possible with those involved in your program is also essential to establishing trust. For instance, host a preseason cookout. Use it as an opportunity to address parents, players, and cheerleaders. Introduce them to your goals, beliefs, and program. Having a preseason informative social event is a great way to prevent problems throughout the season. Let them know you want to develop a relationship with them and their child because your goal is to create an elite young person who is successful both on and off the court.

We typically have our preseason cookout on a Sunday in August so that our players who are participating in a Fall sport can attend the cookout. We invite returning freshmen, sophomores, juniors, and seniors, their parents and families, as well as the cheerleaders. We introduce every player and cheerleader. At the picnic I present all aspects of our program in detail. I discuss September and October open gyms, our four-man schedule, and the right number of classes needed for a player to be eligible to play. The goal is to make sure that the parent and players know we have a system in place to provide academic assistance and address issues that affect their child's performance. We can set up tutoring sessions to handle any problems with classes. We usually provide tutors in history, English, chemistry, and physics. I also let them know once the team is set for the season, we check our players' grades every grading period year-round and periodically during the grading period to address any deficiencies and ensure academic success.

At the preseason cookout, we also talk about the character-building sessions we will have throughout the season in which I invite businesspeople, administrators, law enforcement personnel, and even a judge to talk about the players' future in college and the work world. Again, I let parents and players know what the ramifications might be regarding eligibility if players misuse social media or are involved in legal issues. Our goal is to impress upon our young players their actions during the school year could definitely impact their college or employment opportunities after they graduate.

We also discuss our fund-raisers in the fall and our booster organization. We review the first official date to commence the season. Also, sports physicals are explained and the deadline for their submission is given. If a team member is unable to find a professional to give a sports physical, we supply places where they can arrange one. Try to be as comprehensive about your program as possible. While the website will also have much of this information, this meeting with the parents, players, and cheerleaders provides them an opportunity to ask questions and get clarification.

This preseason cookout is also a great way for parents, especially the parents of younger players, to meet one another and start to build relationships within the parent group.

Regarding establishing trust, the best advice I can give you in this regard is to get involved with as many community organizations and attend as many social events as possible. Being highly visible in your community through volunteering at community socials such as chili cook-offs, senior or veterans' lunches, nonprofit activities, and fund-raisers will provide a bridge between you and your community. Their feeling of trust for you and your program will follow and they will be willing to invest their time and financial support to ensure its success.

Be and look prepared. Be a man of integrity. Never break your word. Don't have two sets of standards. Stand up for your players. Show them you care on and off the court.

—Red Auerbach
Hall of Fame NBA Coach and Executive

CHAPTER 10

Commitment and Patience

**Your commitment and patience will
pave the pathway to success.**

Stay committed to coaching and be in it for the long haul. Lasting in the coaching profession has its own challenges. In many communities during the basketball season, you as the head coach will be one of the high-profile professionals in your community. You will probably find your name and picture appearing on many different social media platforms as well as in print. Therefore, you must be sensitive to the impact your presence and actions as well as words can have on your program, staff, school system, community, locally, and even possibly on a larger scale such as regional, statewide, and national.

Only three percent of adults have clear written goals. These three percent that commit to their goals accomplish five to ten times as much as people of equal or better education and ability. Know your goals clearly, precisely, and passionately and make them your constant companion. Set your goals high and never for one second think you won't reach them.

Ask for advice when you feel as if you need clarity. Seek help from other coaches who have gone through something similar to what you are facing. They can give you advice on what worked and what didn't work for them. They won't come to you. As an old proverb states: "Forewarned is forearmed."

Coaching is a huge time commitment. When you talk about commitment to coaching, the vast majority of you will be married and have a family during your career in coaching. This is challenging. Coaching requires you to be away from family for extended periods of time. I was fortunate to have two sons. To remain committed as a coach and to still enjoy family time together, I found a creative approach to be useful. During my time away due to team commitments, I tried to focus on planning social events for the team and include my family in the team's events. We would go bowling, and I would have my sons along. We would do film sessions and have food at the same time. As my sons were growing up my family interacted with my players and teams. Even after my sons were grown, I still have the players over to my house four or five times a year to share casual meals including pizzas or subs. As a result of my experience, I think that you can, as a parent, combine your team's social events with your family, and create a win-win situation.

A coach must exhibit patience when interacting with student-athletes. Your goal is to develop habits in them that become second nature. You want their habit and instinct to be one and the same on the court so that there is no lapse between a thought and an action. However, it takes a minimum of twenty-one days to form a new habit—a minimum of twenty-one days of consistent correct action. If you must rid yourself of an old habit to develop the new one, it will take even longer. You can see that this doesn't happen overnight. Filming is very helpful here and patience is essential to achieve the desired end result.

Basically I am a very impatient person. However, in my coaching career I have learned to develop some level of patience. I realize if we introduce a new drill, it is going to take time to develop the new skill associated with it. When I am really convinced regarding what would be great for our program, I introduce it. I have learned to use that twenty-one-day minimum as far as expecting great results. I tell my players that they will not become proficient in this new skill overnight. Therefore, when you talk patience as a coach, it means patience in your team, patience in your program, and ultimately patience in your future. You must impress upon your players that if you focus on the new skill, persist in practicing it, really invest your energy in it every single day, and do it at game speed, you will make that skill a reality on the floor.

I have learned a lot from talking to parents of my players. One parent told his son if you are going to commit to being really good at something, including basketball, you will need to give up something in order to focus and make that commitment a reality. As a coach, explain to your players that to achieve elite status as a basketball player, you will have to commit your time to basketball. When you come home from school, you may have to limit time on video games, texting, or email. The benefit of focusing your quality time on basketball will be so well worth it.

As I stated earlier, mental toughness can be developed. You should never state or even imply that a student-athlete cannot develop mental toughness. Mental toughness requires effort on both your part as a coach and on the part of the student-athlete. It may take longer than you expect, and that is why commitment and patience are necessary on the part of the coach and the student-athlete.

Commitment separates those who live their dreams from those who live their lives regretting the opportunities they have squandered.

—Bill Russell
Hall of Fame NBA Player and Coach

CHAPTER 11

The Coach as Role Model

You must model what you want your players to be.

I believe that I must be a great role model as a coach, father, and in every aspect of my life. And I will go one step further. I expect you in the coaching profession to be a great role model to the players you coach. By this I mean exhibit a strong work ethic, have a strong character, make right decisions 24/7 for the best of everyone, be transparent, and build strong relationships. I firmly believe with all my heart that these qualities will make you the kind of role model that will have a strong and lasting impact on your players and your program.

I expect my players to be elite in every facet of their game and in their life. My philosophy is if I am going to preach something to my players, I had better live it. If I am going to expect something from my players, then I better expect it from myself. Push yourself to reach and maintain elite status as a person, a coach, and a role model.

As a coach, you will be subjected to social scrutiny, especially in this era of social media. Therefore, choose your words wisely and always be cognizant of the effect of your actions. Be aware of situations that could expose you to public scrutiny and attempt to limit those situations. If you are a great role model, however, you will have very little to fear.

I believe my job as a coach is to develop the student-athlete to their full potential and that I must be their role model in this regard. Your passionate commitment to your role in this process will have a lasting impact. In time, the players will come to realize this is your goal, and they will appreciate it. As one of my former players, Stephen Lombardo, recently stated,

> What I have always respected about Coach K is he always found a way to bring the best out of you. He helps you find another level you are not even sure is there, and makes you find that untapped potential. Sometimes you think you are giving your all, you are giving 100 percent, and he finds that extra 10 percent that you just are not aware is there. Sometimes it is even more than you feel you could possibly ever give.

I want my players to be in better shape than any team in the state of Ohio, so to be consistent with my philosophy, I stay in the best physical shape I can be. If you tell your players to be in the best shape possible, make sure you do the same thing.

I am thoroughly convinced that success is tied to a person's mental state. It is essential to keep yourself and your team focused and positive. You may consider offering your players a moment of silence before the game to reflect, meditate, or pray if they desire. This allows a person to tap into their inner strength.

Be a positive influence on your student-athletes. Keep a positive attitude. Positivity is important if your players are to play to their highest ability. Having a positive attitude is especially true regarding injuries. One of the toughest things for a coach to do is to address an injured player who is going to be out for a period of time. To the player, it is almost like their whole world has come crashing down. I recently had to meet with an injured player, and I told him, "I believe that God put you into this situation to see how you are going to handle it and how tough you are. I want you to come to practice and be as positive as you have ever been in your life. What you have to believe is that your injury is all for the good—that you will be bigger, stronger, and tougher when you come back. And you will come back. Your playing time will be taken up by other players who, at tournament time, will be better players because of your situation. So, it is a win-win. You may not see it now, but I see it clearly."

Be a resilient leader. Impress upon your player that the only one who can stop you is you. Remember, most coaches don't get fired for lack of strategic knowledge but, rather, for leadership deficiencies. You control your program. Your assistant coaches and players are feeding off you, your energy, and your character. How you deal with frustration and adversity are probably the most important lessons you can impart on everyone in your program. They are looking to you for guidance 24/7. They will model your behavior.

A coach should be a role model and always exhibit positivity which is also important when it comes to handling losses. How you address the loss of a game is absolutely paramount for your success during the year. One of the things that I have been so impressed with through the years is that we seldom lose more than one game in a row. If and when we do lose, my immediate response is this is only a good loss if we learn from it, and we come back stronger than ever. When we do lose, we focus in on what we did wrong and what changes can be made. This approach teaches your players the value of mental toughness when faced with frustration, disappointment, and doubt.

I also address the captains in regard to being role models and tell them how much responsibility and power they have on the court with their teammates. As you mold, tutor, and become close to your captains, and build a relationship with them, you will become a strong role model for them. Then they, in turn, are role models for the younger players. I impress on the captains that they have control in practice. I stress to them their importance that, as role models, they compete in every drill, compete every second, and compete on every possession.

Model what you want your players to be by exhibiting the qualities you want to see in them. Model the mental toughness you expect in your players. It has to start with you as head coach: your expectations, your goals, and you being the best coach as a role model. In the book, I talk about how part-time players don't make it. If you are going to have an impact as a coach, you can't be a part-time coach and pick and choose when you want to exhibit quality characteristics. Being a coach as a role model is not a part-time task; it's an all-in commitment and a way of life.

Being a role model is the most powerful form of educating.

—John Wooden
Hall of Fame NCAA Coach

*Please refer to Section 6, Chapter 38 for more information on the impact of a coach on their players and program.

GBC

It is not easy.
An elite coach fosters and supports
mental toughness in his players.
He plots the course for them to pursue
and achieve mental toughness.
He sets them on the path and pushes them forward.
He develops their full potential.
He sets the bar high.
An elite coach is a role model at all times.

CHAPTER 12

Coaching Your Own Child and Other Special Coaching Situations

It is important to set boundaries and establish parameters immediately.

The special circumstance of coaching your child places unique demands on a coach. When coaching your child, establish boundaries. For example, talk basketball until you get home but once you are at home, no more basketball discussions. Make your home a safe haven and set rules. The rules we followed in our home were that we were allowed to talk basketball anywhere else—at the gym, in the car, and at social events. That approach worked for us. Even if we wanted to talk basketball at home, we didn't. We waited. It worked out well when we kept to those rules. Sometimes it will take a while to establish this new "habit" regarding communication with the members of your family, but it will work. It will minimize any negative impact of your role as a coach on your parental relationship with your child or vice versa. It will also prevent your role as parent from negatively impacting your ability to coach.

I would strongly recommend that you sit down with your child before and during the time when you coach them and discuss your role as their coach and parent. My oldest son, Cole, and I had an understanding that I would be tougher on him than any of the other players. That would negate anyone from saying that I favored him or that he was getting special treatment. I think that it was tough on him at first. Cole was successful as a player. He started all the games, and in his freshman year, our record was 20-5. We won our conference and advanced to the regional tournament. A reporter asked Cole at the end of his freshman year if he had the opportunity to coach his own son, would he do anything different than the way his father had coached him. He answered yes, he would not be as tough and would be softer.

In Cole's junior year, we went to state, and a reporter once again asked him if he was coaching his own son, would he coach like I had coached him. His answer this time was he wouldn't do anything different, except maybe be a little tougher! I think that this answer reflected his maturity and his understanding why I did what I did and that it was best for him. At that time, Cole led the state in scoring and was first team All-State. He was also recognized as one of the top fifty players in the country.

My younger son, Conner, was a little different. He had the luxury of playing with his older brother for one year when Conner was a freshman, and Cole was a senior. I believe this relationship helped Conner ease into my coaching philosophy of being tougher on my own son. Also, when Conner was in seventh and eighth grade, he was on our team bus and being at all the games made the transition a little bit easier for him.

I also would explain and reiterate to your child that it is your strong belief your child's relationships with his teammates will have a major impact on how smooth their career will become. Transparency, loyalty, and work ethic on your child's part will be paramount to the camaraderie of the team. Coaching both my sons was made easier because of the friendships they had developed through the years. They had great camaraderie and great support from their friends and their friends' parents. The friendships also extended into the city of Mentor and the school system as well.

Needless to say, I am totally sold regarding the importance of the support that relationships with other people can provide when it comes to coaching your own child. Strong relationships with teammates and their families can help your child be more secure as a member of a team and less self-conscious as the child of a coach.

During your career as coach, you may find that you are coaching the child of a close friend, board member, the administrator of the school system for which you are working, or even one of your assistant coaches. Parameters of working with your own child have to apply to them as well. You can address questions about basketball and advise them that their child will be treated like everyone else's. You will answer any of their questions about the season, and then they must trust you and leave it to your discretion. Remember, I recommend you have an assistant coach present when you meet with or talk to a parent whenever possible.

It is wise to discuss your role as a coach and their role as a parent before their child starts in the program as a high school player. Set rules and parameters as soon as the child enters your program. Let your lower-level coaches know your position on these issues as well to ensure consistency at all levels.

Explain how your program works and the relationship of coach to parent and student-athlete. The earlier you do this in your relationship with the parent, the better. Complaints by administrators and board members about coaching style get coaches fired more than anything else.

When coaching your child or in these special circumstances, be a mature, tough coach. It is important to give correction in such a way that the student-athlete understands that the goal is to improve their game. Be consistent. Playing time is at the discretion of the coach. The student-athlete earns their playing time. Being a member of a basketball team is a privilege and not a right.

Finally, when my oldest son was about to enter his freshman year at Mentor High School, I reached out to a couple of head coaches in Northeast Ohio that I knew well and who had coached their own sons. I asked them what worked, what did not work, what they would do differently and what they would do the same. Their guidance helped me to set parameters regarding my role in coaching my sons. It worked extremely well. So, if you find yourself in this situation, my advice to you is to reach out to coaches who had also had this unique experience of coaching their own child.

A coach is someone who can give correction without resentment.

—John Wooden
Hall of Fame NCAA Coach

When I asked my sons if they wanted to include a message in this book about their experiences with Mentor's basketball program and comments about being the son of a head coach, I received the following heartfelt messages. Without input from me, both my sons expressed in these honest and personal reflections that they benefited in many ways from their relationship with me as their father and coach, as well as from their interactions with their teammates, and with those involved in my program. Cole is currently playing in the American Basketball Association, a semi-pro league, and Conner's football jersey #5 was retired at Mentor High School on September 24, 2021.

REFLECTIONS ON BEING THE COACH'S SONS
COLE KRIZANCIC'S MESSAGE

Growing up, my brother and I learned from an early age what it was like to be a part of the Mentor basketball program. The high school gym became more like a second home for us, and the people involved became more like a second family rather than just a team made of up players and staff. I can remember looking up to numerous players as role models as a kid, just hoping one day I can be in their position and get the chance to play for my dad at Mentor. I also realized the amount of time, hard work, and dedication it took to have success at that level. My dad has built the Mentor basketball program on the philosophy that we will be tougher (mentally and physically) and outwork any team that we play. His teams have not always been the biggest or the most athletic, but he has made it his mission in life to get every ounce of talent out of his players to have them become the absolute best they could be. This is definitely challenging for some at times, myself included, but it's what separates Mentor from most of the other programs around the state and country. If you don't want to be pushed to be the best version of yourself, in basketball and in life in general, then Mentor basketball is not for you. It has to become your mentality.

With this also comes a great deal of confidence he instills in his players. I can remember coming in to play as a freshman, playing teams much bigger than us and I felt as though I didn't belong at times. Teams would come up to Jaron (Crowe) and me asking "where is your varsity team?" on numerous occasions throughout various summer leagues and shootouts. However, the confidence my dad had in myself and teammates allowed us to compete against any team that we shared the court with, often to the surprise of our opponents. This confidence only grows as you develop as a person and a player, which I've always believed is a major reason as to why his teams have achieved so much success over the years.

As he often says, you enter the Mentor basketball program as a boy, but you leave as a man. After graduating, I look back and realize how special it was to play for my dad and I would not change a thing about it. It was not always easy, but my time at Mentor was filled with many more ups than downs and memories that I know will last a lifetime. Although I may not have realized it while I was still playing for him, I am so grateful for everything he has done for me and I know for a fact I would not be where I am today without his guidance.

CONNER KRIZANCIC'S MESSAGE

When my father asked me to write an entry for his book, I was deeply honored. As I jotted ideas on my whiteboard, I asked myself, "What were the most important things my dad taught me?" The list quickly grew as my mind filled with so many life-changing moments and memories. It took me time to find the words to express my emotions, but I found it rewarding to distill them down to three lessons that impacted me the most. These principles shaped the exemplary life my dad has led. The accomplishments stretch from being a phenomenal role model to taking teams to state championships. My team as well. I live and breathe them each day.

Dream Big and Strive for Greatness

Every day, achieving his personal best is something my father embodies, not for glory but rather for the private revelations that come with personal growth. He extracts the best from everyone, helps people define their big dreams and goals, and maps out ways to achieve them despite how difficult they may appear. He sees life's obstacles as opportunities to do more than just survive. On the other side of them, one can thrive.

He taught me that mediocrity was never an option because anyone can be average or achieve the minimum requirements to get by. Playing it safe is easy and ultimately less fulfilling, so he pushes people out of their comfort zones to ensure they strive for achievements they previously thought were impossible.

That certainly was the case for my team at Mentor High. Most high schools would have been happy with a district or regional championship, but not us. We had one goal in mind, to win the first state basketball championship in school history. Even after losing two 17-point leads to Shaker Heights in the regular season, our dream of holding up the trophy in Columbus never faded until it became our reality. It was in our mind's eye long before we ever set foot on the court, thanks to my dad.

The Power of Hard Work

My father taught us to find a home inside ourselves, knowing our inner-person and being in touch with our highest and best selves. The more we focused on our potential and *not* our shortcomings, the more we advanced physically and mentally. We learned to understand that strength and resilience come from within. To realize that when we hit a mental, emotional, or physical wall, it wasn't time to quit—it was time to dig deeper and breakthrough to the next level. He ingrained in us that there are no shortcuts in life and that true greatness and lasting-legacy rarely come easily and always with some sacrifice.

I was always amazed at my dad's work ethic from the time I was a young child. He practiced what he preached, putting hustle behind his muscle, and accomplishing all he set out to do. Regardless of how busy his days were, filled with teaching, coaching, traveling, or even on vacation, he would get at least one workout in per day. He will always be the hardest worker in the room, leading by example and inspiring others to rise higher. I believe that his ability to experience such impactful days is rooted in his intentionality. He sets the tone of his mind and the day before his feet even hit the floor. I was fortunate to absorb this kind of energy and example from a young age.

I will never forget when the University of Toledo football coaches came to watch our basketball team practice the day before a game. The Rockets coaching staff were scouting a few of us, debating who, if anyone, would be offered a scholarship. They anticipated a lighter routine given our play the next day and were amazed by what turned into a Marine-style workout as they watched from the sidelines. Play or no play, we trained as if every day was the most important day of our lives. Because each truly was. We learned the value of stacking our accomplishments and pushing the limits of our personal best.

My dad and his staff of genius coaches had set up ten workout stations. Each one was three minutes in duration, consisting of defensive slides, sprints, push-ups, weighted ball jumps, and other taxing exercises, so I did what I knew to do—train hard. After watching our team practice non-stop for two hours, the Toledo coaches called me over to speak with them. The first words out of their mouths were, "If you're used to this type of work, we want you to become a Rocket." The next day, a few of us were offered full athletic scholarships. Our team agreed that the discipline and training needed to master those stations were a top reason why we won a state championship and received such accolades. We outworked everyone, following Coach K's lead.

Believe in Yourself

My father also taught us to live from the inside out, knowing that you must first believe in yourself for others to believe in you. He armed us with the knowledge that everything we needed was residing inside of us. We simply had to tap into that place of knowing to find the strength and desire to carry on. The confidence he instilled in us freed us from worrying about the "how's" and taught us we could accomplish great things with unwavering determination and hard work.

Whether you call it the law of attraction or faith, my father understands the importance of an unshakable foundation. He empowers everyone around him to rise to their fullest potential, always leading by example. He preaches maintaining an almost delusional belief in yourself without fearing failure. From his perspective, failure is one of life's greatest teachers. The lessons embedded within our mistakes allow us to improve, be empowered, and come back stronger than before.

Everyone on our state championship team believed in themselves because my father had etched it into our minds. Helping us control our mindset was a top priority, as was encouraging us to play full-out and take chances. As most may know, my dad can get fired up on the basketball court, but not many things grind his gears more than someone not taking a shot they should have taken. He gave us the green light and confidence to take the big shots from anywhere on the court, down to the buzzer! We always knew we could make up for it on the other end of the court if we missed it, giving us peace of mind and freedom.

This book highlights many of the facets that make my father the gem he is. His commitment to himself and the teams that count on him, his no-excuses approach to life, seeing weakness as an opportunity to change, pushing beyond comfort zones, and embodying mental toughness. Although words can't truly capture everything he is, my wish is to convey the honor and credit he deserves. My father has impacted so many lives as a coach, teacher, friend, mentor, brother, and son. Esteemed by his peers and beloved by his family, my brother Cole and I are blessed to call him dad.

SECTION 1:
HOW TO BE AN ELITE COACH

Overview

Exercise Mental Toughness

- Start with a vision and stick to it
- Assemble your staff
- Establish a strong booster program
- Build relationships
- Take control and assume responsibility
- Make difficult decisions early
- Communicate
- Establish boundaries
- Establish trust
- Set the bar high
- Engage in personal and professional growth
- Embrace change
- Stay committed—never give up
- Develop positivism and patience
- Seek help
- Limit social scrutiny
- Understand unique demands of coaching your own child and other special coaching situations

See appendices A though K at the back of the book for further information and relevant documents.

SECTION 2

HOW TO BUILD AN ELITE ORGANIZATIONAL CULTURE

It takes time to create excellence. If it could be done quickly, more people would do it.

—John Wooden
Hall of Fame NCAA Coach

Creating an elite basketball program—a culture of winning—is so much more than winning games. It is formulating and sticking to a winning philosophy and establishing a culture that provides the fertile ground for mental toughness to get a firm grasp in the psyche of players to allow them to flourish. It is creating an identity that is so distinctive that it exudes a unique quality setting it apart from all other programs.

Believe—miracles do happen.
The smallest Division II school in the state,
the long shot, and a team nobody gave a chance to win it all,
claims the ultimate prize.
Expect to win because of *preparedness, communication,
great work ethic, dedication, practice,* and *focus.*
BELIEVE IN YOURSELF.

CHAPTER 13

Determine Your Winning Philosophy and Stick to It

Create your style of play that will bring you wins.

Create and establish a winning philosophy. Determine what you want to focus on and create your style of play that will bring you success and therefore victories. My winning philosophy is run and press and shooting the three. The unique nature of this philosophy is highlighted by the following comment from one of my former players, Caleb Potter: "Coach Krizancic developed a system that no one has been able to replicate. No matter what year it was, we were state title contenders. Our chances of getting to the state were high every single year."

Once you establish your winning philosophy, stick to it and do not abandon it. You may be tempted to abandon your philosophy when you experience a losing streak because your confidence in your philosophy will be shaken. Early in my career, I considered changing our philosophy, but I was conscious of the great advice from successful mentors to tweak and never abandon what you know and believe in. Therefore, our basic philosophy as a program has remained a constant.

This consistency has made all the difference. Our program believes we "never rebuild, we just reload." The 2020–2021 season was a magical year: undefeated in regular season, state semi-finalists, and #! final Associated Press ranking. We had ten seniors who played, so as a result, only one junior actually got playing time as the eighth man in the rotation. That meant that we had only one player returning who actually had playing experience. In addition, because of COVID-19, only twelve varsity players practiced, and they were required to stay separate from the junior varsity players. This again affected the level of play to which our JV student-athletes were exposed. Our 2021–2022 record was 9–6 after fifteen games. For the first time in over twenty years, I was questioning whether we had really "reloaded." However, we stayed with our core beliefs and mentality. We were a very young team but worked harder than we ever have and did everything we could to get that shot at a state title. Our underclassmen grew up quickly and played as veterans. The result was a tremendous run to end the season. We won eleven in a row, league champions, district champions, and when we played the regional on March 10, there were only nine DI teams left out of two hundred. It was probably one of the top three runs in my coaching career. I can't say enough about my players and my staff.

DIII Collegiate Hall of Fame Basketball Coach Mike Moran shared the following observation about the validity of my approach to creating a successful program, season after season. Coach Moran noted: "Most basketball games are won before the game clock starts to tick, because of the head coach's organization. Coach Krizancic has won nearly 700 games! There is no need to say anything else!"

Realize that your philosophy worked for so long. If something in your style of play is not working, it may be beneficial to review the films. Staff and players alike can observe the positive aspects of your style of play. Remember, films don't lie. With this reaffirmation of the strong foundations for your philosophy, your confidence in it will return.

During the season and off-season, take the opportunity to tell your players what in the program worked and this way you can reinforce the positive.

Stress it is not the first or second effort but the third, fourth, and fifth effort that will make you into an elite team. Your culture must exude mental toughness. This mental toughness must be the fabric of your culture in every aspect. Every team member associated with your program at every level must be committed to this "attitude".

Expect to win as a consequence of preparedness, communication, great work ethic, dedication, practice, and focus.

Believe in your ability to win. Don't believe for one second that you could ever lose this game. Pressure comes from either being unprepared or playing not to lose instead of playing to win. Therefore, you must prepare to win. Your self-confidence controls your success. No success will come your way and no one will believe in you, if you don't believe in yourself.

Expect to be the best. Expect to be elite.

Coach Pat Summitt summarized this philosophy in four words: "Achieving starts with believing."

As the head coach, you must develop your winning philosophy. In developing your winning philosophy, you must consistently coach toward the upper range of your players' talent, skill, and ability, regardless of the specific circumstances in which you find yourself.

I received the following description regarding our winning philosophy from one of my players in an email the night before the district championship in 2013 (we went on to win the state title in 2013). Although this was written in 2013, I read it during tournament time every single year since then to motivate the team and focus their efforts and remind them what our program is all about during our tournament season. It noted many of the motivational sayings I had told the players throughout their careers:

My Motivation

Live with the pain of discipline today, so you don't have to live with the pain of regret tomorrow.

—Jim Rhone
Entrepreneur, Author, and Motivational Speaker

At the time, I never knew who said it; all I remember is my coach repeating it to us in the locker room time and time again. When he talked about you working hard, he talked about working harder. He told us eventually we would "get it." You will understand to be elite in everything you do. He would question our manhood and ask, "Why would you leave the gym if you weren't 100 percent confident in your shot, your handle, your defense, your game? When you have the opportunity to make a dream become a reality, why would you ever choose to be average?"

Coach K told us the mental is to the physical as four is to one. The will to win is the way to win, and without the will, there is no way. When talking about team success, Coach K said, "We can't win with boys, we won't lose with men." To do this, you have to be willing to give up what you like in order to achieve success in the things you love, and when you "get it," it will click. What you will realize is that what lies behind you and what lies ahead of you is insignificant compared to what lies within you. Destiny is not a matter of chance; destiny is a matter of choice. When you cross the locker room to the court, you knew as a player on his team, to believe in yourself, to believe in your ability, and that no one—absolutely no one—works or plays harder than the Mentor Cardinals. (Jeff Foreman, before the 2013 State Tournament)

BELIEVE IN YOURSELF.

All really successful coaches have a system.

—Jim Valvano
Hall of Fame College Basketball Coach and Broadcaster

Set your goals for your program high.
This is a regional game at Cleveland State University. Our
goal is always to get to Regionals and then to State.

CHAPTER 14

Establish Your Culture Right Away

Your culture must be defined and evident.

The coach sets the philosophy of the program based on their vision. A coach's philosophy is the result of searching for a purpose. Once a coach determines what actions and practices are necessary to achieve that purpose, a culture is created. Because the culture of a basketball program is a result of the coach's philosophy or vision, it is important for the coach to establish the right culture, the winning culture, right away. It must be defined and evident.

Our program has been successful because our culture is not just our tradition. It's the people and players who carry the culture on. It is essential that outsiders know what our culture is immediately.

In addition, our program has defined goals. We believe in teaching values of discipline, learning, understanding, and decision-making. We believe in developing the whole person. Our players are sound academically and strong athletically with the competitive edge and ability to be a productive member of society.

Define your goals and be specific. Once you have established your program goals and culture, never stray far from them. Minor adjustments will always happen, but the core will not change. The vast majority of the time, changing your philosophy when you don't win doesn't work. Continuity is of the greatest importance. Due to the magnitude of the various levels of commitment to your program, once established, total change is not advisable. However, your program can, and should, be modified when necessary.

Every single individual must be aware of your culture and be committed to it. Make sure everyone feels they are a vital part of the program. When you win medals, get one for everyone in the program, including the support staff. Exhibit your titles and plaques in the locker room as a reminder of how much you must work to win. Our locker room walls are decorated with colorful wooden plaques representing all of the Ohio High School Athletic Association district, regional, and state final titles and national rankings we have achieved. These serve to remind us of what the Mentor Boys Basketball program is capable of achieving and what we expect to achieve.

Your team's philosophy and culture should be so obvious that any outsider coming into contact with your basketball program should immediately be aware of your culture. Who you are, what you stand for, and why you are successful should be evident. Our program established our culture by creating a packet which is distributed at our summer camps and to our student-athletes throughout our program. This packet describes Mentor's program and our expectations in great detail. We say, not arrogantly but confidently, "We don't rebuild; we reload."

A program with a culture of mental toughness leads to success in a basketball program. Developing mental toughness in your student-athletes is definitely a game changer.

In my thirteenth year as head coach of the Girard High School Indians, my team was facing the Villa Angela-St. Joseph Vikings in the regional final. The Vikings was the team expected by many, if not everyone, to win the 1993 Division II State Championship. At the time, Coach Babe Kwasniak was the junior point guard for the Villa Angela-St. Joseph Vikings.

Kwasniak thought there was no way the Girard Indians would beat the Villa Angela-St. Joseph Vikings. Much to Babe Kawsniak's surprise, the Girard team walked away with a 78-57 win over the Vikings in the regional final and proceeded to win the 1993 State Division II Boys Basketball Championship.

In an interview twenty years later on the anniversary of that win, Coach Kwasniak reflected on the similarities in our coaching styles as they had evolved over the years. He concluded, "Coach and

I both believe you can teach mental toughness." *See News Herald articles by John Kampf, December 12, 2013, updated September 18, 2018, and "VASJ, Mentor ranked among Ohio's top basketball programs of past 10 years" by Nate Barnes, April 18, 2020.*

My accomplishments in winning state championships at the Division I and II levels and Coach Babe Kwasniak's state championships at Division III and Division IV highlight why this culture of mental toughness is so crucial.

I have addressed the concept of culture quite often in this book and I believe that "culture" is more physical than "philosophy". You can feel the culture of a program. You cannot feel its philosophy since philosophy concerns how one mentally approaches something. The impressiveness of the culture of a program is directly proportional to the vision and commitment of the coach. When you are around our program and our team, the best compliment you can give me as an outsider is that you **feel** the culture of Mentor basketball. **You feel the toughness.**

> *I think the most important thing about coaching is that you have to have a sense of confidence about what you're doing. You have to be a salesman and you have to get your players, particularly your leaders, to believe in what you're trying to accomplish…*

—Phil Jackson
Hall of Fame NBA Coach

**Encourage your alumni to support your program.
Recognize them at an Alumni Night game's halftime.**

It's About Making an Impact

The following is a transcription of a podcast that aired on **Talk Back Fans** on March 21, 2021 at 9:36 AM. It demonstrates the type of elite culture I encourage you to create in your program.

"As I walked into the press room postgame one word circled in my head... Impact! Little did I know that these guys were thinking it too. Watching the Mentor Cardinals on the floor as the clock struck midnight on their Cinderella season, I sat and watched as they embraced each other and the finality of the moment. Teammates... friends, it's not cliché to say this was a very close team. Brothers in Basketball! All the hours, all the sweat, all the wins and sadly this one loss came to the surface as emotion of a job well done even if the destination they sought was just out of their reach. It was palpable in that beautiful arena in Dayton yesterday... You could see it, hear it, and even to the guys blessed to cover it like us, you could feel it. Lots of players say "it's about team first" but this group of kids lived it. They recognized that success comes from being a part of the greater whole and less about individual accolades...this is very rare air in today's sports culture. But it was senior guard Luke Chicone, a four-year varsity player and the leader of a team of leaders, who fought back that emotion at the podium and delivered in a moment that is one of the most difficult in all of sports, answering the bell of the press when things don't go your way. He was asked (I'm paraphrasing) to sum up his time as a Cardinal. Without hesitation he talked about the effect Coach Bob Krizancic had on him not only as a player but as a young man. He stated that he would like to coach someday because he would like to have an impact on players the way Coach had impacted him. It was genuine, and heartfelt and showed how important the connections that are made in sports truly are. The wins and losses come and go...that's part of the game when you keep score. But in the end, its's relationships you build that have a lasting impression long after they flip the lights off. These young men, these great coaches...this prominent program may have been silenced in their quest yesterday, but they will always be heard. Where they go from here, be it on to the next level or wherever their lives take them, they will always be linked to each other and their community…one game outcome doesn't change that. There is no substitute for the real thing and this team had that no matter what the scoreboard said. They are and always will be Brothers in Basketball… Talk about having an impact!"

—Pat Langdon

**The goal of this book is not to just make an impact
but to make a MAJOR impact
on your life, your philosophy, and your game.**

CHAPTER 15

Create and Maintain a Quality Feeder System

Consistency is of the utmost importance.

Creating and maintaining a feeder system will supply your program with a strong base to build on. Of utmost importance is the existence of a consistent comprehensive grade three through grade twelve program.

In September and October of my senior year at Youngstown State University, the Girard Recreation Department hired me to start a youth basketball program for grades four, five, and six. I set up rosters, schedules, rules, practices and hired coaches. This was five years before I got the head-coaching job at Girard High School. The elementary players from my initial year then became ninth, tenth, and eleventh graders in my first year as head coach. I experienced firsthand the value of a consistent year-to-year approach to the game of basketball.

You must set up a system of checks and balances to ensure that your philosophy and fundamentally sound principles are followed throughout each facet of your program. Any inconsistencies which are found need to be rectified immediately. Each facet must mesh to ensure consistency. From year to year your program must maintain the same consistency.

Start each season by meeting with your coaches and re-defining your system. As head coach, go to the youth basketball program practices. Invite their teams to your skill sessions. Encourage your varsity players to attend practices at the lower level. You need to impress upon younger student-athletes they need to develop mental toughness, learn to handle frustration, and more importantly, overcome it.

Knowing your time is valuable, it is important to invest the time to build relationships with feeder-system coaches. Players in those programs will hopefully play for you someday.

To be consistent your entire feeder program (grades three through six, middle school, freshmen) must learn your offense and defense. Knowing your system is a great start. Knowing your plays is not nearly as important as executing your plays. It's all about execution.

Also, foster community interest in your program by running summer camps for youth in the area. Participants are divided into groups by grade. Groups will consist of participants in grades one to two, three to six, seven to nine, and ten through twelve. In our program this feeder system learns our rules of offense and defense. Again, this instills the elements of your program in potential student-athletes from an early age. Learning to execute your system and plays is a distinct advantage for these players in your program and can be a game changer in future seasons for your program. Overall basketball IQ is enhanced.

I personally run the summer camps and have created certificates that are presented to the participants in the summer program to encourage their development and interest in the sport (Refer to Appendix C). I am totally convinced that, beside the development of basketball skills, another positive effect of participation in youth basketball camps is establishing friendships and the feeling of camaraderie with the other campers. Therefore, I demand that every camper in every station be introduced by first name to every other camper and must learn their name. We switch stations during the week, and by the end of the camp, they have met and learned many new names of many new friends. Knowing the names of the other campers breaks the ice and facilitates the development of friendships with the other campers who share their interest in the sport. Parents have expressed appreciation for this opportunity their child was given to develop possible new friendships.

The importance of establishing a strong feeder system was exemplified by the 2020-2021 team that ended the season with a trip to the final four and with a 25-1 record. Five of our seven top players that season played together on the same travel team throughout their youth.

As noted throughout this book, the best way to develop potential as a player is to compete against elite competition no matter what age. So, involvement in a quality feeder program provides the kind of competitive environment and consistency which will enhance a player's future prospects in playing at the high school varsity level, and even at the next level after high school.

As an elite head coach, your primary goal is to impress upon the feeder system coaches that their most important role is to give their players the opportunity to compete in the highest-level tournaments available. By doing so, they will put their players in the best possible position for future success.

Basketball is a beautiful game when the five players on the court play with one heartbeat.

—Dean Smith
Hall of Fame NCAA Coach

NH

GBC

With a quality feeder system, you can achieve the consistency your program needs to be successful.

The chart below shows the progress made in the Girard program once a quality feeder system was established in 1975-1976. It takes time to turn a program around and establish your identity.

SUMMARY OF GIRARD HIGH SCHOOL BOYS BASKETBALL RECORD BEFORE AND AFTER FEEDER SYSTEM DEVELOPMENT

1953–1980
AVERAGED 6 WINS PER YEAR
NO GRADE SCHOOL PROGRAM

1980–1981
1 WIN—19 LOSSES
PLAYED ALL UNDERCLASSMEN

COACH BOB KRIZANCIC DEVELOPED COMPLETE PROGRAM (GRADES 4 THROUGH 12)

1981–1982
11 WINS—9 LOSSES

1982–1983
20 WINS—4 LOSSES

1983–1984
13 WINS—10 LOSSES

1984–1985
17 WINS—5 LOSSES

1985–1986
22 WINS—3 LOSSES

WON DISTRICT CHAMPIONSHIP

CHAPTER 16

Set the Pace—Be Positive

Tough times define you.

As William Jennings Bryan once said: "Destiny is not a matter of chance; destiny is a matter of choice. It is not something to wait for; it is something to be achieved." Invest time to create and improve your program. Be aware that you must expend consistent and constant energy to achieve a goal, and that energy is either given or taken. As the head coach, you need to be the one "giving" the energy. When you walk into a gym or team meeting, you must have the most energy, and it must be evident. On day one of official practice of the season, let it be known you are the coach, the parent figure, and the leader. Everyone in your program at every level must follow your lead.

To be truly competitive, your players must practice at game speed. You will be doing your players a great service by pushing them to their limits during practice. Practices develop habits of strategically evaluating and responding to actions on the court. They also provide an opportunity for your players to anticipate their teammates' actions and develop a sense of trust among the players on your team. If your practices are tough, your players will take the floor during games with the confidence needed to prevail against skilled opponents. By demanding your players play and practice at a sustained high energy level, you are on your way to developing mental toughness.

Tough times as a coach will invariably include weathering storms. In your coaching career, the probability is high that you will have to weather a storm or two. Your program may come under attack because of an indiscretion by a player, a booster, a person close to you, or an assistant. Chances are that you will face one of these situations when your program comes under fire. You have to weather the storm for your benefit and that of your basketball program. You have to be prepared to weather the storms that will undoubtedly come your way. From unforeseen events in my early career, I learned that you need to have a firewall. I needed to be a good person in every facet of my life. I always advise my players to make great decisions all the time. I can tell you that I am not a saint, but I try to make the best decisions that I can make in any situation.

I learned that the solid relationships that I have built helped me to weather at least three storms during my forty-two-year coaching career. That is why in this book, I am so adamant about cherishing your close friends and also building relationships with not only your players and staff, but also with the people in the community. They will be your support when the storms come in. People in your community will be much more apt to be on your side knowing that you are a good solid person and are a person of your word. When you do run into that storm, be as truthful as you can. **Don't hide** from it. Don't run from it. Your character and your integrity will get you through it.

I learned so much from these storms. They permanently affected my approach to my chosen career of coaching. I instinctively became more conscious of what was going on around me. I quickly understood the scope of my responsibility as head coach and, as a result, became much more vigilant.

It's often adversity that's needed to shine a light on our most significant growth opportunities. It can be more difficult to grow and develop when skies are blue, and life is utopian—but with storms comes potential. Show me a storm that you come out of, and I'll show you an opportunity to achieve things you didn't think were possible.

—Paul Epstein
Former NFL and NBA Business Executive,
Author, and Founder of Purpose Labs

Tough times for a coach can include dealing with injuries. For example, a couple of years ago we had to deal with a tough injury to one of our best starting players. He shattered a finger, and his chances of playing were fifty-fifty at best at tournament time. He ultimately missed four weeks of the season. When you deal with an injury, while you feel bad, as a coach you must control your emotions. Make sure all your players don't see one second of you feeling bad for either the player or the team. The injured player must understand they are getting better and coming back to play and they will be playing with a better team around them. Immediately tell the team the player will be out an extended period of time and hopefully back by tournament time. Be positive. Explain to your team this is a great opportunity for them to step up and get playing time. As a result, the team will be stronger overall and will have more depth. Conversation with your players should be positive. In 2013, when we won the state boys basketball championship our starting center, Brandon Fritts, was injured and did not play in the first fifteen games of the season. The players who received Brandon's minutes improved their game, and we were a better team at tournament time. So, look at the positive and not the negative every single time you have to face dealing with injuries. Brandon not only recovered to help us win the state championship, but he also played football for the University of North Carolina.

Our first loss was devastating in the 2021 season. It was especially devastating because we were undefeated and were one game away from the state title. The finality that the season was over was a terrible feeling for everyone involved. The locker room was extremely emotional and at that time I told my players that if it hurts that bad, then it meant that much to you. When we talked to the players, we focused on being undefeated, number one in the final AP poll, how much they accomplished and how proud their parents, the community, and the school were of them. We boarded the busses to return to the hotel and the coaches met as a staff at 11 PM. For the first ninety minutes, we talked about all the great things that happened this past season. At 12:30 AM our discussion totally changed to the future and the upcoming 2021-2022 season. We discussed personnel, what we had to work on, and got excited for the future. I was extremely impressed by the way my staff handled the loss, grieved the loss, and looked forward.

As the head coach, you must set the pace for the upcoming season and end the prior season on a positive note. Remind your players to accept that the tough times will define you. As Hall of Fame NFL player Archie Griffin noted regarding tough times, they won't stop you unless you stop yourself. "It is not the size of the dog in the fight but the size of the fight in the dog." Talk about the goals for the upcoming season and what the team can do to meet those goals. This approach to the team creates a bridge of positivity and focus that will carry your program forward from season to season.

Everything negative—pressure, challenges—
is all an opportunity for me to rise.

—Michael Jordan
Hall of Fame NBA Player

NH

It all starts with you as head coach—your attitude, your commitment, your energy!

CHAPTER 17

Develop Your Program– Evaluate and Adapt

When something in your program doesn't work, adjust but keep the core intact.

Once you have a clear vision of what you want to accomplish, be tenacious in developing an elite program. Seek out opportunities for growth by playing elite teams. My philosophy on "how to get better the quickest and most efficient way as a player and as a team" is to play against bigger, stronger, and older players and play the best possible teams in the state during the season. If your system isn't working, make adjustments in your program, but do not discard your basic philosophy. Always keep the core of your program intact and make adjustments in small increments. If you must fine-tune your program, seek input from your assistant coaches and your captains. You may be shocked at what you hear initially, but ultimately you will adapt. That is why constant, open communication is critical in developing your program.

Be passionate and committed to the end product. In developing my program, I am guided by the concept: "Desire plots the course, courage goes the distance, and commitment finishes the race." In developing your program you need to put in more time and effort than expected. Enforce upon your student-athletes that if they think they will only be practicing two hours at a time, they are wrong. They need to realize they need to be committed to putting in time before practice and after practice and even on off days. It is extremely important to your program that your players put in as much quality time as the vast majority of teams in the state. We tell our players that we must outwork everybody in the state of Ohio for us to be successful.

The 2020–2021 season, our record was 25-1, state semi-finalists, number one in the final AP poll for the state of Ohio, and without a doubt one of the hardest working teams I have ever coached. The majority of our practices ran from 2:45 PM to 5 PM daily and at least three days a week the majority of our varsity players came back to the gym at 8:30 at night and put in at least ninety more minutes working on skills and shooting. I was never so impressed with a team's commitment to excellence. I have always been inspired by the effort and commitment of all my players and it continues to get better and better.

Sometimes a reality check is needed so your players and coaches know where they are with respect to their level of play. In our system, we use a players' evaluation form to accomplish this (see Appendix C).

In developing your program, if there is something that you believe will work to your benefit, look to the businesses in your community and your program's booster club for support and assistance. You may also obtain aid from your school system or even local banks, as I did with my drug and alcohol-testing program that I mentioned earlier in this book. The key is if you have an idea that you believe would benefit your program, don't abandon it. It may make a world of difference to the quality of your program and make a significant impact on your team members.

When developing your program, in-season tournament play is important. You as head coach must be vigilant in searching for possible tournaments for your team and marketing your team to those tournaments. There are two different kinds of in-season tournament play. One type of in-season tournament, such as the Beachball Classic in South Carolina and the Arby's Classic in Tennessee, covers some or most of your expenses. The other type of in-season tournament, predominantly during the holidays in warm weather states, is one in which you must cover most if not all your expenses including travel, lodging, meals, and sometimes entry fee. Our program has been to the Arby's Tennessee Classic six times, and every time we return we are a better team because of the bonding and the great competition. If attending an out-of-town in-season tournament is not in your budget, then consider a local tournament. In my early years at Girard, we even started our own four-team tournament and called it the Christmas Classic so our players would get that experience of competition and especially tournament competition.

Your players may need to obtain employment during basketball season. As a coach, you can approach employers in the community and discuss the possibility of your players obtaining jobs they can work around their basketball schedule. I routinely meet with proprietors and owners of small businesses who now employ many of our players. The players can achieve some level of financial independence and responsibility for themselves and still not miss out on the other positive benefits of being in our basketball program. This is a win-win in that you find jobs for your players who need work and also get the opportunity to dictate the hours that they do work. Many employers have supported our basketball program because of the positive experience they have had with one of our players as their employee.

Finally, in developing your program you need to implement rules and regulations on the use of social media. For instance, consider a rule requiring your players to stay off social media during basketball season unless approved by a coach. If you do use social media, do not use Twitter, Instagram, Facebook, Snapchat, or any other social media to make a comment about an opposing player or team. The end result is you will be protecting your players from the negative possible fallout of social commentary which may come back to adversely impact themselves, the team, the school, or future employment. You will instill in them an approach to social media that will serve them well for the rest of their adult lives.

Your program must have an overriding purpose which is clearly visible, and which teaches lessons beyond winning.

—Don Meyer
Hall of Fame NCAA Coach

Basketball Program

I. Coaching Philosophies

    A. Discipline
    B. Fundamentally-Sound
    C. Better Conditioned Team
    D. Smart Role Players
    E. Defensive Pressure
    F. Percentage Shot (Shot Selection)

II. Strategies for Developing a Program

    A. Cohesiveness Through Entire Program
    B. Junior High Program
        1. Discipline
        2. Defensive Fundamentals-Man - to - Man
        3. Ball-Handling
    C. Off-Season
        1. Weight Training Program
        2. Play Against Best Possible Competition
        3. Shooting
    D.. Get as Many People Involved as Possible

III. Game Strategies
    A. Play Our Game-Control Tempo
    B. Total Organization
    C. Take Advantage of Others Team Weaknesses
        1. Mismatches
        2. Speed
        3. Heighth
    D. Intimidate by our Style of play

IV. Community & School Involvement
    A. Open Pep Rally
    B. Senior Citizens
    C. Fan Involvement

V. Public Relations

    A. Meet the Team Nite
    B. Tip-off Dinner or Breakfast
    C. Posters
    D. Excellent Rapport with Media
    E. City Officials

This is an outline of a Basketball Program similar to what I used as a foundation for our program. We have slightly modified this original plan over the years. Note the defined goals!

CHAPTER 18

The Synergy of Relationships

The continued success of an elite winning program depends on many people and organizations.

Once you have the core established (values, philosophy, and identity) you can concentrate your efforts on attaining elite status for your program. You now need to branch out and generate increased support for your program.

You as head coach and creator of your program are the spark that keeps the interest and support for your program alive. Your continued effort is required. However, you cannot create an elite athletic program on your own. As noted in previous chapters, it requires the enthusiastic and continuous support of many people and organizations.

Therefore, for the well-being of your program, when it comes to relationships more is better. Create and develop positive, healthy relationships with those you come into contact with and with everyone involved in your program. Establish, develop, and value those relationships.

In addition, it is important for you to realize the greater the number of people who carry a positive impression of your program, the more support you will have. They will be present at games to provide encouragement and support for your team and will attend fundraising activities to generate financial support as well. Their involvement in your program will ensure that your program, and especially your team, can be competitive and make it to the mountaintop year after year.

The term for generating this ever-increasing support is **synergy** which is based upon the concept that the whole is greater than the sum of the parts. As educator, author, and businessman Steven Covey said, "When properly understood, synergy is the highest activity in all of life."

I believe that cultivating relationships and synergy are synonymous in our program. I am of the firm belief that the sum of all our supporters and our relationships make our program greater than all other programs.

To develop such strong support, it is therefore extremely important for you and those involved in your program to invest time in the off-season and summer. While the team devotes time to preparing for the challenges of the upcoming season, you as head coach can enthusiastically educate others about your beliefs, your goals, your philosophy, and your program. In addition, your assistant coaches, players, their families and friends, and countless others with whom they interact can also spread the word about your program and spark interest. These activities exponentially grow the ranks of your fans and supporters by positive comments in their conversations. They can highlight the successful program you have created and its positive impact on student-athletes and the community. A personal invitation by them to view a website or attend an upcoming game or function can be extremely effective.

Once established, these relationships must be acknowledged as valuable assets of your program and are essential to its continued success and longevity. Your program must strive to maintain and grow its level of support throughout the season and from year to year. You can keep their interest alive by communicating through emails, your website, newsletters, and press guides. Your booster club is an important source of information for your parents, school, community, and supporters. They can send out mailers, post on social media, and maintain a website reflecting upcoming fundraisers and events.

While communication is key, invitations to the community to participate in activities such as summer camps for youth, golf outings, and community car washes keep the program and your goals for the upcoming season a priority for parents, students, and the community. Again, your booster program is essential in this regard.

Another significant element to maintaining support for your program is to express gratitude to all those who dedicate their efforts to its success. Distributing small gifts of appreciation, such as team t-shirts, mugs, and drinking glasses are a great way of saying, "Thanks." Impress upon your supporters that they are an important part of your program. When Mentor won the state championship in 2013, I ordered championship rings for those who had substantially contributed to the success of our team. I did this to express our total appreciation.

Making every single supporter feel important is essential to building a great program. Our culture is not just our tradition. It is the people and players who carry it on!

At the end of the day, if it's all about the ring and the trophy, you lose the most valuable thing, and it's the group of people and the relationships that are established, of people working together to accomplish something they couldn't accomplish on their own.

—Billy Donovan
NBA Coach

When the Girard team won the state championship
in 1993, the community support was phenomenal. To
my team's amazement, twenty-five thousand people
lined the street as our bus proceeded to the high school
and the whole gym was packed when we entered.

CHAPTER 19

Be Transparent with Your Words and Actions

You must take action to convey your character and the quality of your program to everyone.

Early in my coaching career, I learned that everyone will have an opinion about you and your program, including parents, administrators, and your community. Your words and actions determine how people formulate their opinions about your program. By being involved in community events your character and the quality of your program will become known to everyone. Our program is involved in activities such as judging the chili cook-off at the Community Senior Center, helping unload food trucks at United Way, assisting seniors to move for the Council on Aging, or overseeing developmentally disabled students from a neighborhood school play basketball.

Always educate your community regarding your program. The proper use of an up-to-date presence on social media is important for your program's existence and longevity. Developing and maintaining a website can be provided by your booster club.

Regarding your program understand and enforce that first impressions matter. It must be obvious to anyone on their first impression you have an elite program. This first impression must confirm you exude mental toughness and a strong work ethic that is second to none. Every aspect of your program must reflect this, and everyone associated with your program must be held to this high standard.

Uniforms, shoes, and accessories such as gym bags, practice shirts, hoodies, and knit caps contribute to the team's identity and self-confidence. This is also an area where your booster organization can help. Hang pennants and display trophies in the locker room where all those entering are reminded of past achievements and the winning tradition of your program. Use motivational material to keep your team mentally focused on striving, achieving, and having positive outcomes. You can send out positive, motivational communications to your team through social media like Twitter. I have found by doing this daily they have made a difference in motivating team players. On the wall in our locker room, I have hung a poster showing Coach John Wooden's *Pyramid of Success*, and I refer to it throughout the season to remind our players of what they need to do to be successful.

One of my favorite motivational sayings is, "Envy our past; fear your future!" To my players, one of my favorite motivational sayings is "Don't be arrogant, but be confident."

It is extremely important to constantly acknowledge your players who are on the bench. These include players such as your sixth, seventh, eighth, and ninth men on the team. Make them aware that you appreciate and know how hard they work, the effort they put into practices, and improvements they have made.

Being transparent with this action is important. Your bench players will be getting less playing time. The last thing you need is to have your bench players not give maximum effort in practice because they are not getting playing time.

Since you demand so much of your players, it is also important to be transparent in your actions towards their parents. I learned this in my early days of coaching as I closed my practices at first. After much thought I realized that parents needed to understand my words and actions, so I made a change in my program and allowed parents to watch practice as long as they did not interfere. Then I made practices totally open as long as the parents called me and let me know they were coming. I realized this transparency was important so parents would know that I did not have any hidden agenda. Through my actions and transparency, everyone realized I am an open book.

Transparency breeds legitimacy.

—John Maxwell
Author, Speaker, and Pastor

SECTION 2:
HOW TO BUILD AN ELITE ORGANIZATIONAL CULTURE

Overview

Emphasize Mental Toughness

- Create a winning philosophy—expect to win
- Establish the right culture right away
- Believe and invest time
- Seek out opportunities for growth by playing elite teams
- Set the pace and be positive
- Be tenacious
- Be passionate and committed
- Create and maintain "elite" relationships
- Be open and educate the community about your program and involve community leaders in it
- A consistent "feeder system" is essential
- Develop the system, evaluate, and adapt
- First impressions matter

See appendices A through K at the back of the book for further information and relevant documents.

SECTION 3

HOW TO DEVELOP A STRONG FOUNDATION FOR SUCCESS

The ideal way to win a championship is step by step.
—Phil Jackson
Hall of Fame NBA Coach

An elite basketball program requires your involvement in your program not only four to five months or even seven or eight months of the year, but rather year-round. You must monitor your program and your players the entire year. Even if they are in another sport, you need to guide your players to increase their strength, skill level, explosiveness, and speed.

This section provides a month-to-month breakdown of what we do as a program. It presents basketball skill training, summer ball, scheduling, and booster club fundraisers. With the support of our booster club, we are even engaged in team activities in the summer with such events as a golf outing and cookout. We have taken our team to science museums and engage in community service. It is a year-round program designed to attain elite status.

There can be no coasting. Your energy level has to be high twelve months of the year.

CHAPTER 20

Off-season

Develop a habit, an attitude, of mental toughness.
Mental toughness is the psychological edge or advantage
to overcome frustration and adversity, along with the
confidence and presence to compete at the highest level.
There should be a "no fear" factor in your game and in life.

April

You cannot change the past, but you hold
the power to shape the future.

Remember how I stressed the need to develop and recognize important relationships? I recommend that you work with the booster group to arrange for a banquet in the beginning of April, about two to three weeks after the last tournament game. The purpose of this banquet is to honor the team and its accomplishments during the season that just ended. You should recognize the contributions of the cheerleaders, team managers, athletic trainers, and booster club officers. This banquet also provides you with an opportunity to talk about the upcoming off-season of April through November.

This is a time to impress upon the team members the importance of grades, ACT/SAT scores, and community service. For all players we provide ACT/SAT classes one hour prior to open gym twice a week. You can explain AAU programs and their role in teaching student-athletes the fundamentals of the game and providing them with all-important playing time. In addition, to serve as an extension of your program, advise them to get involved in an AAU program that highlights man-to-man defense, running, and discipline. You can inform them how AAU works, the number of players on a team, the cost, as well as pros and cons.

Explain the off-season and how it affects basketball. Advise the players of jobs available through local businesses who will work around practice schedules and how jobs affect their off-season time.

Lastly, you can share that you expect the team to begin to get stronger and more explosive in April through the use of additional training at area facilities. We have used independent training facilities in our area as well as the P90X approach to strength training. The P90X strength program calls for six consecutive days of workouts, three of weights, stretching, yoga, plyos, and Kenpo X. Strength and conditioning training does change from year to year based on recent developments in the field. It is important for team players to get involved in a program that measures progress both in their physical strength and in their basketball skills. Also during this month, a demonstration is presented for parents and players regarding bands, core work, use of equipment, and proper strength and conditioning.

In April, you should also meet with your staff to review the past season. During this meeting suggestions can be made by team players and personnel. Use this time to make minor adjustments. Determine if there are any incoming freshmen who are ready to play for the junior varsity or varsity squads. For those players you have identified, schedule meetings with parents and players. Discuss with them the possible promotion from ninth grade play to prepare them for the summer months, preseason, and season. In promoting a freshman player to the junior varsity or varsity level, I want to be sure they are ready physically, mentally, academically, and socially.

Regarding meeting with parents and players, I want to impress on you something that you should never forget. As mentioned before, anytime you meet with players or parents, have an assistant with you if at all possible.

Next, during the meeting you will be discussing the first day of open gym with parents and players in attendance. You should review next year's scheduled opponents and most importantly the state's requirement to be eligible to play. The OHSAA requires five full classes. In addition, our players take a strength and conditioning class in the last period of the day as well as a nutrition class.

During our April open gyms we encourage the presence and participation of alumni home from college and former area basketball players. We also encourage local high school players to participate as this will have a more positive impact on our open gyms. I notify local coaches by email or text of dates and times of our open gyms.

During these open gyms, a coach should address all players in the gym before every open gym and stress the difference between cheap fouls and playing hard. Stress that cheap fouls will not be tolerated whatsoever. The rules in open gym are man-to-man only with no fouls called. The reason no fouls are called is to develop toughness. This is the reason we explicitly say: no cheap fouls. During these open gyms we typically play four-on-four on three different courts.

Another method you can use to develop mental and physical toughness in your players is how you define a "win" in games played during open gym. To finalize the game and validate the win in open gym, we use a creative approach. The last player to make the "game-winning" point must make an additional free throw. If the free throw is missed, that team goes back two points, and the game continues. If you win the game a second time and miss the second free throw, that team automatically loses the game. Approaching open gym this way makes the person who scores the last to be the most important player. In addition, it puts game pressure on the players during open gym in April, long before the season begins. It also gives you a strategy as to who scores the final point in open gym.

The following are important activities for **April**:

1. Have a banquet to honor the team.
2. Order extra medals for all players, coaches, and support people.
3. Begin strength and conditioning program.

4. Open gym and 4-man sessions begin; play man-to-man, four-on-four, and three-on-three with no fouls called to develop mental toughness.
5. Get as many players as possible on AAU teams.
6. Meet with new booster officers.
7. Identify incoming freshman who may be able to play at JV or varsity level.

May

Greatness is not built in a day; greatness is built daily.

Training kicks into high gear in May, as does involvement of the players together as a team. In May, the weather is your friend, and student-athletes are now more available to train with the school year coming to a close. This is the time to work on improving each player and creating a cohesive team.

Team activities such as car washes are great for getting the group to engage in meaningful activities that not only benefit the group financially but also develop camaraderie. The presale of car wash tickets guarantees revenue or donations and also ensures team cohesiveness.

Strength and conditioning training is also increased at this time. This should include core work incorporating the use of resistance bands for squats and squat thrusts. It is time to engage in some meaningful competition.

Open gyms provide an opportunity for our student-athletes to compete against our ex-players and players from other communities. You must call around to other schools to see what teams are available and the quality of players for this competition. Summer leagues and shootouts in your area are also a great opportunity for your student-athletes to develop their skills.

May is also time to get ready for summer camps that you run for lower grades in your school system. These camps are important as they provide the feeder groups we talked about in other areas of this book. Remember, consistency in your program from level to level is essential. These camps are typically three weeks and for grades K-2, three to six, seven to nine, and high school levels. You can let the community know about these camps by publicizing them in newspapers, camp flyers, and school websites. I discovered using technology was one of my deficiencies and rely on my younger coaches when it comes to using social media and technology to our advantage. This includes advertising our camps as well as promoting our team and players.

May is also the time to prepare the scrimmage schedule that you will play in November. The goal is to arrange scrimmages with diverse teams while providing the best possible competition. No three-way scrimmages, however. In my opinion I try to stay away from three-way team scrimmages. This is because I do not like my team sitting out a quarter. At the end of a three-way team scrimmage, it always seems you did not get the complete work out you had planned.

During May when your players are playing in their AAU games, it is advisable that you as their coach attempt to attend those games.

A coaches meeting is highly recommended in May. Use this time to discuss the top ten to twelve players, the summer programs, and personnel. We discuss what improvements players have to make. We also use this time to secure alumni and players to coach summer games. We also rate our top ten to twelve players at this time.

In May we meet again with parents and players individually and discuss expectations regarding skill, strength, explosiveness, and attitude. We reinforce the importance of their academics such as the players' GPA, and ACT/SAT. We also impress upon them the need to develop leadership skills, and to be involved in community service.

Finally, May is the month to let the college coaches know your players' AAU schedule from May through July. Also inform the college coaches of your team camps, the summer league schedule, and your open-gym schedule.

The following is an example of what a head coach can expect to address in the month of May as leader of the team and program:

My athletic director called me with the news that Cincinnati Princeton invited us to a tournament this Christmas. With Mentor's commitment to playing in the tournament, three of the four best teams in the state of Ohio would be competing at this event. My athletic director knew that this invitation meant a lot to me and asked if I was interested. I said that I was, but that I would need to address the cost of travel, hotels, meals, and incidental expenses. I immediately conversed with our booster officers and within 45 minutes we committed to playing in this high-profile Christmas tournament. Committing to this tournament was dependent on a number of factors. Our athletic director inquired as to whether my team was able to play the already scheduled game against Warren Harding, a team of highly skilled players, and then commit to a two day tournament schedule of two additional games against other highly competitive teams after a four hour bus ride to get to the tournament. Fortunately, the athletic director and I shared the same level of commitment to the goals for the program: high-profile showcases and a high-profile Christmas tournament. Also, because of the costs involved, a great working relationship with the booster club was a necessity. Once we were committed, this involvement in such a prestigious Christmas tournament sets the tone for the season as it provides the team with a great incentive to work hard during the off-season.

The following are important activities for **May**:

1. Organize summer elementary and middle school/junior high camps.
2. Open gym and 4-man sessions continue.
3. Contact alum and area college players regarding open gyms.
4. Participate in community service events.
5. Commit your team to summer leagues and June shootouts.
6. Start to assemble your November scrimmage schedule.
7. Send college coaches the June and July schedules of your players.

Concentration and mental toughness are the margins of victory.

—Bill Russell
Hall of Fame NBA Player

All year long, but especially in the off-season, we work
hard on fundamentals: shooting, defense, and ball
handling. We want to be fundamentally strong.

CHAPTER 21

The Importance of Summer

**Basketball players are made in the summer
and perform in the winter.**

June

Never mistake activity for achievement.

—John Wooden
Hall of Fame NCAA Coach

Basketball is in full swing in June as you are now able to play in leagues, basketball shootouts, and in various camps. It is time to focus on perfecting your players' game skills. Stress to your players that during practices and games there should be no wasted possessions. Stress also no wasted dribbles (i.e. east to west vs. north to south). Finally stress that you must become a "five-tool player." Explain the concept of "five tools"—shoot the three, drive to the basket/create/finish, pass to open teammates, handle the ball, and play defense. Defensively, we stress to our players that you should be able to guard a big man or a guard so that you are flexible. Flexibility is essential to being an effective player. We don't label.

June is the time to stress strength and conditioning. Your student-athletes should be serious and spending two days a week in agilities, for instance the sand pit, ring of fire, and medicine balls. Core work is also in these workouts to develop the needed muscle tone and flexibility. You must also impress on your players during the summer season that they should play with game speed, explosiveness, and mental toughness. This makes them game ready.

Basketball skill development requires at least two hours a day of practice in the gym with just your team members. We also get together once or twice during the summer to rate our players. We attend shootouts and team camps at the University of Toledo, the University of Cincinnati, Cleveland State University, the University of Akron, Denison University, and various other locations depending on the quality of teams participating. June is also the time to demonstrate and work on shooting drills. These drills may include five-minute drills, Mullins drills, Gonzaga drills, and The Ohio State University drills which should all stress game speed shooting.

My players were asked in a questionnaire by a local paper after winning the state title in 2013 what their most favorite part was about Mentor basketball and what they would remember. The players confirmed that playing in summer leagues and shootouts, they gained so much more than just advancing their skill set. They talked about June and July, and in addition to the hot weather, they spoke about the large number of games, the overnighters at basketball camps and shootouts, and the camaraderie that is developed as a team. These experiences are what they valued most. On the inside of their championship rings, this group of players had engraved the word Brotherhood.

The following are important activities for **June:**

1. Engage in quality competition—leagues/shootouts.
2. Run summer feeder camps.
3. Schedule 1-2 overnight camps to promote camaraderie.
4. Promote booster club golf outing and seek sponsors.
5. Engage in skill sessions with your players.
6. Have your staff rate players 1-2 times in June.

July

The best competition I have is against myself to become better.

—John Wooden
Hall of Fame NCAA Coach

In July make a personal appearance at local AAU games in which your student-athletes are playing. During the AAU summer games there is a limit to the number of teammates from the same school that are allowed to play on each team. Therefore, this is an informal opportunity for you to meet the parents of AAU players from other programs and interact with their coach.

Our players' involvement in football has changed how we conduct summer practices. This is especially true in July, when football practices begin. Due to the overlap of the summer commitment of our players, developing a great relationship with your high school's football coach is essential. This interaction between the head coaches from each sport makes it easier for two sport players to honor their commitments. This eliminates players' concerns about pleasing both coaches.

Make sure to continue your conditioning program in July. Our basketball players find it beneficial to attend football agilities practice two days a week at 7:00 a.m. As mentioned above, agility stations include the sand pit, ring of fire, resistance bands, medicine ball, and agilities. These agilities have been found essential for both sports. We have found when players engage in these agility drills, they improve their footwork, defense, change of direction, speed, coordination, and explosiveness.

Regarding your players that are participating in other Fall sports, wish them good luck. Make sure to discuss their status with the team so that they have no questions as they begin their Fall season.

July is also the time to have a second car wash to help defray players' in-season costs. Following the car wash have a cookout which is a great way to end the summer season. These cookouts are usually held at a park in the community. In addition, July is most likely to be the month when the booster club organizes a golf outing.

Explain the dead period and what the players can do to enhance their game. The dead period consists of the upcoming time where no formal or informal basketball activities can occur with any of the coaching staff. In Ohio, the entire month of August is the dead period. Stress this dead period is a wonderful time to see what independent development the players can achieve. Explain they have thirty-one days to become more skilled, get stronger, quicker, more explosive; and increase their flexibility.

So, June or July, and especially July, is when your players develop overall toughness. When they are playing two, three, or four games a day during basketball camps, the weather is hot, and there are no breaks. They are developing character, toughness, and great relationships with their teammates.

Remind your players that:

To play the game is great; to win the game is greater. To love the game is the greatest of all. "No fear" and passion to compete must be what you're about.

The following are important activities for **July:**

1. Attend summer fundraisers.
2. Watch your players' AAU games.
3. Prepare for the 31-day dead period in August.
4. Communicate with multi-sport athletes and their coaches.
5. Continue skill sessions for players.
6. Film summer league games and have a few film sessions with your team.

August

If it doesn't challenge you, it doesn't change you.

—Fred DeVito
Fitness Expert and Entrepreneur

Embrace change!

August is a good month to judge the work ethic of your team members. The Ohio High School Athletic Association {OHSAA) rules prohibit coaches from interacting with players regarding their basketball skills during the month of August. This is known as the dead period. Players must work on their skills independently. We encourage our alumni who are currently playing basketball in college to interact with our players and work on developing our players during August.

During meetings with the players, reiterate the requirements to be on the team. Remind them that during the school year team members must take five full classes, and strongly advise them to take six classes the first semester of the school year. Tell your team members to give a copy of their class schedule to the coaching staff to verify they are enrolled in five classes. This is important because we have found at least three times, team members had counted Phys. Ed. as a full class. Had we not caught this error, it would have rendered that player ineligible to play in the second semester. The sixth class ensures that, should this happen or if they fail a class, the player would still be eligible to play. In addition, the review of our players' class schedules stresses our program's focus on the importance of academic achievement as well as athletic competition.

Enforce that players must be enrolled in a strength and conditioning class during the school year. We emphasize the goal of working out must be to gain strength, speed, and explosiveness. Explosiveness is a high priority. We recommend our players work with resistance bands and continue skill work on their own at various local gyms and sports facilities. We also provide jump and stretch boards to the players to take home in August. In the past we have used programs such as FlexBands, P90X, and Dick Hartzell's Jump Stretch.

The end of the summer season is a good time to bring everyone together. Having a cook-out is a good opportunity to accomplish this. Invite the incoming tenth, eleventh, and twelfth graders, as well as any ninth graders joining the team and their parents. This is a great time to meet and socialize. Reiterate September and October expectations and the requirements to qualify for inclusion on the team. Again, stress players must take five classes and meet the required grade and GPA expectations. Let them know there will be ACT/SAT help available to them and a study table. At this cookout introduce the officers of the booster group and allow them to present their organization, goals, and fund-raisers.

Make sure the parents and players are informed regarding curfew times and when they start. In preseason this may be optional, and parents can opt in or out for their child until the season begins. In my experience usually 100 percent of the parents are on board. Also, during this cookout discuss the perils of drinking, drugs, sex, social media, internet, cell phone, and pictures.

At this cookout, remind everyone it is time to consider athletic physicals. Because the season is still two months from beginning, this gives players advance notice to make appointments.

Obtain permission to include the parents and players on the phone lists. Provide the emails of coaches, players, and the athletic director, and especially include the incoming freshmen and sophomores from whom permission is obtained.

Also introduce to the group how they will receive notice about games, practices, and changes to the schedule. We use the One Call Now system. This system presently costs the booster club $120 per year. This service allows one parent and one team member to be included. Make participation mandatory to ensure its effectiveness. It is a wonderful system where the coach can place one call to the system and direct this communication to specific people or the entire group. This makes communication easy and efficient. As a backup. our varsity players are in a group text with our varsity coaching staff.

Finally, impress upon the team members the importance of showing support for other teams at the school by attending other Fall school activities, including athletic and academic events.

Summer is the time you find out your players' and team's strengths and weaknesses. Once you do that, you have the next four months to change those weaknesses into strengths and prepare yourself to compete at your highest level.

The following are important activities for **August**:

1. Stress to your players how essential it is to develop a great work ethic on your own.
2. Attend the team cookout and outline the program.
3. Strength and conditioning programs should be in full gear.
4. One Call Now—get new names and parents' information.
5. Review class schedules to ensure eligibility.
6. Remind players to arrange for physical exams.

If you're not getting better in the summer, you're wasting your time.

—Chris Bosh
Hall of Fame NBA Player

Cleveland.com

CR

The exhilaration of tournament wins can probably be attributed to how hard you work in the summer.

CHAPTER 22

Fall Preseason Planning

This is the time to get into great basketball shape-increase strength and improve skills.

September

A winning effort begins with preparation.

—Joe Gibbs
Hall of Fame NFL Coach

In Ohio, you are allowed to start your Fall preseason open gyms in September. You are allowed four-man workouts and it is a perfect time to get into great basketball shape. Other than that, coaches are not permitted to give instructions to the players during open gyms, although they can be present.

As previously mentioned, to be truly competitive, your players must be on a strength and conditioning program. A number of your players may be on their own programs. As a coach, you must check on their progress. All good strength and conditioning programs measure results, such as vertical jump, increasing the weights lifted, explosiveness, and speed. I recommend you stop in and watch your players work out at their respective strength and conditioning facilities. At this time meet with and talk to their strength and conditioning coach.

The Fall preseason, including September and October, is a chance for your team captains to act as captain-type mini-coaches and gives them an opportunity to exert their authority. Captains of the team can help develop young players. They set the tone to get other players in the gym to do extra sessions such as shooting, ball handling, and strengthening exercises to improve their game skills. Captains are in charge of open gyms. They are responsible for keeping order and drawing the line when playing hard enters the realm of cheap and dirty. Therefore, as was mentioned before, the end of August or early September is the time for coaches to meet with the captains of the team. At this meeting, have a heart-to-heart conversation and delegate more control to your captains. Express to them that as a result of their actions and leadership they can make a vast difference in their team and in the season by being engaged in these next two months.

After summer basketball leagues, basketball shootouts, and three months of high-quality basketball, we believe that the beginning of September is the time to rate our players again. The coaching staff and players each rate the top 12 players in priority order. We found the coaches' and players' ratings have always been extremely close. This gives our players a great indication of where they are in our program (See Appendix F).

During this time of the year, we make sure all our team members understand how important community service is for admission into the next educational level after high school. We set up opportunities for community service for our players at such places as the Mentor Senior Center, where they help serve lunch and the Council on Aging, where players assist the elderly. They also help at Broadmoor School for the Developmentally Disabled and participate in their homecoming game in October. To show appreciation for senior members of our community our team visits Heartland Home for the Aged on Valentine's Day and some holidays. During these visits, each individual player spends time with a senior.

We also emphasize the importance of nutrition at this time. We do not want to wait to stress nutrition until November because we have then lost valuable time needed to develop good habits. We impress upon our players that proper hydration and nutrition can greatly enhance their game. We set up a meeting with a nutritionist regarding what to eat, when to eat, and weight gain. We also make certain our players understand that they can replace everything they've lost in competition within forty-five minutes by ingesting proper proteins and fluids. Your high school staff will usually have an instructor well-versed in nutrition to address this with your team members.

The month of September is the time to set up speakers to address the power of choice in important areas of life as well as communication and leadership skills. Speakers we have used in the past in this regard include the Mentor chief of police, a municipal judge, a counselor for an addiction and drug-dependency program, our superintendent of schools, and physicians from area hospitals. Speakers may also include business leaders for professional sport organizations such as the Cleveland Cavaliers, veterans of foreign wars, presidents of the United Way, and our own state representative.

During the Fall preseason open gyms continue. Core work, resistance bands and other strength and conditioning drills are still important. We also start to run more and do full court ladders. A great preseason conditioner is three-on-three full court, but we also run four-on-four and five-on-five during this period.

Curfew is set at 11:30 p.m. on weekends, and players are not allowed to use their cell phones to call in. They must use their home phone or their parents' cell phones. As was mentioned before, curfew in September and October is optional, and we make sure that each parent knows this by making an announcement at our August picnic. In the past, no parent has actually ever opted out of a curfew set for September and October. Parents actually love it.

Seniors are reminded of opportunities provided through the Greater Cleveland Basketball Coaches Association game and Fall Showcases. We highly encourage our seniors to play in as many Fall Showcases as they can to get exposure from college coaches. I recommend the showcases that have a significant number of college coaches in attendance. Our booster club will usually cover one or two entry fees per senior attending.

During this time study tables are ongoing two to three days a week (one hour prior to open gym), and the senior team members are assisted with preparing for the ACT and SAT. Coaches and qualified parents help players with subjects such as math, science, chemistry, biology, and social studies. Another important feature of our program is geared toward preparing our student-athletes to further their education and for employment opportunities. Communication and leadership skills are addressed by a professor from a local community college. We also conduct mock job interviews for this purpose.

The following are important activities for **September**:

1. Coaches rate the players.
2. Start 30-minute talks from outside speakers on life skills.
3. 4-man sessions and open gym continue.
4. Check grades and schedule tutors for academic assistance.
5. Distribute ACT/SAT prep material and make sure juniors take the test in the Fall.
6. Initiate proper nutrition and hydration habits.

October

Failure is not fatal, but failure to change might be.

—John Wooden
Hall of Fame NCAA Coach

October is the time to focus on public relations in preparation for the upcoming season. Through the booster club we publish an annual poster of the team. These are distributed to local businesses in the area as well as to those who support our booster program. In addition, it is time to address game programs and media releases.

It is also time to order basketballs and make sure we have adequate practice equipment. When working with your booster club, if they have the financial ability to absorb the cost, inform them of the number of polos, fleeces, and warm-ups for this season's team.

The 11:30 p.m. curfew on weekends for the team is still in place in October.

During October, we sponsor elementary school basketball clinics every Saturday for grades one to two and three to six. Our players are required to assist at these clinics to help perpetuate our program.

As we are still providing study tables for our players one hour before every practice, October is now the time to check grades of the players. This is the time to identify the players who are academically struggling and possibly becoming ineligible to play.

Another important condition affecting eligibility to play is the requirement for athletic physicals. These physicals must be turned in at this time to the coaches in preparation for the upcoming season.

Scrimmages and in-season games require bus trips, and schedules for traveling must now be set up in advance. These bus trips can be set up by designated assistant coaches. After travel schedules are completed, we have a coaches' meeting to review the season practice schedule, personnel, and basketball drills.

Because continuity is of utmost importance to a successful basketball program, October is the time to start monitoring seventh and eighth grade practices. Every coach in our program must be implementing our program's game plays so student-athletes become skilled in their execution.

Advise your staff of opportunities for professional development that present themselves at this time. October is the month for Coaches Clinics, for example, clinics by Nike, the Greater Cleveland Basketball Association, or various colleges.

Do not forget open gym is still taking place. This is the time to continue conditioning, core work, and resistance bands.

Also, a schedule needs to be finalized for our team pregame meals. Dates must be set with local restaurants and catering businesses. Again, the booster club can assist in this regard.

Agendas and transportation need to be arranged for the Christmas tournament. At every Christmas tournament to which we have been invited, we have faced some of the best teams in the state and country.

The following are important activities for **October**:

1. Continue the lecture circuit of professionals to your athletes—30 mins.
2. Make sure you have 5 quality scrimmages and referees for November.
3. Attend coaching clinics and remind your staff.
4. Continue curfew.
5. Constantly remind players that their physicals must be turned in by the end of October.
6. Attend Fall sports games.
7. Continue monitoring grades.

I believe that good things come to those who work.

—Wilt Chamberlin
Hall of Fame NBA Player

Plan in advance for such items as uniforms,
warm-ups, fleece, shoes, and equipment. They
contribute to the elite identity of a team.

CHAPTER 23

The Significance of November

Getting Ready for the First Game and Regular Season

You will never regret working too hard; you will always regret not working hard enough. You cannot get back time.

November is a very important month. This is the time to select your team, release players, and define the roles of each team member. Most importantly for the season ahead, this is the time to reemphasize your philosophy of hard work and teamwork with your team members.

Releasing players from your program is probably one of the most difficult things you will have to do as a coach. Do not make the mistake of keeping players because you like them or because you think that they will be devastated by getting released. It is so much worse if they stay on a team, do not get a lot of opportunities, and work tirelessly without reward. With that being said, in the past we have retained some players because we knew it would be good for them. You have to be dead honest, and transparent in regard to their playing time and their role on the team.

You will have twelve to fifteen players who will think that they can start and be in the game rotation. By the third or fourth week in November, you will have to pick your starters. In addition, you must designate who will be your sixth, seventh, eighth, and ninth rated player. There will be some players who will not get playing time, but that is just the reality of the game. Again, being transparent and open and explaining the reasons for the decision will ensure that your players understand. Explain to them this may not remain all season. I discuss with players that the majority of years I have coached, the starting lineup can change, as well as the rotation. Be aware some players will become complacent, and others will work harder than they ever have. Some players may move into the starting lineup, and some may move into the rotation. Persistence, dedication, effort, and execution will determine a player's involvement.

Films are helpful as films do not lie. Sit down with your team and go over what you expect as far as hustle, toughness, skill level, who should be getting the shots, and what a good shot consists of. Make sure as you go into the season, these issues are clear and there are no questions whatsoever. It will help you as a coach, and your players as well, to know what they need to do to get playing time and to be a better player.

Players have been released at all levels of the game. Remember, Michael Jordan was released as a sophomore in high school. He didn't get a lot of playing time his junior year. Michael Jordan came back and arguably became one of the greatest basketball players of all time. Remember people develop at different stages in life. Some players develop and are strong in eighth or ninth grade; some aren't ready until the first or second year of college. If you do release a player, or a player does not get playing time, you need to tell that player what they have to do to earn it. We have had numerous players who have been released at every single level or have remained on the bench and received zero playing time, in seventh, eighth, ninth grades, or the junior varsity level. Some of these players advanced their work ethic, increased their basketball skills, and developed a high level of mental toughness. Again, the strength factor will be totally different each year, depending on the time and the effort players commit. Some students that are released maintain their passion. Whatever you do as a coach, do not take this passion away. Every time someone leaves your program, make sure your conversation and your relationship end on a positive note.

Some players and teams will make great strides in November. We strive to make sure that it is our players and our team that get better. You must stress to your players that:

Alone we can do so little—together we can do so much.

—Hellen Keller
American Author and Educator

Finally, if we are prepared, the game will take care of itself.

As a coach, you must constantly push and teach. Games are short, time is precious, so you must work diligently. During our practices, we use a seven-second shot clock. We demand our players get off a high percentage shot within seven seconds every time we touch the basketball. We insist on a fast-paced press and run offense. Also, stress to your team that they have to play with no fear.

In many coaching articles related to mental toughness, out of the top fifteen categories on "how to be tough," only one stresses offense. Therefore, we start out stressing and focusing on defense and the little things. Next, although it has already been covered, schedule a players' meeting to review rules, expectations, as well as family and personal information.

At this point in the season, it is time for another coaches meeting. This meeting involves the middle school and ninth grade coaches. Review with them the scouting schedule and out-of-town teams. We get a progress report on the players whose development we should be watching, and also ask if there is anything the coaches need. At the end of November meet individually with each of your coaches. Assign each varsity coach two or three players and explain to them that they are responsible for communicating with these players. We expect each individual coach to work with these student-athletes to improve their basketball skills, academic performance, and their ability to communicate so they are on their way to becoming elite student-athletes.

Of utmost importance when meeting with all your coaches is to review with them that all players are to play man-to-man defense, handle the ball, and there is to be no labeling. This would be an excellent time to review the posters and media releases with all team members and coaches. Points of emphasis in the first few weeks of November are there are no tryouts during this time. In practices stress punctuality, crispness, communication, and mental toughness. In our program on day one, we start immediately with our run and press mentality and establish our identity.

During scrimmages stress rebounding, eliminating turnovers, maximum effort, and not taking any plays off. Emphasize no wasted possessions and high percentage shots (can you make six out of ten from that spot?). Develop these skills by playing one-on-one, one-on-two, five-on-ten, and three-on-eight. We always put our players at a disadvantage, hence, the three-on-eight and five-on-ten. It is always a smaller number of varsity players against a larger number of junior varsity players.

Demonstrate power moves, the box drill, the transition drill, and the hesitation drill. Our box drill is always a full court drill.

Remind your players of Michael Jordan's work ethic and his focus on getting it right that led to his exceptional level of play.

It is also at this time that your mandatory curfew is in place. A curfew time is set by consensus of the coaches and captains of the team. It is usually between 11:30 PM and 12 AM midnight.

The following are important activities for **November**:

1. Release players to get down to appropriate numbers.
2. Coordinate with all coaches at every level to ensure system cohesiveness.
3. Develop captains/leaders.
4. Set the tone and mentality.
5. Stress execution every day/every drill.
6. Use scrimmage films and stats to evaluate your team and players.
7. Send out media guides to all alum, college coaches, and supporters.

Don't measure yourself by what you have accomplished, but by what you should have accomplished with your ability.

—John Wooden
Hall of Fame NCAA Coach

Playing in a quality Christmas tournament simulates the crowd, pressure, and all the emotions that will occur in March Madness.

CHAPTER 24

Regular Season: Focus on Execution and Detail

Position your team for tournament play.

As a coach, you have control over your independent schedule, but not the league schedule. December is a great month when you can try to get into a holiday tournament. You can arrange to play better teams to increase the skill level of your players. You can play against the best competition possible. In the past, through our players' hard work and the support of our booster club, we have been fortunate to play in Holiday Tournaments in San Diego, Utah, Phoenix, Tennessee and in numerous other tournaments. We have played in basketball showcases at Huntington Prep, Walsh University, Baldwin Wallace University, and Cleveland State University. Playing in these holiday tournaments and showcases matches us up with some of the best teams in the state and nationally. Christmas tournaments in December are the easiest way to take your team to the next level and allows for the development of team identity.

You must simplify the important goals of your program's culture at this time. Stress to your players that the second you are satisfied or feel you have accomplished your goals, that is the time when other teams will pass you by. You have to focus on the mountaintop as your goal. At times it may seem as if you are taking little steps, but each step is getting you closer to the mountaintop you are shooting for.

Execution is the key to everything. You can have the greatest plays in the world, but they must be executed. Stress to your players they are not going to win because they come to practice from 2:45 to 5:15 p.m. or from 5:30 to 8:00 p.m. Stress that as a team, we are going to be successful because of time you put in on your own, before practice, after practice, and on weekends. You have to have that close bond with your teammates, so you want to come in and spend the extra time. This will make you better and create togetherness among your teammates.

My son Conner also played football for Mentor, and so did his friend Mitch Trubisky, who has played with the Chicago Bears and Buffalo Bills and is currently with the Pittsburgh Steelers. They probably spent almost every day in the spring and summer, with Mitch throwing thousands of passes to Conner to practice executing their plays. Teammates who have this type of great relationship will develop their skill levels together. Knowing the timing off the pass, off the dribble, and the plays you are going to run makes all the difference in your team's execution of your plays.

When you do deal with an injury to a player during the season, turn that negative into a positive and see it as an opportunity for other teammates to step up, and use that individual's playing time to make the entire team execute so much better.

December

Failing to prepare is like preparing to fail.

—John Wooden
Hall of Fame NCAA Coach

During December embrace the vision of what your team can be. The mental aspect of your players' approach to playing the game is important at this time. You must remind your players they are capable of the highest level of play. It is now time to start playing like it. You must get into their heads. This is what is important in December.

Twenty-five to thirty days of practice and preseason scrimmages are done. It is now the beginning of regular season games, and now each game counts towards the success of your season. It is most important to constantly tell your players what they are capable of doing and doing it at the highest level. I tell my players I envision the absolute best of what they are capable of doing on the court. The problem is they do not see themselves playing at the highest level. You need your players to have confidence in themselves and in their teammates and to be mentally tough. This allows them to face and overcome adverse situations.

Remember most people say the mental is to the physical as four is to one. I personally believe that it is more like ten to one. When you critique your players, the volume of your voice may increase in order to make a point. I stress to my players, "When I look at your capabilities on the court, I see you are capable of playing at your highest level." Do not let them be comfortable. Keep the bar for your players' performance high. Once they hear it from me, as their coach, it means so much more. When they believe that they can do it now, they push themselves. To achieve the highest level of skills of which they are capable, they must continue to develop it in practice. To assist your players with developing these skills, they can review marquee players on various pre-recorded programs and try to emulate their success. By mastering the skills they observe, players will develop the belief that they can play against the best on the court.

It is important to realize that the month of December is the time to actualize the goals and expectations of your team. By working on, and hopefully mastering, these goals in December, the team's competence will show in February and March. December is also time for the head coach and staff to assess chemistry within your team. You, as the head coach, can go to HUDL stats or your individual stats to determine which five players perform well together as your starting team. This will enable you to evaluate the impact a player's presence or absence has on the game. After three or four games, you will be able to determine which five players you need on the floor in "crunch time."

December also provides an opportunity for season-related team activities. To continue the promotion of our program, we arrange an alumni game to take place at the last home game around Christmas. Most of the current grads are home for winter break. Therefore, at that game, all alumni players in attendance are introduced to the crowd between the JV game and varsity game. We arrange to have pizza and soft drinks after the game to allow players and coaches to reconnect.

In December, also discuss and prepare for possible community events for your team to attend. We play in an exhibition game with a local school for the developmentally disabled at which we introduce the other school's players. Our players are involved during the month of December in serving holiday lunch at the local senior center. This is the time to prepare for any Christmas Tournament and to take time to scout upcoming opponents via the internet. It is also important to finalize team dinners, which are the night before all Friday or Saturday games.

Another way to energize your players at game time is to honor someone special to the players by dedicating a game to them. We do this with every new varsity group. By sharing their inner feelings and giving a tribute to someone important in their lives, the teammates share a special personal moment.

There are times in December when we have found it necessary to deviate from our strictly enforced curfew of 11:30 PM. This occurs when we have played an away game. We realize that our players will be finishing the game later in the evening and returning home even later. Therefore, our curfew is changed to midnight on those evenings to make it possible for our players to go out and get a bite to eat after the game.

The following are important activities for **December**:

1. Attend some middle school/junior high games.
2. Communicate and build relationships with middle school/junior high coaches.
3. Take your team to a local pro or college game.
4. Talk individually with some of your key players and let them know what you think their strengths and weaknesses are at this point in the season.

5. Send out holiday wishes to all former players, families, and supporters.
6. On New Year's Eve, remind your players about making great decisions, socializing with people that also make great decisions, and have the players call the **head coach** for curfew.

January

At the end of the day, let there be no excuses,
no explanations, no regrets.

—Steve Maraboli
Behavioral Scientist, Speaker, and Author

In January, you do more in-depth scouting. It is time to watch more films, fine-tune roles, and establish minutes per game. Remind your players that, as Hall of Fame NFL Coach Vince Lombardi said, "the price of success is hard work, dedication to the job at hand, and the determination that whether we win or lose, we have applied the best of ourselves to the task at hand."

Get creative to maintain your team's energy level. Around the last fifteen days of January, you will find that monotony begins to set in. It becomes tough to be motivated in the middle of the season. Therefore, boredom is inevitable. Practices are monotonous. As coach, you must keep their interest. To do this, get creative. During the last couple of weeks of January, we do things together as a team to maintain their sense of camaraderie and help them get through the boredom of practices. We know that we have to get through it. We try some innovative things. In the past we have set up a volleyball net and played for the last fifteen minutes of practice. We have also replaced watching films with playing and listening to the latest genre of music and allowing them to hang out together. The purpose of this change in routine is to let the players relax, build relationships, and break up the monotony. This also lets the players know you have a human side too.

Call your local professional or college teams and ask to be their guest at their game. We typically do this as a team in January on a weekend date when no game is scheduled. On a Saturday or Sunday, when we do not have a game, we sometimes arrange to go bowling as a team. During January at the end of a film session we watch ten to fifteen minutes of a motivational movie. Finally, I host a Saturday morning brunch at my house for players, coaches, staff, and parents. Whenever possible, we also try to involve parents to develop relationships and be transparent.

At the end of January, there have been a number of seasons where we have a player who has exhibited a significant amount of dedication, energy, and hustle. As a result, they have gained the respect of the team, the staff, and me. In this instance I have elected to name that player an additional captain. Not only does this make the player feel appreciated, but for future teams, each player knows that even if they are not chosen as a captain at the beginning of the season, they can attain that status through their efforts.

In January, we have invited middle schools to our high school gym to practice. We have four teams (two seventh and two eighth) and give them overlapping blocks of time. This allows them to meet the varsity players. This is also a time when you can work ninth-grade players and junior varsity players alongside your varsity players. If your eighth-and ninth-grade teams have a postseason tournament, you and your players can show support by attending. Prepare for a junior high/middle school basketball night at which you introduce the junior high/middle school basketball players at halftime. Invite them to come into the locker room after the game. Finally prepare for a night to recognize your feeder program participants. We have a Mentor Basketball Association night when the second- through sixth-grade leagues are present and they are introduced with their coaches after the JV game.

At the end of January meet with your captains to evaluate what they have done in their role as captains and what they need to do further. Start the process with your senior players and current senior captains to evaluate four potential team captains for the next season. Give the senior captains two weeks to evaluate the leadership qualities of your one, two, and three priorities as to who should be captains next year. The prospective captains for the following season will be announced in February.

The following are important activities for **January**:

1. Get creative at practice to avoid boredom.
2. Have players make hi-lite films for college recruiting; update stats on your players and send to college coaches.
3. Stress sleep, nutrition, and hydration.
4. At a varsity game, introduce your junior high/middle school teams and feeder program players.
5. Have coaches and senior players make their list of three prospective captains because next year's captains will be named in February.
6. Meet with your staff to determine if any player exemplifies the work ethic, dedication, and commitment deserving of the honor of being appointed as an additional team captain.

February

It is the little details that are vital. Little things make big things happen.

—John Wooden
Hall of Fame NCAA Coach

In February, as the season winds down, begin to prepare your team for the postseason tournament.

Continue intense focus on repeated execution of your plays. Execution and confidence are the keys to winning tournaments. With your staff, review teams in your district and potential tournament seeding. Review the teams, the draw, the tournament dates, and prepare a strategy with your staff. Regarding tournament dates whenever possible, we choose not to take the bye. I like playing early and getting on the court to keep our team fresh. By playing an early game, you are allowing your players the opportunity to familiarize themselves with the surroundings and your tournament strategy. You should provide your players with every opportunity to execute your plays. We spend much more time in the film room and in the gym shooting. Our coaching staff does a very thorough job of scouting every possible team that we could play.

Continue to get heavily involved in team bonding activities through scouting, team dinners, and reviewing films. It is absolutely crucial you scout, and you know what you have to do to win basketball games against tournament teams.

In the last four or five games in February, put in offensive and defensive out-of-bounds plays as these will become important to win games in March even though you have only been doing these in the last few games in February. We also notify the seventh, eighth, and ninth grade players about AAU opportunities and place them on teams so they can develop their basketball skills.

During the last few games of the season, we formulate our entire scouting report of all the teams we have scouted. We also review offensive and defensive plays we will use against potential opponents. While other teams will scout you, it is more important that your players believe in what you do. Your team needs to execute 100 percent, and your players must be confident in the strategy you have presented.

Once you know who you will play that is the team you prepare for. Install the offense, defense, out-of-bounds plays, end-of-game situations, and every facet of the game you may need to use in the tournament. Executing these plays is more important than if the opponent knows your plays. This is why I am not concerned about who sees our plays because it is all about us and our ability to execute our plays.

The following are important activities for **February**:

1. Review the draw and strategy with your staff; consider not taking the bye.

2. Make sure you know the schedule of all the possible tournament teams you may play for scouting purposes.
3. Review films and continue shooting drills.
4. Get heavily involved in team bonding through scouting, dinners, and film.
5. Have the JV and ninth grade practice together.
6. Notify seventh and eighth graders about AAU for spring.

You can practice shooting eight hours a day, but if
your technique is wrong then all you become is very
good at shooting the wrong way. Get the fundamentals
down and the level of everything you do will rise.

—Michael Jordan
Hall of Fame NBA Player

GBC

During a time-out, make absolutely sure that all five players
going out on the court know exactly what they are supposed
to do. As we leave a huddle or time-out, we instruct our
players to talk to one another and make sure that everyone
knows what they are doing so they can execute correctly.
Everyone has to know what they are going to do the second
they walk out onto the court. If one person is in doubt
or doesn't know, it will probably destroy everyone.
I have learned this the hard way.

CHAPTER 25

March Madness, Tournament Play, and the State Championship

Our success is going to be measured at every level.

We have left nothing to chance. We are prepared in every facet—on the court and off the court, in the classroom, and health-wise.
It is a mindset—a mentality.
This is what Mentor believes in.

At this time of the year you stress, "There is no room for error!" This is a time of the year where we try to be foolproof about absolutely everything we do. We again talk to our players about the importance of nutrition, getting the right amount of sleep, colds, flu, and anything that can impact how well we play as a team. On the scouting end, we really dig in, and we make sure we know opponent's tendencies. We understand what our opponents are going to run offensively, defensively, press wise, press breakers, and out-of-bound plays. Our players watch films regarding individual matchups and possible matchups.

On the night before tournament games such as district, regional, or state, we study older films from previous years where we won district, regional, or the state titles. We also review films of games we have played against the number one team in the country and the number four team in the country. I find this definitely gets the team motivated. The films allow the team to get a clear picture of what tournament play is like regarding the crowd, intensity, energy, and pressure. Our past successes have helped us win future games. I will even read texts and emails from former players for motivation and advice.

The night before our tournament game we have a pregame meal together. This continues to promote togetherness and camaraderie. We also have a pregame meal on a Saturday or non-school game day. Once we reach the district tournament level, we have become a truly tight-knit family with meals being brought in to allow us to have longer film sessions. Our goal is to create the tightest possible bond between the players, and also a unified mental approach to the game. As a result, when we present ourselves to each opponent as we progress through the tournament, we have become a formidable force with "no fear" when we step on the floor.

Curfew at this time is extremely important. For this part of the season, we set an earlier curfew time. Earlier in the season, players will call assistant coaches for curfew time check-in. At tournament time, I personally make these calls just to get a read on their emotions and talk a minute or two about how important the game is. From these calls, the players clearly understand what is on the line. During tournament time, we add the night before every game to the curfew requirements.

Any day school is out, such as for a Saturday game, we will participate in a walk-through. We will arrive at the gym between 11:00 and 11:30 a.m. and walkthrough offenses, defenses, and review our scouting report. We then allow our players to shoot and have them feel mentally and physically that they are in the best position possible for success in tournament play. After each victory, we spend ten to fifteen minutes talking about our next opponent and what lies ahead of us. We make sure our players recognize we are not done until after we win the state championship game.

The following are important activities for **March**:

1. Watch past films of big-time games that give the sense of energy, crowd, and intensity the players might see.
2. Keep it business-like after each tournament win; keep emotions in check.

3. Leave nothing to chance; have the players reiterate to you verbally exactly what you need to do to win.
4. Emphasize to your key players how important their composure and energy are to the other players on the team and the outcome of a game.
5. In my belief, this is the time of year where coaching in big games can make the difference in a win or a loss; make sure that you are prepared in every way possible.

Physically tough/mentally tough—you get that reputation when you compete and dominate other tough players, not by dominating a weaker player.

What lies behind us and what lies ahead of us are insignificant compared to what lies within us.

—Ralph Waldo Emerson
Essayist, Poet, Lecturer, and Philosopher

One of the greatest feelings in high school basketball is knowing you are going to the state tournament. Celebrate for the night and get back to work the next morning.

CHAPTER 26

The Power of Support

**To achieve and maintain elite status, it is important
to establish and maintain a quality booster program
dedicated solely to your basketball program.**

The kind of support you need to sustain an elite high school basketball program is dependent, in large part, upon the presence and commitment of your school's basketball booster program. It is important to establish and maintain a booster club dedicated solely to your basketball program. The value to your program can be summed up in three words: opportunity, equipment, and camaraderie. In order to be highly competitive, your team must play the toughest competitors available even in the off-season tournaments, which often requires overnight travel. Equipment is also a necessity and this requires additional funds. And, finally, your team will play best when the bond between the individual players is strong. Therefore, social opportunities provided by a booster program serve this purpose well.

Former Cardinal Cage Club President Rick Martucci offers some insight into what makes a booster club successful:

> We enjoyed a great deal of success with the Cardinal Cage Club in the time I was involved. There are two things you must have to be successful as a booster club: 1) a sound program and 2) a dedicated organization.

You need a program that the community can get excited about and support, that includes sponsors, school administration, fans/students and, most importantly the coaches and players themselves. The coaches and players need to believe in what they are doing and show that to the public. Be engaged as this makes fundraising much easier. One of the most surprisingly successful fundraisers we did every year was scheduling several car washes over the summer. It was very simple. Players would commit to selling tickets to family and friends. We also put up flyers and put ads in the paper as well as local community publications (this was before the internet). We would select locations for the car wash that were high traffic, high-visibility areas. Not only was this a great success financially, but it was a tremendous opportunity to build community support: the players would take pictures with fans and engage with customers/fans of all ages. We even washed a fire engine one time.

You must have a booster organization that is as passionate and committed to the team and program as the coaches and players are. The biggest challenges for any organization or business are to make sure everyone is pulling in the same direction and make sure you understand the club's priorities, which are aligned with the team's priorities. While I may have been the "president" of the Cardinal Cage Club, the real work was done by those parents and supporters handling the fundraisers, community relations, financing, player support (meals, uniforms, equipment, etc.) and school relations. My role was to facilitate—to ensure that everyone had what they needed to succeed and to make sure we all kept the program moving in the right direction. Communication is key, especially between the booster club and the coaching staff, and in turn, the school administration.

If you find that there isn't a booster program already in existence for your sport, you can create one from various organizations within your community. Parents of current and former players and businesses within the community can be the base of your organization. That would be a great place to start. Please refer to Chapter 3 for more information on the booster club organization and its functions.

Since the majority of the booster club officers are new each season, I inform them as to the businesses and restaurants that have been supportive in the past. I also ask the officers if they have any new suggestions for sources of support for the program within their realm of friends and acquaintances. I inquire as to whether they know of any new businesses we can reach out to. This enhances the networking capability of our program. I impress upon each new group of officers that our goal as a program is to maintain our alumni base and keep our program as a very tightknit, large, ever-growing family.

I immediately incorporate into my discussions with the officers the underlying principle that once you are involved with our Mentor basketball program, you are a valued part of it. **Once a Card, always a Card.** Even after a student-athlete graduates, they and their parents will always be considered a part of the program. I stress to the booster club that the strength of the club is directly proportional to the number of followers and the support that people are willing to give. This is the way to keep the program strong, united, and powerful from season to season. As I said before, "When it comes to relationships, more is better."

I personally meet with our booster group regularly to keep them informed of our team's record and address any needs that arise. One of our important meetings, however, occurs in August or September when I meet with the officers and I propose a skeleton budget of the upcoming year's needs. At this time, I will know the Christmas tournament and showcases we will be participating in and be able to relate the approximate cost of those expenses to our boosters. I will also propose potential paraphernalia such as travel gear, polos, shoes, and other foreseeable needs of our players for the upcoming season. Your school may or may not pay for new uniforms on a rotating basis. At some schools, the booster club may have to cover the costs of new uniforms. This is the same with practice gear and practice equipment.

I also make it a point to attend every booster club event. This is your responsibility as coach. As of the time the book is being published, our boosters raise an average of $30,000 to $40,000 per year. After expenses, our golf outing profits between $5,000 to $7,000. Our "Night at the Races" or "Reverse Raffle Dinner" brings in $10,000 to $14,000. Our membership drive raises $5,000 to $7,000. Various other fundraisers contribute $7,000 to $10,000 per year to our program. Other fundraisers include three-on-three invitational tournaments, AAU basketball tournaments, and monthly raffle drawings. The Mentor Cardinal Cage Club has become one of the best booster organizations in the state of Ohio. This is a testament to our phenomenal parents and supporters.

In addition, you should encourage your program's basketball alumni to become involved with the team's booster club.

We are stronger together than we are alone.

—Walter Payton
Hall of Fame NFL Player

GBC

An elite athletic program, such as the Mentor Boys Basketball Program, can have a major impact on the community by bringing people together to support one another.

SECTION 3:
HOW TO DEVELOP A STRONG FOUNDATION FOR SUCCESS

Overview

Support the development of mental toughness year-round.

Off-season

- Postseason—April and May
- Summer—June and July
- Dead Period (in Ohio)—August
- Preseason—September and October

Regular Season

- Month of Preparation—November
- Game Time—December through the third week of March
- Tournament—The end of February until the end of March

Year-Round

- Prepare for the season monthly and plan every aspect with attention to details
- Engage your booster organization

For month-specific lists of important points, see the respective month in the previous chapters.

See appendices A through K at the back of the book for further information and relevant documents.

SECTION 4

HOW TO DEVELOP ELITE STUDENT-ATHLETES

Basketball players are made, not born.

—Unknown

Only a small difference separates the physical abilities of good athletes and great athletes. Great athletes have and use their mental toughness/mental attitude. The goal of the coach and program should be to develop the whole person: athletically, academically, ethically, morally, and socially.

As a coach, especially a young coach, make sure you realize dealing with high school players is a journey for both you and your players. It is my experience that your players will eventually understand that the basketball skills you are instilling are actually life skills.

CHAPTER 27

Develop the Whole Person and Emphasize Self-Control

Guide the student-athlete to develop habits that will contribute to their future success.

When it comes to your team members, strive to develop the whole individual. This includes the athletic, academic, ethical, and social aspects of a player. These elite individuals exhibit poise, confidence, maturity, and mental toughness. Such a person is likely to be highly successful in life.

In truth, the only limitations anyone has are the limitations they place on themselves. We make sure our players set their goals high and, more importantly, believe they will reach them. I am a strong believer in the importance of setting deadlines for goals. There has to be a sense of urgency connected to goal setting. Goal setting is essential to success on the basketball court as well as later in life.

Guide the student-athlete to engage in habits resulting in personal responsible behavior. Be proactive regarding social issues that affect your players. It is best to do this through a blanket approach, addressing them all in a team setting. Address issues such as sexuality, teenage pregnancy, drugs, alcohol, and choices that can lead to life-altering results. Be open to counseling your players. Make them feel at ease in approaching you. Remember, you are a coach but also a parent figure. Assure your team members you will only give them sound advice. Young people sometimes need a parental figure in their lives. Even if they are eighteen years old, they still need guidance.

No matter whether a student-athlete is a starter or comes off the bench, treat all players the same and offer help to all. As a coach, you can only play so many, but all deserve your time and attention. Make each player in your program feel important.

You can prepare your players for success on and off the court by emphasizing self-control. The question is,

How competitive can you be without losing your discipline?

—Doc Rivers
NBA Coach

Team rule-setting is a tool that you can use in this regard. Curfews are important as they create players who are capable of controlling their impulses and do not succumb quickly to peer pressure. Putting your team members on a curfew is a good idea. Nothing good happens after midnight. I tell my players repeatedly what I myself have heard many times: "Show me your friends, and I'll show you your future." Advise your team members to associate with goal-oriented and motivated individuals. You may trust your players, but you do not know their friends.

You are the average of the five friends
you spend the most time with.

—Jim Rhone
Entrepreneur, Author and Motivational Speaker

You must guide the student-athlete to learn to deal with and control the emotion of frustration. So much about success as a student-athlete is about dealing with struggles and losses. They must learn to be positive when they feel deflated and try again even after they have made a mistake. However, they must also keep their emotions in check. I have heard from other coaches many times that our players play through mistakes better than any team they have ever seen. Be mindful that you are an influence in their life; therefore always be a positive influence.

A great team starts with great leadership. Two actions that can undermine your team are hazing and bullying. In previous chapters, we talked about building strong captains and being very transparent with them. We address everything with them. We don't avoid controversial issues and we talk about this with them year-round. Our captains and every one of our players know that hazing or bullying won't be tolerated for one second.

We stress team cohesiveness. There has to be mutual respect among all the players on the team. Otherwise, all the efforts to develop camaraderie will be eroded. Impress upon your players that respect is earned, not given. Discuss the need for empathy and to put yourself in the other player's shoes. Sometimes a younger coach fails to address an issue until it becomes a problem. It is far better to identify potential problems before they arise and avoid a distraction to the successful pursuit of a winning season.

You can't be a great team unless you have a great locker room. As coach, you will only be in the locker room before and after games, at halftime, and maybe before and after practices. The majority of the time, only the players are there. Again, your captains are essential in maintaining a positive and supportive environment in your absence. They must understand that to be an effective leader, they must be respected by the team. However, the respect of teammates has to be earned. Stress that the locker room should be a place of integrity, dignity, and respect.

Remind your team members of the importance of a strong work ethic. "First on the floor, last out the door" is a great motto to impress upon them. Instill in your student-athletes the belief that motivation beats talent. To develop this mindset in your players during the season, always play the best teams whenever possible: preseason, in-season, and in the summer, so you are ready for tournament play.

Community involvement on the part of the players is important all year-round. This imparts an experience that the student-athlete has value extending beyond the basketball court. It provides them with a perspective that they are not the center of the universe. At the same time, it instills in them a sense of personal worth. It also develops the student-athlete's self-confidence in diverse social settings. On occasion, one or two student-athletes accompany me to speaking engagements in the community. This experience is a win-win for the attendees, the players, and our program.

In our program, players perform self-assessments throughout the season and measure their progress in achieving higher skill levels. Through self-assessment and focused effort, a player who is not confident becomes confident in their abilities when they make progress, and their accomplishments are acknowledged. I suggest that you offer each player your input so they can accurately recognize where they are as players and where they can improve. You can assist them in developing emotional intelligence so that they become aware of how certain situations make them feel, why they feel that way, and how such feelings help or hurt them. Encourage your players to assess their own skillset and help them create a plan to improve through small, incremental changes. As a coach, you can provide your players with valuable feedback and support them as they turn their weaknesses into strengths.

Use the preseason wisely. As a coach, you can also arrange for community involvement in the development of the student-athlete. Securing speakers from the ranks of businesspeople, judges, chiefs of police, and spiritual leaders can impress upon the student-athletes the need to make good decisions and prepare them for the future. We keep the sessions to twenty-five to thirty minutes maximum. The speakers alert our players to life issues and the negative ramification of actions they might take. I also reach out to the parents to ask if they have a preference as to someone who might want to speak to our team.

Teaching your team members to make good decisions is a part of developing the whole person and emphasizing self-control. Impress upon your players that their choices in life have to be good choices 24/7 (24 hours a day, 7 days a week) and they should be wise in every decision they make.

All coaching is, is taking a player where he can't take himself.

—Bill McCartney
NCAA Football Coach

CHAPTER 28

Stress the Power of Choice

Impress upon each player the power of choice. Student-athletes must learn to take every opportunity every day to become a better athlete and an even better person.

As motivational speaker and consultant Dr. Denis Waitley explains, "there are two primary choices in life: to accept conditions as they are or accept the responsibility for changing them." Be a changer, not a complainer. Each player must be committed to step on the floor with unbelievable confidence and play through mistakes. As was written by Dr. Reinhold Niebuhr in 1932, "God grant me the serenity to accept the things I cannot change, the courage to change the things I can and the wisdom to know the difference." Wisdom comes from experience. Educator, author, and businessman Stephen Covey challenges us to "be part of the solution, not part of the problem." Help each player identify and develop personal goals. Never be afraid of setting your goals as high as possible. You cannot change the past, but the future is whatever you want it to be. The key is you. Student-athletes must be open to doing what they need to do and doing it right.

I was fortunate to play Division I college basketball for Coach Dom Rosselli at Youngstown State University. He taught me if you were going to do something, don't leave the gym until you do it right. Your players must learn that details are the difference between success and failure. They must learn to focus on the details even when revisiting the same issue makes their mind numb. It's all about choice.

Another key to success is being able to prioritize your goals. Impress upon the players that you are always free to choose the task that you will do next. Your ability to choose between the important and unimportant is the key determination of your success in life and work. I am a firm believer in motivational speaker and author Brian Tracy's concept of "eat that frog." This means to do the tough tasks early in the day, preferably in the morning and do your tough, most strenuous drills, early in your practice. Our defenses and presses are always at the forefront of our practices.

Henry Ford, industrialist, businessman, and founder of the Ford Motor Company, stressed that when addressing difficult situations, "don't find fault; find the remedy." If a student-athlete has a hard time during practice or especially during the game, you must come down hard to impress the need for change. Then, soften the blow with a kind gesture or a word immediately afterward. This reinforces that, armed with a new experience, improvement is imminent.

The student-athlete must believe in their capacity to improve. In truth, until they try, they have no idea how hard they can play! The longer I coach, the more I realize that toughness, especially mental toughness, and true leadership has to be constant. So many players are "part-timers": they pick and choose when they want to play and when they want to lead. These part-timers are destined to be part-time players, at best.

Remember, your former players can also be tapped as a source of inspiration and motivation for your team and any "part-time" players. I love when my former players come into a practice or before a game and relate to my current team how Mentor basketball affected their lives: the mentality, seeking to be the best, overcoming frustration, setting their goals as high as possible, and most importantly, believing that those goals are within reach. This personal message from my former players is so much more effective and powerful than anything I could deliver myself.

Finally, seek input from your community leaders to stress the power of choice. By arranging for experienced professionals to educate your players regarding life's challenges, they can impress upon your players the importance of the choices they make. Choices can change the course of one's life.

Remember this, the choices you make in life, make you.

—John Wooden
Hall of Fame NCAA Coach

CHAPTER 29

Promote Community Involvement

Community involvement provides experiential education.

Even though we have mentioned in previous chapters the importance of community involvement, I feel it is important to expound on this subject. Community involvement with our players provides an opportunity for experiential education, a different sort from that found in the classroom. It also has an element of preparation for applying to college after graduation since most colleges look for community-involvement hours when considering an applicant for acceptance into their schools.

Community involvement is important all year-round. Community service provides a perspective that the universe is large, and players are only a small part overall. Players need to realize the world does not revolve around them. At the same time, community service instills in your team members a sense of personal worth and the importance of building strong relationships. The coach can get in touch with the community-service director at your high school and, in our case, a social worker. Advise them that the players are available to be involved in the community. The staff at the high school can let you know how the student-athletes can get involved.

Our student-athletes give back to the community by visiting a local nursing home with Valentine's cards for senior citizens and we serve them lunch. They spend time with the seniors and also play pool with them. We have done this the last Friday of every month for twenty years. When student-athletes interact with senior citizens, it connects the senior citizens with your program and the game.

As we have mentioned before, the team also plays an exhibition basketball game with developmentally disabled students from a local school. Our student-athletes also attend this school's homecoming which is their students' annual social event. The team members help out in any way they can, even occasionally by showing dance moves on the floor. Our players also invite their players to attend our games. This allows the developmentally disabled students to feel they are an extension of our team and are important and involved. Community involvement imparts a positive experience for our student-athletes that can also meet the community-service requirement for acceptance into some colleges.

At our August team cookout, community service is always one of our major topics. I invite parents to join in our work, such as assisting at food banks, helping seniors move, and serving senior citizen dinners. I have found such involvement promotes bonding not only in our parent group but in the organization as a whole. As always, our program is a family.

Nurture relationships with your players and community leaders so they will respect your program and serve as mentors to your student-athletes. Be involved in the community. Seek out character-building opportunities for your players. Presentations by successful individuals can impress upon the student-athletes the need to make good decisions and prepare them for the future. Our efforts in preparing our student-athletes for the future and their role in the world have made an impact. Our players have gone on to have successful careers and be positive contributors to society in many ways (see section 6, chapter 38).

The true athlete should have character, not be a character.

—John Wooden
Hall of Fame NCAA Coach

As head coach, establish strong bonds with the community by arranging your team's involvement in community service. Our team participates in a homecoming game and dance at the Broadmoor School for the Developmentally Disabled.

CHAPTER 30

Foster a Strong Work Ethic

**Working hard with a purpose separates
the good from the great.**

It is important for the student-athlete to know your system and culture. The student-athlete must also know that the program is bigger than they are. It is important to stem their egos early in your interaction with your players. Impress upon your players that when you cheat on drills, you decrease your skills. It is important to execute drills until those habits become skills. Players must choose to give 100 percent whenever they are on the court. That's what separates the elite from the average.

Explain that working hard is one thing, but working hard with a purpose is what separates the good from the great. It isn't what you do once in a while that counts; it's what you do day in and day out. Hard work is what you do religiously every day to improve your game and that is what makes the difference.

Stress that true success comes from knowing that you did your best to become the best that you are capable of becoming. You must leave everything on the floor—in practice, in games, in life. Then you and success will travel hand in hand.

As a coach, you are dedicated to working with your players. However, after a few minutes, you can tell which players are motivated and which are not. By filming practices and scrimmages, you create an opportunity to call in the parents and the player and watch the film together. These films will show the effort or lack thereof.

Releasing players is a tough decision, but it must not be put off. If you retain players who don't show effort, it will hurt your program. This attitude can spread to other players and is why you must make your decision early.

With that being said, it is wise to keep less talented but motivated players. When you find a student-athlete who exhibits a strong work ethic and can motivate the team to perform their best, it is wise to keep such a person even if they are not presently one of your top nine players.

Finally, you must be sensitive to the needs of your student-athletes. The student-athlete may have the desire to fully participate in your program, but the means may be lacking. Many times, as a coach, you will be made aware of obstacles to the player's commitment or their ability to participate in various aspects of your program. This may be due to circumstances beyond their control. Sometimes money to pay for food, equipment, or transportation is lacking. In my years as a head coach, I have learned some players have experienced unimaginable home situations. These may be seemingly insurmountable to the young person. Together, we have been able to come up with a strategic plan and to put the individual on a path to success. I have found, to my amazement, that a student-athlete who seemed to be a slacker and who was accepting the repercussions, was actually exhibiting an extraordinarily strong work ethic and was dealing with outside issues which they did not share with me. If you have followed my advice in the earlier chapters regarding developing relationships with community leaders, you have positioned yourself to intercede for your players.

While this is up to you, I would entertain the idea of visiting a few, if not all, of the players in their home during the season, along with their parents. In addition, younger players' parents and those just entering your program may not understand the magnitude of your program. As I have stated before, it may be extremely beneficial for you, and especially for the younger player, to meet the parents and player at their house. It will facilitate a discussion regarding what their roles and responsibilities will be. The parent(s) and player must understand and support your goal to develop their child as a whole person and not just improve their child's basketball skill set.

The vast majority of the information that parents receive is from their child and you have no way of knowing what is being passed along. A conversation with the parent(s) and player will make your program totally open and transparent to them. It will educate you regarding any issues which may impede the student-athlete's full participation in your program. Again, it is not a bad idea to take another staff member with you.

Your team is a family! It is important for parents to be onboard with your program. This will help ensure they will be supportive of your efforts. The development of great habits requires consistent effort. You, as the coach, need parent(s) and the player to understand the dynamics and the positives of a strong work ethic. When their child does develop a strong work ethic, it will give them a competitive edge in basketball as well as in every aspect of their life.

Hard work beats talent when talent doesn't work hard.

—Tim Notke
High School Basketball Coach

CHAPTER 31

Reward Motivation

Reward and reinforce the positive.

It is widely accepted that comfort is the enemy of success. A person's desire to change must be greater than their desire to stay the same. In order to grow and improve, a person must embrace change. Comfort zones and satisfaction hinder a person's progress. If you have easy days, you're probably not very successful or goal-oriented. Teach your players to wake up with a purpose and attack the day! I often use the motivational phrase, CARPE DIEM! (Seize the day!).

No one can change what they refuse to confront and therefore a person must accept reality. Some players are "in denial" about their actual skill level and, as a result, never realize their full potential.

I believe a quick way to develop a player's skills is to open them up to the need for change. This fosters motivation. Throwing them into the fire is the best way to do this. By this I mean that you put the student-athlete into practices without compensating for any deficiencies they may have. In doing so, you create an experience in which they must face the challenge of learning on the fly. They become painfully and undeniably aware of areas where they are lacking in skill. We don't coddle our players or move at a slow pace to accommodate them. The players quickly realize that they don't know what they need to do to be successful.

We have found as a result of this experience that our student-athletes develop much more quickly into a complete player. The learning curve increases when they recognize and meet their responsibilities on the court. That is the reason it is so important for them to play bigger, stronger, and more skilled competition.

Success is waiting for your players, but they have to achieve it. Success doesn't happen by accident; they must compete and believe. They must compete in every drill every day.

Captains, as extensions of the coach, should motivate their teammates, especially younger players. Captains should stifle any negativity immediately. This is important to ensure a positive and confident mindset in every player on the floor.

Players must have passion and drive to be successful. It has to be what their heart wants. There is no room for excuses. The player must set their plans for success. They must be reminded, as I do with my players, that the only one who can stop you is you. As Hall of Fame baseball player Babe Ruth wisely remarked, "It's hard to beat a person who never gives up."

If a player truly hates to lose, it will be obvious by their effort in practice and the extra time they put into changing their deficiencies into strengths. It takes a different amount of time for different people, but every day players can improve. During the regular season, time is short and of the essence. A coach must be positive and patient to ensure their players stay motivated. It keeps student-athletes open to growing athletically, as well as academically, socially, and ethically.

As mentioned many times before, make sure you recognize achievements with positive reinforcement. Use your positive reinforcement to motivate players who are not receiving a great deal of playing time. Constantly acknowledge how hard they work, the effort they put into practices, and improvements they have made. You control so much of what you want in your program.

The winners in life think constantly in terms of I can,
I will, I am. Losers, on the other hand, concentrate
their waking thoughts on what they should have
or would have done, or what they can't do.

—Dennis Waitley
Motivational Speaker, Writer, and Consultant

GBC

Reward the positive. Reinforce the positive.

CHAPTER 32

Encourage Resilience and Perseverance

Always find the positive in the negative.

Resilience and perseverance are essential to managing and executing changes one must face in life. As a coach, you are first responder when a student-athlete's efforts fall short of their goal. It may be when they miss a shot or when they are at the free throw line and winning the game depends on making the shot, and it just doesn't happen.

How you react and help them through it can influence how they react to the stressors of everyday life as an adult. You are helping them form habits they will take with them long after leaving your program. The true test of any student-athlete or team is how they react to adversity. Winners are survivors and will find a way to achieve success. This is as true in basketball as it is in life. Remember, you are planting the seeds for mental toughness that will serve your players well in all their future endeavors.

You discipline those under your supervision to correct, to help, and to improve. not to punish.

—John Wooden
Hall of Fame NCAA Coach

One of the most difficult challenges for a player is when they suffer an injury. This is especially true when they realize they have to be out for a certain length of time. To the player, it seems like their whole world has come crashing down. As a coach, you must be totally positive so they, in turn, keep a positive attitude throughout their recovery process. This positivity is absolutely essential for your player's psyche and morale to be able to persevere through the rehabilitation of their injury. I impress upon my players that while this injury may seem to be devastating to the student-athlete, there is a positive side for them as well as the team. Tell both the injured player and the team this challenge will reveal their resilience and perseverance.

Student-athletes can and must learn to recover from and adjust to misfortune or change. They can develop the ability to make a continued effort to achieve something despite difficulties, failures, or opposition. They must learn to focus on the present, plan for the future, and forget the past. You can help them do this by continuously reminding them whatever happened in the last quarter or that last game does not define their future. Stress to your players that their regrets should never outnumber their dreams.

In the following personal reflection, one of my former players, Jonah Waag, explains how mistakes he made in his attitude and actions almost caused him to lose sight of a promising future. Participating in the Mentor program turned him around:

> I had a troubled high school basketball career. I received DI offers as a freshman, and so I was cocky. I stopped working on my game and stopped focusing on the sport. This was a big mistake. I lost my DI offers. After losing my offers, I thought I'd never touch a college court. Then I met Coach Krizancic and he took me in even after knowing my mistakes. I was never coachable 'till I met Coach K. He brought me into his program and built me into a man. He could have looked the other way, but instead he taught me to never quit, always go 100% in practice, and to be mentally tough. He took me, a troubled kid, and

turned me into a man. I only spent one year playing for Coach K, but that one year has impacted
my life. Coach K doesn't coach…he teaches. I
will never forget my one year in Mentor. I am
where I am today because of Coach K.

—Jonah Waag (currently at Lake Erie College)

Even losses should be turned into positives. After every loss,
review why the loss occurred and challenge the team to come back
stronger. After a loss, magnify and focus on what your team did
wrong and how you can correct and improve it. This is a great example of how they can use resilience and perseverance throughout life
when faced with undesired results in their endeavors.

Student-athletes will come to see their future is in their hands.
You must remind your players that it is their choice every single day
to get stronger, more skilled, develop their fundamentals, and overcome weaknesses. Perseverance is the key.

Sometimes you learn more from losing than
winning. Losing forces you to reexamine.

—Pat Summitt
Hall of Fame NCAA Basketball Coach

In my coaching career, as of this writing, we have been to the
regional level nineteen times with a resulting fourteen losses. It is
heartbreaking for the team to lose at any level, but even more so
when they reach the regional tournament level. As you know, on the
positive side, winning nineteen district titles allowed us to advance to
the regional level and learn from our regional losses. Our experience
of going to the regional tournament and learning from our victories
and defeats enabled my program to ultimately win the boys state
basketball titles. Most players who succeed in the face of seemingly
impossible conditions are players who are resilient, persevere, simply
don't know how to quit, and never make excuses.

It's all mentality. I have found through my coaching career that making my practices so much tougher than the game has paid huge dividends. There are so many times that our players at the end of practice thought they had given everything they could in the two-hour session. Then we put three more minutes on the time clock and put our starters down ten points. They have to give their maximum effort to win the three-minute session or have to run more splits. I think that by doing this, you plant the seed that the players are able to persevere and their resilience is at a high level. Making practices so much harder than games is the key to developing these assets. When one of my players was asked this year about the difficulty of playing four games in a row, the player's response was "Heck no, games are so much easier than practices!".

Winning means you are willing to go longer, work harder, and give more than anyone else.

—Vince Lombardi
Hall of Fame NFL Coach

CHAPTER 33

Strength and Conditioning— Forming New Habits

You are what you repeatedly do so you better do it right.

If you want to change, change your habits. Habit and instinct are important qualities to develop if you are to be a successful basketball player. Habit and instinct should be one and the same. It is a question of stimulus and response with no lapse in between. Players and coaches must be patient in developing new habits as it takes a minimum of twenty-one days of consistent action with no lapse in between for muscle memory to be established. Repetition of correct form is essential.

To be the best player you can be requires skill, strength, toughness, and conditioning. These are crucial if you are to achieve your basketball potential. Skill requires technique and form. Once they are shown proper technique and form, players should work to master these independently. Strength is developed through personal training and conditioning. Physical toughness involves body contact in keeping another player from gaining an advantage on the court. This may involve a closely guarded position or boxing out another player. This can only be practiced with another player. Finally, one way to increase the speed of your game is to play tougher, quicker, and stronger players.

Regarding strength and conditioning our student-athletes may secure their own personal trainers and use workout programs geared to their specific needs and abilities. However, no matter what program is followed, the goal is to improve the individual student-athlete's overall health, skills, and abilities on the basketball court. As stated earlier, any work out or skill program must be measurable.

When it comes to basketball skills, it must be noted that the role of bigger and taller players has evolved. "Big men" are now asked to shoot the three, handle the basketball, and run the floor. As a result of these desired skills, the traditional "big men" have actually gotten smaller in college and the NBA. So even if you are a "big man", you need to develop the skills of a guard. You need to be a more complete player no matter what position you play. This is why we never label anyone in our program because of height. As a coach you need to develop a complete skill set for every single student-athlete on your team.

Developing these new skill sets will require forming new habits through strength and conditioning. To ensure that the strength and conditioning program in which the student-athlete is engaged is making a difference, it is necessary to periodically check skills such as vertical jumping ability and speed on a treadmill to assess their ability to cover the court. Also monitor weight gain, muscle mass, and body fat. Look for improvement. In two to five months, they should be a better athlete.

Not being an expert on strength and conditioning myself, I rely on experts in the field. I have learned that supercompensation is an extremely important concept to master as the head coach. You want your athletes to be at their peak at game time. Monitoring your players' performance during practices will allow you to become familiar with what your players can tolerate. Therefore, at game time, equipped with this knowledge, you can facilitate performance at their highest level. The last thing you want is a fatigued or tired body at game time. In my forty-one years, I have learned the key to getting your players' bodies to their strongest and quickest capabilities is how you work your players daily in practice. You can work on skills and fundamentals as a break between hard practices. Otherwise, the body will react in a negative fashion. Remember, the body needs time to recover.

I recommend that fourteen to fifteen year old players and their parents seek professional guidance from someone who is an expert in the field of strength and conditioning. They will impart their knowledge regarding the anatomy of the human body, how to develop strength and conditioning, and increase the strength of core muscles. These professionals should incorporate the importance of hydration and nutrition as well as timing of various exercises into a program they are proposing. They should also discuss potential injuries and rehabilitation through physical therapy. Consulting with professionals will ensure that updates in this ever-evolving science of developing the human body to its peak performance and optimum health can be incorporated into your program.

Excellence is not a singular act but a habit.
You are what you repeatedly do.

—Shaquille O'Neal
Hall of Fame NBA Player, quoting Will Durant, Philosopher

CHAPTER 34

Address the Importance of Sleep, Proper Nutrition, and Hydration

Adequate sleep, proper nutrition, and hydration are essential if a student-athlete is to perform their best during practices and games.

It is common sense that sleep deprivation is detrimental for anyone, especially for a student-athlete. Student-athletes need guidance in this area because they think they are invincible. In your role of coach, it is very important to stress that sleep deprivation affects mental sharpness as well as physical stamina.

Nutrition is also a key factor. There have been advances in the area of sports and nutrition. Strength and conditioning experts are often also nutritionists. I have personally brought in nutritionists from our local health system as well as our school nutritionist. We have also consulted with the head of our high school's home economics department. Do this at the beginning of the season. If the student-athletes have questions, you will have a ready resource that will be willing to guide them during the season.

It is important to have a good meal prior to the game. This meal should be eaten three to three and a half hours before a game and should consist of high protein food. Hydration is also key to performance. Anytime you are thirsty, you are two liters deficient in your fluids. Teach proper hydration. It can stop illnesses. You must stress to the student-athletes that they must drink fluids early and often. They should start their day with sixteen fluid ounces of fluid, preferably water, and make sure they drink at every meal and before, during, and after practice. This will enable them to avoid heat-related illness. It also will help them sustain performance during grueling practices and games.

Our team has two athletic trainers from the Cleveland Clinic who are well versed on the anatomy and physiology of the human body. When they address any muscle pull or small ailment, their first question is, "Are you staying hydrated?" Through the years, the lack of hydration became an issue when it affected the kidneys of one of my players. The player was a first-team all-stater, and missed a month of the season due to the kidney problem resulting from dehydration. This is why we stress hydration, hydration, hydration.

There are many sports drinks currently on the market. Sports drinks, such as Nooma®, Gatorade®, Powerade®, and All Sport®, as well as Pedialyte® products (among others), can give you needed hydration and even an energy boost during your activity. These are designed to rapidly replace fluids and to increase the sugar (glucose) circulating in your body's circulatory system.

Many of these sports drinks also come in the form of gels, powders, and chews. I would highly recommend that you as a coach or parent confirm that what they are taking meets your approval. I realize that there are energy drinks and other forms of hydration that may not be conducive to your student-athlete competing at their highest level. If there is a question of hydration or especially cramps during a game, our athletic trainers and team doctors recommend Pedialyte® for athletes as a treatment. Advise parents to make sure that their child is totally hydrated before the game. Whenever we run a camp, I tell the participants that any time you are thirsty, you are probably two liters down of liquid, and you never want to get there.

It is wise to drink sixteen ounces of water one hour before exercise as it takes one hour for the fluid to be absorbed into the body. During practice student-athletes should consume twenty to forty ounces of fluid per hour, and make sure you schedule fluid breaks during practice. Immediately after exercise, drink twenty-four fluid ounces of water for every ounce of body weight lost. Weighing before and after practice is one way to ensure that lost fluids are restored.

Snacks are another area that needs to be addressed. There are heathy and unhealthy snacks. Pretzels are a healthy snack mentioned by our trainers due to their high carbohydrate content (energy source), low fat content, and salt (helps the body fight dehydration). The student-athlete must snack on foods that provide the most energy over the longest period of time. Foods containing a great amount of sugar are not a wise choice. They will at first produce a feeling of great energy, however, after a short period of time the body will metabolize the sugar causing a feeling of loss of energy.

As a coach with forty-two years of experience, I would highly recommend that you ensure any coaches in your program are educated in the areas of hydration, proper nutrition, and sleep deprivation. Also impress upon your student-athletes the pitfalls of dehydration, improper nutrition, and sleep deprivation so that they are in the best shape for the rigors of practice and games. In doing so, you will instill in them lifelong healthy habits.

Take care of your body from the inside out.

—Blake Griffin
NBA Player

CHAPTER 35

Prepare for the Future

Set up a support program for your players.

A coach can set up a support program around basketball practice sessions that addresses courses student-athletes are currently taking in high school. In addition, sessions can be arranged to prepare the players for college entrance exams, the college application process, and even looking for employment after high school graduation.

Impress upon your student-athletes they will benefit if they are not only skilled at basketball but also make a positive impression on their coaches, and potential college coaches. Your team members' toughness, work ethic, attitude, and leadership will make a positive impression as they are building a reputation that can benefit them after graduation. To showcase our student-athletes we invite college coaches to watch our open gyms and practices. I suggest you do this for your team as well.

We have developed an aspect of our program that guides our student-athletes in understanding the economic responsibilities of everyday adult life. When we travel in the summer or during the season our players dine in restaurants. Our players will have a per diem spending limit. We teach our student-athletes that a typical meal and beverage should cost about $ 10.00 to $ 15.00 and that they should be sure to leave 15 percent to 18 percent gratuity. We want our players to understand the dynamics of budgeting.

Also when traveling, we are strict on how players manage their time. This includes being on time for breakfast where the entire team eats together, lunch, and being prompt for our transportation. When we talk about being "elite," the responsibility of time management is a very important factor.

Better three hours too soon than a minute too late.

—William Shakespeare
English Poet, Playwright, and Actor

In our program, we have arranged tutoring sessions throughout the season to assist our players in their academic standing as well as in preparing for the ACT/SAT. We also make sure our players take the SAT and ACT in their junior year. To ensure they get the best possible score, we have ACT and SAT preparation sessions in the fall. We are well aware that college entrance requirements are everchanging and some do not currently require college entrance tests. We also bring in local businesspeople to talk about the hiring process and hold mock interviews so the players are prepared for applying for jobs.

Regarding recruiting, you need to be aggressive in getting your players known to college coaches and programs. Your players should be able to make their own HiLite films on software such as HUDL (with the help of the coaching staff). Twitter and other social media platforms can also be useful in promoting your players throughout the season and postseason. You can update Hi Lite films or social media periodically. To get additional exposure for your players, film scrimmages or summer games and post them on "YouTube" for various college coaches to observe.

In our program we send out a preseason press guide to all local universities and media outlets. We insert a page for our senior players who have a chance at playing at the college level. In this day and age, to attain a scholarship I feel that a coach must be proactive and aggressive and get their players' names out early.

Seek opportunities to show you care. The smallest
gestures often make the biggest difference.

—John Wooden
Hall of Fame NCAA Coach

GBC

**My players don't care how much I know
until they know how much I care.**

SECTION 4:
HOW TO DEVELOP ELITE
STUDENT-ATHLETES

Overview

Instill Mental Toughness

- Develop the whole person—athletic, academic, ethical, and social
- Set rules
- Recognize a strong work ethic
- Schedule community service
- Involve the community
- Use the preseason wisely: condition the body, mind, and character
- Stress the power of choice
- Don't find fault; find the remedy
- Monitor your players' strength and conditioning
- Address sleep, nutrition, and hydration
- Prepare your players for the future—college, ACT/SAT, life skills, and recruiting
- Encourage relationship building

See appendices A through K at the back of the book for further information and relevant documents

SECTION 5

MENTOR'S ELITE SYSTEM: HOW WE WIN

We don't quit, we don't cower, we don't run. We endure and conquer.

—Kobe Bryant
Hall of Fame NBA Player

As the head coach, I have found you must work to prove you are worthy of your student-athletes' wholehearted allegiance so that they buy into your leadership. Once your team members commit themselves to following your lead, they will dedicate themselves to passionately preparing to pursue and achieve your vision.

My experience is that when we are prepared, the game will take care of itself. And when we learn to play together and learn to play hard, the winning will take care of itself.

In the 2020 MaxPreps' "Top Ten Most Dominant High School Boys Basketball Programs of the Last Ten Years," published on April 16, 2020, the Mentor Boys Basketball Program ranked seventh out of 827 schools and second in public school programs out of 700 in the state of Ohio. These statistics are based on the ten-year period that began in 2011 and ended in 2020. It should be noted that in both 2010 and 2021, we went to the state tournament. Both these years are outside the ten-year period noted in the statistics above and so are not included in the rankings for that decade. These statistics reflect the success of our program.

CHAPTER 36

Our Philosophy

Play the absolute best.

I have always agreed with NBA Coach Brad Stevens' perception that TGHT: The Game Honors Toughness. Play against tough players and develop a mindset that will elevate your game to new heights. Without it, you will just be average.

You cannot be elite unless you play the elite teams. Dominate your opposition. Compete. Prove yourself. We look for opportunities to develop the skills of individuals. To build confidence in yourself, your team, and your program, you have to put your team to the test. You must put yourself in a situation that shows how strong, skilled, and prepared you really are. You must establish and exhibit your quality of play. As mentioned previously, we schedule elite teams as independent games and Christmas tournaments to prepare for postseason.

This is why we want to play against the best teams in the state of Ohio. Christmas tournaments or showcases always attract elite teams, so you want to establish your team as elite. At the time this book is being prepared, I have accepted an invitation for our players to experience the elite competition that will be offered in the Cincinnati Princeton Christmas tournament for the 2021-22 season. The other two teams participating are Cincinnati St. Xavier and Cincinnati Taft. We ended the 2020-21 season rated as number one in the state. St. Xavier was ranked number three in the state. Cincinnati Taft went to the state tournament and has two nationally ranked players coming back. Cincinnati Princeton's Guard committed to The Ohio State University. We feel this is the best holiday tournament in the state. Participating in this tournament will give our players something to work towards and look forward to attending as the season begins and ultimately a taste of what truly competitive play entails. Our attendance at this prestigious tournament would not have been possible without the support of our athletic director and the Cardinal Cage Club.

You can dress a maximum of fifteen players in tournament play. Any players who will not receive a lot of playing time at Christmas tournaments or showcases are given the option of going to the tournament or showcase or staying home and participating in our home JV tournament. Allow them to choose between going and watching elite teams and players versus getting playing time for themselves.

Our goal is to be a tough team. Tough teams never lie down. They never concede defeat. Tough teams overcome hostile environments. Tough teams celebrate and dominate the non-glamour stats. Tough teams have one or more players who give their teammates courage. They have rosters filled with driven, self-motivated, high-motor players. They rally and persevere in the face of hardship and challenge. These types of players cultivate an aura of toughness in all they do, year in and year out.

Our winning basketball strategy is based on a strong work ethic. We foster the belief that you must work hard, run, press, and play fast. Our philosophy is that we outwork every other team we will potentially compete against. We stress that we are the hardest-working team in the state of Ohio.

From Coach Glenn Bower at Girard High School, I learned the value of a hard-nosed philosophy based around full-court pressure and an up-tempo style. From my Youngstown State University coach, Dom Rosselli, I learned no detail is insignificant. Execution in games, and especially practices, requires perfection.

Mentality is a word we use often. It is the mentality to press like winning the state title depends on every possession. The mentality of a scorer is when you catch the ball you have only two options: get a high-percentage shot for yourself, or create a shot for someone else. It is the mentality of absolutely wanting to be the lockdown defender, knowing that every possession is important. It is the mentality of working extremely hard in practice to prepare for the game. It is the mentality of not being afraid to take a shot or drive to the basket after you've missed a shot. It is the mentality of believing in yourself and your ability.

We stress it is not the first or second effort, but the third and fourth effort that will make us into an elite team. Mental toughness is the fabric of our culture and every aspect and every person associated with our program at every level must be committed to the attitude of mental toughness.

Consistency has also been our hallmark. We have a feeder system from grades three through nine that ensures that the student-athletes coming up through our system know our type of play and our coaches at each level are committed to it.

We believe that motivation, discipline, and toughness beat talent. If you want to prove your work ethic, change your weaknesses into strengths. When you do that, you reveal your work ethic to everyone. As a coach, you must find the individuals who want to be motivated. It is extremely difficult to motivate someone who does not want to be motivated.

Investing quality time is important. Everything must be done at game speed during preseason. So many young players practice at their pace, not at game pace and therefore are just wasting their time. When it comes to putting in quality time to improve their game, 80 percent of the players work at a game pace, but 20 percent do not. As a coach, you must put your time into those who are willing to invest significant time to improve their game skills. For those who are not practicing at game speed, I recommend that they watch film of a game vs. their practice efforts so they can experience and visualize the difference.

For us to be the best and compete with over eight hundred schools in the state of Ohio, we need to be ultimately prepared and the hardest working. We have a tournament tradition which is to get to the state boys basketball championship every year. To reach this goal, we must have a strong work ethic characterized by a willingness to work hard, to care about you playing your best, and no matter what, maintaining a positive attitude. This means doing more than expected at any given time. Knowing what it takes and the willingness to sacrifice gets you to the mountaintop.

Every mountaintop is within reach if you just keep climbing.

—Barry Finlay
Award-winning and Best-selling Author

Playing for Mentor is a privilege; it is not a right. We play athletes who deserve to play.

We value a "good loss." With every loss we endure, the first comment is, "The only way this can be a good loss is if we absolutely learn from it." We call the coaching staff together to discuss the loss. Next, we call the captains in with the coaching staff and then discuss it with the whole team. It is imperative you address any problems and deficiencies with the team and the captains immediately. Do not delay even one or two days to review the loss. Reviewing a good loss helps to ensure that positive changes will occur.

I believe as essayist, lecturer and philosopher Ralph Waldo Emerson noted, "the speed of the leader determines the rate of the pack." You might have one or two strong leaders out of four. You need strong young individuals as leaders. Everyone can lead when things are going in a positive direction. However, the captains and coaching staff must lead when things become negative. The quality of captains on our Mentor High School basketball teams has had a lot to do with our continuing success as a team.

Change is inevitable, so embrace it. Change is the law of life. When the three-point shot was introduced in the 1987–1988 season, we embraced it, we ran with it, and we dominated the competition. In 1988, our point guard at Girard High School, Nick Cochran, was mentioned in USA Today for successfully making eleven three-point shots in one game and leading the state in three-point shots made that season.

Those who look only to the past or present are certain to miss the future.

—John F. Kennedy
35th President of the United States

It may sound simple, but you must stress team effort. If one person is not playing at the level we need them to play, our press will not be effective. Everyone has to do their job for positive outcomes on the court to occur. Everyone must possess and exhibit leadership qualities—getting people to think, believe, see, and do. It means possessing the vision to set the right goal and the decisiveness to pursue it single-mindedly. Enforce upon your student-athlete if they think they will only be practicing two hours per day, they are wrong. You need to impress upon them that they need to invest time before and after practice and on off days.

A winner is someone who recognizes his God-given talents, works his tail off to develop them into skills, and uses them to accomplish his goals.

—Larry Bird
Hall of Fame NBA Player

I have discovered our success can also be traced to how strong the bond is between the members of our team. The bond between the players on both Girard High School and Mentor High School state tournament winning teams was exceptional. In close games, they knew what one another was going to do and how hard each of them was going to play for one another. Engraved on the inside of each of the players' championship rings were the words "Together" and "Brotherhood" respectively. I firmly believe that the strong bond between our team members allowed us to be victorious.

Former player Ian Kipp, currently at Kent State University, shared the following as he reflected on this bond that exists in the Mentor program: "Mentor basketball showed me what it was like to be a part of a true family, not just a team, all thanks to a group of guys who put winning before themselves. I walked away from Mentor basketball with lifelong friends and an unbreakable mindset."

I want to emphasize that although I do delegate a lot to my assistants and captains, everyone realizes that the tone is set by me as the head coach including energy, motivation, and responsibility.

I also believe we have been highly successful in our program because our coaching staff and players have always shared an understanding of what to do in adverse situations. Overcoming adversity is paramount. During tournament play, you have to be prepared in every facet—on and off the court, in the classroom, and health-wise.

After each game we win, we spend fifteen minutes talking about our opponent and what lies ahead of us, making sure our players recognize we are not done until the state tournament.

IT IS A MINDSET—A MENTALITY.

This is what Mentor believes in. This is our philosophy.

"Good teams become great ones when the members trust each other enough to surrender the Me for the We."

—Phil Jackson
NBA head coach

218

NH

2013
Mentor Cardinals under Coach Bob Krizancic win the state title.

Mentor has established a long-standing tournament tradition.

Mentor's Tournament Tradition

TOURNAMENT TRADITION

Now is the time of year for some to fall and for others to
rise to the occasion. Some more often than not -
continually rise above the others. It's called Tradition,
and better yet - Tournament Tradition. It's pride above all
else. It's knowing what it takes and to be able to
sacrifice to do whatever it takes to reach the mountaintop.
Some teams have that, it's in the uniform and inside the
heart, sometimes you don't even know it's there, but you'll
be able to tell it's there. It will surface when you need
it most.

There is only one way to go about the pressures of this time
of year. To stand up and be counted, to be strong in your
belief and goals. To look at a challenge and take it on -
head on, no backing down, guts for glory, no selling out, no
pointing fingers, put up or shut up, life or death! Some
people and some teams are fearful, you can see it in their
eyes and read it in their face. You'll know where you
stand, there is no in between!

There are area teams who know they will be there. Not all
the time, but time and time again they are there - district,
regional and state. People unfairly expect it, the fans
who don't know what blood is spilled, what sweat is expired,
what tears are shed. They say you'll be there, they say
it's your time of year - and they are right - DEAD RIGHT!
You will be there, district, regionals, and state - but only
if you get there together - only if you spill the blood,
only if you sweat the sweat, only if your willing to cry the
tears. You may not know you have it inside you but it's in
the uniform, it's in the halls, it's in the heart -
Tournament Tradition only lives in a few, not in all.
GUTS FOR GLORY, LIFE OR DEATH.......NO SELLING OUT!!!

Contributed by an unknown source

CHAPTER 37

Our Game-Winning Strategy

Offense, Defense, and Pressing—
What We Run and What We Do

Our game-winning strategy is based on mental toughness, preparedness, and our belief in our ability to win.

We always approach the game with a strong focus. We believe we must dominate especially at the end of the third and fourth quarters. Key words that stress strong focus are composure, intelligence, and belief. Our players know we need thirty-two minutes of total focus and all-out hustle to make our scoring runs.

Our program's philosophy is that we want to press, we want to run, we want to wear down our opponents, and we want to create mismatches, especially in transition. We talk about being aggressive, being strong, and having absolutely "no fear." Our players are conditioned to understand that it starts with our pressure defense and full court presses. The majority of our drills in practice are full court. All four presses we run full court are a combination of man-to-man and zone defense, but we are always in our man-to-man in our half-court sets.

Offensively, our goal is to take a shot within seven seconds on every possession. In practices, the majority of our offensive drills are full court, and we utilize a seven-second shot clock. I realize that this is not going to happen every single possession during games, but our players totally understand the pace at which we want to play.

Offensively, we are always looking for a quick mismatch. We look to get picks in transition. We have found it is so hard to hedge a pick in transition, and opposing big men run to the rim and then come out so a pick in transition works almost every time. When we are at the three-minute mark in the fourth quarter of the game, our players totally understand that it is "lay up only" time. We spread the floor and only the players who are high percentage free throw shooters should touch the basketball.

Our players must know how many time-outs we have left and which is the direction of the possession arrow. We have out-of-bounds set plays and press breakers. We must have total communication on substitutions. If we are behind in the score our players understand which full court presses to run and who to potentially foul. We try to save time-outs to the end of the game. However, if chaos happens on the court, you cannot afford to save it for the end of the game. You must address that situation immediately. When you feel positive energy, let the players play through it. Time-outs can be useful to give your players a break, to set up plays, to stop the clock, or to stop your opponent's momentum.

As I have said before, I believe that the game honors toughness and that the mental to the physical is four to one, but my belief is it is much greater. We don't talk about winning; we talk about putting the game away. We do not want the game to come down to an official's call or even be a close game. We look for two major scoring runs in the first half and two in the second half. We constantly strive to wear our competition down and to be mentally and physically stronger than our opponent.

As shown on the following page, I have set up a game day schedule that focuses on the mental preparation for the game. This schedule is designed to prepare our team physically and emotionally. I want my team to be absolutely sure they know what to do. I do not want them to guess. There can be no break between the thought process and the action taken.

The following is our home game schedule:

3:00 p.m. to 4:00 p.m.	EAT PRE-GAME MEAL AT HOME AND HYDRATE
5:00 p.m.	VARSITY PLAYERS SHOOT IN AUXILIARY GYM—HYDRATE
5:50 p.m.	FILM ROOM—WATCH FILMS AND GO OVER PRELIMINARIES—HYDRATE
6:10 p.m. to 6:45 p.m.	SEE TRAINER FOR ANY TAPING; GET DRESSED; WATCH JV GAME
6:49 p.m.	TEAM LOCKER ROOM—FOR THOSE PLAYERS WHO OPT IN, ONE MINUTE OF REFLECTION, MEDITATION, OR PRAYER TO MENTALLY PREPARE FOR THE GAME AHEAD
6:50 p.m.	TEAM LOCKER ROOM-REVIEW OUR GAME STRATEGY: OFFENSES, DEFENSES, PRESS BREAKERS, PRESSES, OBs, AND DEFENSIVE MATCH-UPS
7:10 p.m.	PRE-GAME WARM-UPS
7:30 p.m.	GAME TIME
~9:00 p.m.	LOCKER ROOM—POST-GAME TALK ABOUT TONIGHT'S GAME, CURFEW, AND WHAT'S AHEAD

During Christmas tournaments or Saturday games, the team members arrive at our facility at 11:00 a.m. The players must have eaten breakfast. After they arrive, we proceed to watch films and walk through exactly what we want to do in the upcoming game.

We review with the players whom they are guarding. When we prep for other teams, we tell our players that it is 99 percent of what Mentor does and not what the other team does. It is 99 percent how hard we play, how well we execute, and to what degree we believe in ourselves. It is all about our team. That is our philosophy. We review game films, not of teams that we are going to play but of teams that we beat that are so much more talented. That is how our team and players understand that all this is about us, not whom we play.

If you get tough mentally, you can get tough physically and overcome fatigue.

—Pat Riley
Hall of Fame NBA Coach

SECTION 5:
MENTOR'S ELITE SYSTEM:
HOW WE WIN

Overview

Exude Mental Toughness

- We believe we are capable of winning
- We embrace a strong work ethic: playing is not a right; it is a privilege
- We stress mental and physical toughness
- We focus on winning the state title
- We seek out and engage in opportunities to develop
- We maintain consistency throughout the organization
- We develop and nurture relationships
- We prepare

See appendices G, H, and I at the back of the book for further information and relevant documents.

SECTION 6

HOW DEVELOPING AN ELITE HIGH SCHOOL BASKETBALL PROGRAM PREPARES ATHLETES FOR FUTURE SUCCESS

Show me someone who has done something worthwhile
and I will show you someone who has overcome adversity.

—Lou Holtz
NFL Coach

An elite high school basketball program develops many attributes in its student-athletes, but the most life-altering is mental toughness. Mental toughness enables them to meet and overcome obstacles in their path to successfully reach their goals. They develop a new perspective on what it takes to succeed and the need to be prepared for challenges. Student-athletes develop the ability to handle frustration, nurture relationships, possess a strong work ethic, and gain experience with the media. Most importantly, student-athletes develop the right attitude toward setbacks and strength under stress. They know how to focus on long-term goals and hold a steady course to overcome obstacles in their path.

CHAPTER 38

Testimonials and Inspiration from Former Players

Former players share their insights into the qualities they developed that had a lasting impact on their post-graduation successes.

Former basketball players on Coach Krizancic's teams attribute much of their success after graduation to the habits they developed while playing for him. Coach Krizancic would remind his players, "You can't fake toughness. **Toughness isn't a look, it's an ability**. Toughness doesn't take plays off, and it doesn't take days off. **If you're "tough," you will succeed in life." Mental toughness is the gateway to success. It is a game changer in basketball and life.**

Former players/alum have successfully pursued many different postgraduate paths. The vast majority have finished their college degrees. Among our graduates are coaches, businesspeople, account representatives, attorneys, entrepreneurs, financial analysts, engineers, teachers and school administrators, medical professionals, members of the armed forces (including Army Rangers), and professional baseball, basketball, and football players.

An elite basketball program instills self-confidence in its student-athletes, and self-confidence controls a person's success. The more a person believes in themselves, the better they will become.

Recently, a point guard on our 2013 Mentor State Championship team who was the Most Valuable Player in the state tournament related a story about how being on the Mentor team affected his career. After graduating from college, the player applied to a national car rental company. There were five very impressive candidates for the position. The party interviewing him was in his late twenties and, after the second interview, explained that he had attended St. Edwards High School and still carried the vivid memory of playing Mentor in the regional finals and of Mentor beating them and going on to win the state championship. **He said that he respected Mentor's work ethic and toughness and, as a result, felt confident in giving the job to the ex-Mentor player because he knew that his new hire would bring these qualities to the job.**

Reflecting on their time in Coach Krizancic's program at Girard and their 1993 state championship win, players from that Girard team quickly noted the following:

Philip Huyler was the 1993 Division II state tournament MVP. He relates how his experience at Girard, playing for Coach Krizancic, and winning the state tournament was life-changing. He was later awarded a scholarship to attend Florida Atlantic University where he played Division I basketball and he was MVP twice. Philip's nickname was "Lionheart," which he took from his days playing for Girard. Philip runs his own financial firm with locations in south Florida and California.

> From a very young age, I remember playing basketball on the outside courts with no type of physical training or weightlifting; we were just happy to have a decent basketball to play with. The late Mr. Godfrey McQuay, my very first basketball coach in the Bahamas, believed in me and gave me the confidence I needed to make my dream a reality and to attain a college degree. Mrs. Laverne Beachum of Girard, Ohio made my trip to the United States possible and as a result, I was enrolled at Girard High School.
>
> At Girard High School, Coach Krizancic, our head coach, believed in my abilities and

inspired me to be athletically ready to play basketball at a high level. Coach Krizancic would always say, "Speed it up, Philip. Make it into a track meet and run it down their throats." Coach Krizancic asked if I was ever nervous. Instantly, with no hesitation, I replied *no*. **We were prepared and ready; we were warriors.** We knew we were in better condition than our competition thanks to Coach O'Hara, our strength and conditioning coach.

I clearly remember my teammates coming to me for the first time and asking me if I wanted to go to "open gym." They wanted to see if I could play. I had no idea of what the term "open gym" meant and was amazed to learn that I had access to an indoor gym to practice playing basketball with my teammates because I only played basketball on the outside courts in the Bahamas.

I am so thankful for all of my teammates because they were the ones who accepted and allowed me to be myself at all times. As a team we were like brothers, and that is the reason why we used the word TOGETHER and how it became our mantra, our battle cry! **We were definitely together, and the chemistry was the reason for our success.**

Once I had been exposed to the opportunity to play indoors, **I created a new mantra for myself called the three Cs, which stood for COMMIT, COMPETE, and CONQUER.** As I look back at everything, over twenty plus years later, those lessons and victories are kept within me today. **I am always competing at a high level like there's no tomorrow. I expect to win every day and excel for greatness. Maintaining a positive attitude even while facing adversity, loving your**

teammates, and treating everyone fair that you encounter are other lessons I took away with me. So, as I live my life today, I believe it's important to be a big dreamer and have ambition to fulfill those dreams. Furthermore, when it comes to your dreams and goals, NEVER, NEVER, NEVER **give up, and** NEVER **quit.**

Nick D'Eramo is also in finance: a portfolio manager for J.P. Morgan. Nick offered the following on how playing for Coach Krizancic impacted his life:

> In 1993, I was fortunate to be a senior on the Girard High School basketball team under Coach Krizancic when we won the State D2 Basketball Championship. As time goes by, it's amazing to think back on those four years playing under Coach Krizancic and **how so much of what was learned at either a team meal, film room, locker room, or basketball court helped shape me into the person I am today.** In my mind, I have no doubts that those experiences playing for Coach Krizancic were integral in preparing me for life after high school basketball and my over twenty-year career in asset management.
>
> Toughness is the first thing that comes to mind as a key to our success. Not just physical toughness but mental toughness as well. **The ability to mesh the physical and mental together during times of adversity can create a strong, calming sense of self-confidence.**
>
> Next are togetherness and accountability. I loved my teammates and coaches—not all the time but the majority of the time. When we would break from a time-out, we would say,

"Together." It wasn't just a word; we lived by it. **Coach Krizancic was able to build a family atmosphere where everyone played for one another. Every individual on the team had a role, and every individual needed to be prepared to execute their role.**

Finally, **I learned the importance of being prepared.** Not only were we one of the most conditioned teams in the state of Ohio, we knew whom we were playing. There weren't many surprises when we played the game. We knew the opposing players and the teams' tendencies both offensively and defensively. I manage mutual funds and ETFs for J.P. Morgan in both the passive equity and asset allocation spaces. Playing for Coach Krizancic at Girard impacted my career by giving me the confidence to believe in myself to go after my life goals and to be mentally tough to withstand life's adverse moments.

Keith Swan, who was the fifth starter on the Girard team, is now an engineer developing new vehicles at Fiat-Chrysler near Detroit. Keith recently shared:

Playing sports in general can instill in you a **perseverance to push through tough moments, a willingness to push yourself when no one is looking, and a will to improve and practice that extends well beyond the basketball court. Being a part of such a great team proves that no achievement, no matter how great, is out of reach if you're willing to put in the time and effort it takes to improve every day.** These were all life lessons that were honed during long practices where "good enough" was never acceptable.

I've carried that mentality through my personal life and my career.

Brad Root described the Girard team's brand of mental toughness: "**When the chips are down and you're really faced with some adversity, dig deep and good things will happen.**" He is still conscious of "how great things were and how together of a team we were and close-knit." Root is part owner of a company that leases MRI and CAT scan machines.

Alrashan Clardy, whose nickname was "Beep," was the sixth man on the Girard team. He explained, "**Coach was a great mentor and an excellent teacher of the game. He showed me tough love that I needed at the time.**"

Kris Kelly, who went on to play football at the University of Rhode Island, noted, "You know, **we're a group of brothers,** and a lot of us still keep in contact." Kris works in insurance. He recalled the championship game against Columbus Whitehall-Yearling and being told "No" after asking for help in guarding future pro Samaki Walker at the five-minute mark. "Girard was down by four points at the time. The coaches said that they couldn't sag off any other player. I was told "No" because the coaches believed that I was capable of defending against Walker. **Their belief in my skill level made me believe in myself** as an important contributor to our team and the win. Walker ended the game with only twenty-four points. He did not score in the last twenty-five minutes of the game. I shut down Samaki Walker."

The Mentor players have also been quick to point out the lasting positive impact that playing for the Mentor program under Coach Krizancic had on their careers and lives.

Robert Lombardo, an entrepreneur engaged in real estate finance and development, described what made the Mentor program so special:

> From the beginning, **you could always see the passion Coach Krizancic had**, and that rubbed off on everyone, from the children in his youth

camps to the parents of his students and his athletes. **When you grow up in his system, the first thing he teaches you is mental toughness: working through the pain of whatever life and basketball throw at you and fearlessly pursuing your goals**. Igniting that passion not only took kids from diverse backgrounds and molded them together to create powerhouse teams but also helped unlock the potential of gifted athletes with a hand in the careers of two Mr. Footballs, a Mr. Basketball, a future all-American pitcher, and sixth round draft pick in Kade McClure, a future NFL number two overall NFL draft pick and Pittsburgh Steelers quarterback in Mitch Trubisky, and NBA Miami Heat player Micah Potter. Even extending beyond athletics, his impact is seen in the daily lives of so many of his prior athletes and their successes, not only in their careers but in their family life as well.

Kade McClure, currently with the Chicago White Sox, expressed how the work ethic he developed under Coach Krizancic has paved the way for his successes as a professional sports figure:

> Playing basketball under Coach Krizancic and his staff prepared me for the rigorous days ahead of being a Division I athlete as well as a professional. I attribute my work ethic and commitment to developing my craft as a professional baseball player to the days under Coach 'K'. Our program helped me learn to play for something bigger than myself. We were coached to be successful on and off the court.

For **Collin Barth**, with the exception of his parents, no one else impacted his life as much as Coach Krizancic:

> I'm sure I'm not the only one who feels that way. He was truly the one person that was the major contributor to me growing from a boy to a man; and looking back, he truly treated me, along with every other player he's ever coached, like his own son. Over and over you hear, "I can't win with boys. I need men." **He loves you but challenges you to be your absolute best each and every day both on and off the court. One of his quotes I'll never forget is, "My job is to get 100 percent out of your body that God gave you."** I believe that every time he says it, he means every word, and that's almost a mission statement to his life, and what his gift is, and why God put him here.
>
> His leadership style is unique compared to others, and a lot of people honestly may not agree with it. Almost every player struggles to understand him or read him while you play for him, and it absolutely frustrates you to death. But it's one of those love/hate relationships that you love him, but you're too young and naive to understand why he rides you so hard EVERY DAY. It isn't until the end of your senior year, when your time has run up playing for him, that you understand **what he was doing the whole time**, and that was only **trying to make you the absolute best you could be.** It hits you like a ton of bricks when it's over, that you won't have him screaming at you every day and that you'd give up anything to go back just for a day to go to war with him. The people that are in the trenches with him every day will never forget him and what he did for

them. **Using basketball, he molds you into a man.**

I was an AAU coach for five years and then a college basketball coach for four years, and Coach Krizancic was definitely a part of me choosing to do that. Not only my choosing to do it but how I did it. I always said, "If I can impact my players half as much as Coach Krizancic impacted me, then I'm doing my job."

It was only until my family had some health issues that I came back to run our family's construction company and invest in real estate. But even though it's a different industry, I still run our company with the same foundational values he's instilled in me. Obviously, a different approach because of the audience of adults and not high school kids, but in terms of approach, he will always be there with me no matter what I do and how I operate.

Andrew Valeri also commented on Coach Krizancic's lasting impact:

If had to highlight **what makes Coach Krizancic so special is not his ability to coach the game of basketball; it's his ability to prepare us for life by using the game of basketball as a platform.** I am twenty-two years old, four years removed from the program; and in every aspect of my life, I always compare it to what Coach Krizancic would say, and he would say, "**It's all mentality—everything is.**" And till this day, I strive to control my mind and mentality every day to impact myself and those around me. He also would say, "Show me your friends, and I'll show you your future." **Surrounding myself with integral individuals**

who have a vision is the second-most important lesson I have learned from Coach Krizancic. No number of wins or championships will ever compare to how many young lives he's changed and impacted in such a positive way.

I am self-employed as of now and graduating in May from Otterbein University with a major in business administration and management and a minor in finance. I am looking to start my own ventures and become a full-time investor. **Success at being self-employed requires that I draw upon the Mentor work ethic: don't wait for anything, no handouts, go out and make it happen.**

For **Kyle McIntosh**, playing for Coach Krizancic for four years developed him as a basketball player but even more as a person.

One of the many things I took away from my relationship with Coach Krizancic was the idea of "mental toughness." You would hear that phrase multiple times every practice as this was one thing that he wanted us to understand as we went through the season. This idea of "mental toughness" is something I took with me after graduating from Mentor High School and into my next phase of life at Case Western Reserve University.

After my freshman year at CWRU, I decided to pursue a master's degree in finance along with my bachelor's degree in economics. This started off a little rough as it was difficult to handle classes associated with both degrees at the same time. **During these more challenging times, I would think back to how Coach Krizancic would preach "mental toughness" and how if you really believe you can do something, you can make it happen.** This extra push or drive that I get when I think about the idea of "mental toughness" has allowed me to succeed in my four years at CWRU. In a few weeks, I will be graduating with both my bachelor's and master's degrees and a job offer from Sherwin-Williams. Through these last four years, I can definitely attribute some of my successes to Coach Krizancic and all the lessons he taught me.

Dr. Joe Meyer reiterated that Mentor's work ethic has served him well. He recently received his doctorate in physical therapy.

Coach Krizancic gets his players to understand that **success does not come easy, but if you work hard enough, anything is possible.** During my years in the Mentor program, I grew to understand the value of hard work and what it takes to follow through on achieving your goals. After basketball, I focused on academics, and today I am fortunate to have my dream job as a physical therapist.

Greg Miller, a former high school teacher, varsity basketball coach, and recently named athletic director in the School District of Greenville County, South Carolina, reflected on how the Mentor program stresses the importance of being elite in every aspect of life. He writes:

Perspective is an interesting thing. While some people may see the wins, the championships, or the cup of water, those of us that have been a part of Mentor Basketball share a life perspective that makes us different. Playing for Coach Krizancic goes far deeper than a game. It is a program that prepares you for life. **His perspective of creating Ohio's top basketball program has translated into turning kids from Mentor into men**

capable of achieving what they, without their Mentor program experience, may have never been able to achieve. When you begin playing basketball at Mentor, you learn how to be elite in the game. When you enter the real world, you realize that you have been prepared to be elite in life. **Because of Coach Krizancic's vision, leadership, and caring for others, the true reasons why the Mentor Basketball program is elite is because basketball was always secondary. Building elite men was the core.**

In my life, I still hear Coach Krizancic's voice during times of difficulty and realize that the extra "suicides" didn't kill me, and this tough time won't either. Sometimes I may not be getting the results out of life that I want, and then I remember how to work "game speed." I am able to get back to working with a purpose. I still tell stories of the good old days to anyone who will listen, and I pray that I can impact others the way Coach Krizancic, Coach Grantz, and the rest of his staff have impacted us for all these years. **To truly understand why Mentor Basketball has been elite for so many years, you have to learn to see the perspective of its creator—one with purpose, driven to a standard that many are unwilling to strive for, and orchestrated by a dealer of hope whose purpose was the success of others**. Perspective is an interesting thing, and I am grateful to have had the perspective of playing basketball at Mentor.

To **Brad Gerard**, a math teacher at Mentor High, the importance of relationship and of the experience of belonging to something bigger than yourself is what he values from his days playing for Coach Krizancic and the Mentor Program.

When I think of Mentor Basketball, one word comes to mind—*family*. **Coach Krizancic has created more than just a basketball program. He has created an extended family of players and coaches that spans more than thirty years.** It doesn't matter if you played in the early '90's or the mid-2000s; players continue to keep in touch and come back to see him year after year. Every time, they are greeted with a hug and a smile as if it were a father greeting a son.

It makes you feel like you are a part of something special and unique. When he won his state title, we all (thirty years of players) felt like we won the state title with him. I can't begin to describe how being a part of the Mentor Basketball family has impacted my life, from going into the business world to becoming a teacher and coach in the very same building and gym that I played in. **The one thing that I have taken wherever I have been is the importance of relationships.** I try to develop relationships with my students and former players because in the end, that is what matters. The wins, titles, and successes are great; but when all of that is done, what you have is the relationships that were built and sustained over the years.

Coach Krizancic is still a part of my life nineteen years after I graduated. He came to see my play in college, and he was at my wedding almost fourteen years ago, He knows my four kids, and my oldest son attends the same basketball camps that I attended and worked. I hope he sticks around long enough so my son(s) can become a part of his ever-growing family of basketball.

Alex Edwards, a team captain in his senior year at Mentor, explained how he learned to push himself further than he ever knew and what it takes to be a good, effective leader.

When I first became part of the Mentor High School basketball program as a Freshman, I was terrified of Coach Krizancic. To a young player, he was an intimidating figure who sought perfection out of his varsity roster. When I finally got the opportunity to be coached by him, my eyes were opened. Going into my senior year, I was voted by the prior senior class to be a captain. This is somewhat rare in the light that I had never played a minute of varsity basketball, and Coach Krizancic most likely did not even know my name. My senior year changed my outlook on Coach Krizancic and sports in general. We built a relationship solely off respect for each other.

To this day, I am in awe of the way he consistently breeds success on and off the court. **He taught me mental toughness in that he had ways of showing me that I was blessed with the ability to push myself further than I ever knew.** He challenged me every day, asking whether I would choose to be good or great. He reminded me that not just basketball but life is a mental game; it is all about how you react when knocked down. He taught me to have thick skin and to take criticism in a way that would better me. **Between the lines of the basketball court, he pushed me to my limit every single day but knew exactly when to turn the switch between being a coach and being the person to whom I could go with anything.**

I am a firm believer that success comes from good leadership. Coach Krizancic has over six hundred wins in the Mentor program, as well as two state championships under his belt. Very few coaches can say they have been as successful as him, and it all starts with his leadership. Those willing to take his lessons and words to heart have also been impacted in the way I have. **He has the unique ability to be a father figure, friend, teacher, and coach all at the same time.**

Today I am a finance major at the University of Cincinnati. Coach Krizancic wrote me a recommendation letter during my application process to help get me to college and is a reference on my résumé that has gotten me an internship as a freshman. I am so grateful for the year I got to play for Coach Krizancic. He is the face of one of the most elite high school programs in the state of Ohio and continues year after year to impact the lives of many. Because of his impact on my life, I will forever be inspired to be even half the man he is and to give back to him in any way that I can. Coach Krizancic will always be the most influential coach I ever had the opportunity to play for and learn from. **I aspire to be the leader and inspiration that he was for me to somebody else.** It is not always the talent or the height or the abilities that make an elite basketball program; it's the coach that leads you to success. **I have found that life is all about connections and relationships**, and Coach Krizancic is one connection that I will be proud to mention every single time.

Justin Fritts, the 2012 Ohio Mr. Basketball, was also impacted by Coach Krizancic's coaching style. Justin currently works as a medical device sales representative for Stryker Sports Medicine and is also a player for the Burning River Buckets, an American Basketball

Association (ABA) semi-pro team. He explained that he learned that hard work and the proper mental attitude are key elements to success.

The one quote or saying that still resonates with me today is Coach saying, "The mental is to physical, as four is to one." At the time, I took that saying and applied it to basketball. We were never the biggest or fastest (although we were pretty fast) team on the court—but **what we lacked in physical stature, we made up for with our willingness to compete every day.** I would be pressed to find a team who worked harder in the off-season/preseason than we did. Between summer shootouts, preseason conditioning (brutal), and early November/December practices—the actual season itself was the easy part.

To me, there is only so much you can teach about mental toughness. **Coach Krizancic and company built a program that instilled mental toughness.**

I remember one playoff game where, during a time-out, Coach Krizancic completely stopped what he was doing and told us to look over at the other team. This isn't an exact quote, but he said something along the lines of: "Do you understand why we do things the way we do?" We did not know exactly what he meant. He said, "Look over there, look at them. They just burned a time-out because they can't catch their breath." I remember looking over and seeing two players actually sitting and getting water while the other three were curled over and hands on top of their head, gasping for air.

This was where Mentor basketball flourishes. **"Mental is to physical as four is to one."** I still think about this quote regularly as I now try and apply it to my career in sales. Whether in basketball or everyday life, talent will only get you so far.

Jason Ioppolo, a rising senior point guard, was one of the Cardinal's top returning players when he met Coach Krizancic. He thought he was working hard until he was part of Coach Krizancic's Mentor basketball program reformation. He expressed surprise that only one year in the program under Coach Krizancic made such an impact on his self-confidence and mental toughness:

> I've always thought that playing for Coach Krizancic, albeit only for one year, made a major impact in my life. Here are two areas that can be applied to all aspects of life.
>
> The first is self-confidence. In short, I didn't believe in my abilities quite like I should have before Coach Krizancic arrived at Mentor. His belief in me and relentless passion to get the best out of me every day really flipped a switch in my mind.
>
> Coach Krizancic called me in 1993 to inform me that he was the new head coach at Mentor, and there would be some changes in the program. He made it clear that we, as a program, could be better, and he started to outline what he believed was the outline to success. As a seventeen-year-old senior, I honestly didn't know what team success looked like on the basketball court because I had not played on a lot of winning teams.
>
> What caught me by surprise was when he asked me what type of player I wanted to become and what level of college basketball I thought I was capable of. He went into details involving how to become a better player, team identity, team goals, and our style of play. **He already had my buy-in because he had this passion about helping me become the best version of myself and how our**

team can become the best version of itself. When you aren't used to winning and you're unsure of how to get there, it's hard to believe you can be successful. Coach Krizancic laid out a plan on how to make it happen, provided examples, and had us believing in ourselves even when we met challenges along the way. He arranged for us to play our new league mates in a challenging summer circuit that included the league's toughest teams. It was the toughest summer league he could find, and it changed the mentality of our program.

Every coach has some type of a plan, but Coach Krizancic had a way to create action and instill confidence in his players. **Coach Krizancic's strong belief in his style of play really helped us because we had an identity and something to really believe in.** We thought he was crazy sometimes at practice and in film sessions, but he knew what success looked like and wanted us to see it and experience it for ourselves. Once we started having success, our confidence continued to build and changed our mindset of who we were.

The second is mental toughness. Mental toughness has to be the foundation of the Mentor basketball program since 1993. From day one, Coach Krizancic brought a new mindset to our program, and it challenged us in ways we hadn't experienced before. **From our new style of play to the level of competition he exposed us to made us stare discomfort right in the face, figure it out, and fight through it.**

Both self-confidence and mental toughness are what help us all get through those tough times we have or will eventually have in life. I greatly appreciate what Coach Krizancic brought out of us, and I still hear his voice in my head regularly when I'm coaching. My goal has always been to do the same for the players whom I coach because it can have such a profound impact on their life.

To **Chris Jaklich**, the year he spent as a senior in Coach Krizancic's basketball program set him on the path for success after graduation and gave him insight regarding the relationship between preparedness and success:

> The thing that Coach Krizancic taught me the most was mental toughness. I was only in the Mentor program for my senior year, but that year helped prepare and pave the way for my successful college career. He never let you get too high or stay too low. He had an incredible way to relate to his players. His background in psychology was very evident. **He also pushed the right buttons and would adapt his style of communication to each player. Some needed tough love; some needed a gentle push or positive words. He just knew how to relate to everyone.** To this day, I regard him as the best coach I ever had because he taught you skills that would help you throughout your entire life, not just on the basketball court.

Confidence to face life's challenges is the quality that **Jaron Crowe** gleaned from his days on the basketball court while playing for Mentor and Coach Krizancic. He stresses:

> Playing for an elite high school basketball program like Mentor provides young athletes with much more than simply high-level basketball coaching. It has been ten years since I last played for Coach Krizancic and his assistants at Mentor. I can now confidently confirm that the life lessons and certain character attributes that I gained

during my time at Mentor far exceed the basketball skills/knowledge that I walked away with.

Anyone that is familiar with the Mentor basketball program can confirm that year in and year out, we overachieve to a degree. We are never the tallest, strongest, or most athletic team, but **playing with heart and having confidence can go a long way—not only in the game of basketball but in life itself. My favorite quote that Coach Krizancic reiterated daily was, "Failing to prepare is preparing to fail."** Ten years ago, these were just words on a piece of paper; however, now this quote has much more meaning. I want to excel in every aspect of my life. I believe any situation one may find themselves in, if you are confident, you have nothing to worry about. **Now to gain confidence, one must prepare in a way that failure is not an option. The confidence I once had on the basketball floor from practicing ten thousand plus hours has now translated to the point in my everyday life that, no matter what life throws at me, I am confident enough that I know I cannot fail.** I work for an insurance brokerage firm on our financial due-diligence team. I work on potential acquisitions, so regarding the quote I gave, my work is only as good as how prepared I am. **The long hours I have to put in to be prepared when I go into meetings provides me with the confidence to be good at what I do in my job.** If it wasn't for the work ethic that I have engraved in me, I wouldn't be able to do what I do.

As **Jack Korsok** put it, as a result of his interaction with Coach Krizancic, he learned to understand that the basis for the success of Coach Krizancic's program was his commitment to his players, his passion to excel, and his dedication to bringing out the best in his players:

> Mentor Basketball was a very large part of my high school years while I lived in Mentor. I had grown up waiting and wanting to be a part of such a prestigious and well-known program built by Coach Krizancic and his team of coaches. I started playing varsity basketball when I was a sophomore, which is when I started to talk to Coach Krizancic every day and when I started to build a good relationship with him. One of the most fascinating features about Bob was that he loved every single one of his players, kept up with what they were doing in and outside of school, and tried to help them out as much as he could in both life and basketball. That is the type of coach he was, and I think having that passion for your players like he had was why he has impacted so many people throughout his career.
>
> Coach Krizancic was the definition of a competitor, and he always hated losing more than he loved winning. He was obsessed with being great, and he worked very hard to instill that in his players. **Every day, good or bad, Coach Krizancic would bring the same energy to practice and push us to be the best that we could be. He always used to tell us that we could always push harder, that the body is capable of much more than we know, and that we were strong enough mentally to overcome obstacles and be the best.** I learned many lessons outside of basketball about life during my time with Coach Krizancic. Bob Krizancic helped me grow into the person I am today, and I will always be grateful for the time I spent in the

Mentor basketball program. He always told me that he would be my greatest supporter and my greatest critic and always made sure that things were done right. I will always be appreciative for the lessons learned, memories made, and championships won at Mentor with all my teammates and coaches.

For **Danny Wallack**, Coach Krizancic taught him the value of discipline and building quality relationships:

From day one, I learned the importance of building quality relationships. One of my favorite quotes from Coach Krizancic is "the quality of your life is the quality of your relationships." Coach Krizancic put a large emphasis on the importance of surrounding myself with people who have similar goals and work ethics. I learned that the decisions and actions of those I surround myself with can be a direct reflection on myself.

Furthermore, I learned the difference between pain of regret versus pain of discipline. Coach Krizancic taught me the importance of work ethic and fighting through the pain now so that you don't have to suffer the pain of regret down the road. I am an accountant for Ernst and Young. **I work in teams on a daily basis, and communication is essential. Building quality working relationships with coworkers not only makes work more enjoyable, but it helps when adversity hits, and we need to work through problems. Quality relationships help reduce barriers that are in the way when working to find that solution.** Further, relationship building plays a big role in my growth within the firm. I have to build relationships and earn the trust of my peers so that they are confident I can accomplish my tasks. I work with clients on a daily basis, and my decisions/actions in front of the client are a direct representation of EY as a whole.

Like other ex-players, **Michael Gallagher** learned that setting high goals, working harder than anyone else, and attention to detail are keys to success on the basketball court and in life.

From my years playing under Coach Krizancic and the Mentor Basketball program, I was able to develop and apply a few important values throughout my collegiate and young professional career. The traits that have resonated with me the most throughout my life include **having no fear, to set incredible goals and standards for myself, and then using my work ethic to actually accomplish the goals that I set.**

I was always told that to be elite, I had to not only challenge myself to be the best that I can be individually, but to believe that I could be better than anyone else in the country. In setting such high standards, the only way that those goals could be accomplished was to work harder than I could imagine possible. **I developed a relentless work ethic** to help me be the best basketball player I could be, and I succeeded as an integral part in our team's achieving the goal of winning a state championship.

Now in my life, I've developed new aspirations, and have continued to set new goals to achieve my dreams. I know that to achieve my goals, I need to continue to work as hard as I ever have. After four years of working for Toyota North America as a Buyer and Project Manager in their Purchasing Division, I developed a new dream to pursue. I've since embarked on a new challenge by changing industries and moving to Chicago to work for Kraft Heinz. My new role has me procuring all of the fruit and juices for the company's North American brands, such as Kool-Aid and Capri Sun. One of the greatest lessons I learned from Coach Krizancic is **attention to detail**. We would practice the same plays over and over or shoot free throws after every practice because **we were taught that all the details, no matter how small, could impact a game.** I have used that same mentality and applied it to everything I do. At work, **I need to be meticulous in my calculations, research, and decision-making.** I take pride in my ability to create approvals for management based on my findings. **I trust that because of my effort and attention to detail, my decisions will be accepted, and I am able to positively impact our company** in terms of quality and cost saving.

Brody Nelson was quick to point out that being a part of Coach Krizancic's elite basketball program infused in him mental toughness, a strong work ethic, and a competitive spirit. Brody is a biomedical engineer at Element Materials Technology in Cincinnati. He works with orthopedic total joint replacements and other medical devices. He is also a real estate investor.

Being a part of an elite high school basketball (or other sport) program in high school absolutely prepares one for the life beyond the game.

When I think back to all the things that being a part of Coach Krizancic's program has done for me, the first thing that comes to mind is *mentality*. If you want to play for Coach Krizancic, you will figure out a way to become mentally tough. There is no way for someone to be weak mentally and survive in that program. **Coach Krizancic expects excellence from his players and, some might say, goes to extreme measures to get all of what he can out of his players. There just isn't any way for someone to not have mental toughness and be able to come into practice day after day, year after year, and be pushed to your limits—it's a constant battle with yourself to see how far you can push your mind and body**. However, this mentality that I have taken with me has helped me succeed so far in life. When adversity hits, I have been able to overcome with ease everything so far because they don't defeat me mentally. When some people may give up or crash or become overwhelmed with stress and fail, having an extremely tough mentality allows you to use some of that stress or anxiety to motivate yourself and overcome whatever lies in front of you. **Being under Coach Krizancic really taught me how to deal with stress and deal with criticism and use it as motivation.**

The next thing that absolutely has helped me succeed thus far is my work ethic. Your goal in high school sports is one thing—win a state championship. To play in an elite program is a full-time job, all year round, you have to be working on becoming better with that one goal in mind every single day both during the season and during the off-season. You are fighting for a starting spot against ten other guys every single day. When you aren't working someone else is, that means you are falling behind. It's like there is this goal out there, and you somehow develop this method mentality or grind mode where every single day you need to be doing something to step closer to that ultimate goal. Eventually, it becomes a part of you. It becomes natural to be working toward something in all aspects of life. I took this work ethic, which has just become a part of me, and use it in all of my life. **I finished at the top of my class in biomedical engineering not because I was the smartest but because I worked harder than everyone around me. I am moving up in my career quickly because I constantly am putting in hours and hours week after week of overtime learning more, getting more done—chasing after my goals like an obsession.**

Another thing that has helped me become who I am and be where I am (which ties into the first two things) is my competitive nature. This again is something that is required of you to have or develop when playing in an elite program or more specially for Coach Krizancic. **Every day, every practice, every game, there is a will to win that drives you. This <u>will to win</u> feeds your mentality and your work ethic.** When I think about it, it is probably my competitive nature that feeds everything. **When you crave being the best and can't even bear the idea of failure, you will find a way to work harder and push yourself further than everyone around you. It's the only way to avoid that feeling of defeat.** This competitive nature was pretty much a culture in Coach Krizancic's program. It was well understood we did not stand for losing. This trait doesn't just concern sports. Again it is a part of me. I am competitive in every single thing I do. There is just a drive to be the best at everything. It's there in school, it's there at work, it's at home, it's on the golf course with my friends. Even last night, I was extremely competitive playing Scrabble with my girlfriend.

One of my favorite things Coach used to say is that you do 95 percent of things great. **If you want to be the best, then you need to improve the other 5 percent.** We never dwell on the things that we did well; we always focus on the areas we could get better. I use this all the time. I tell the same thing to the engineers that report to me. **That 5 percent is what drives me.**

Rick, Mark, and Tony Martucci shared that, even after having played for Coach K in the Mentor program two decades ago, the mindset and work ethic developed during that time with him continues to be a benefit in all aspects of life. His ability to teach young people how to push themselves to achieve their goals is an invaluable skill that players past and present carry for the rest of their lives.

*****

When you invest time and energy in young people as a coach, you reap gratitude from your players mature enough to recognize the lasting positive impact you had on their journey to becoming successful, independent, productive adults. **You actually start a human chain reaction of "paying it forward." Your ex-players make a positive impact wherever they go.**

The difference between the possible and the impossible lies in a man's determination.

—Tommy Lasorda
Hall of Fame MLB Player

Confidently meeting the challenges you face on the
basketball court generates an attitude of mental toughness
and a thirst for success in basketball and life.

SECTION 6:
HOW DEVELOPING AN ELITE BASKETBALL PROGRAM PREPARES ATHLETES FOR FUTURE SUCCESS

Overview

Career success is achieved through mental toughness.

- They seek continuous improvement
- They are able to handle frustration, stress, and criticism
- They nurture relationships
- They possess a strong worth ethic
- They have experience with the media
- They are self-confident
- They recognize the importance of attention to details
- They focus on achieving goals
- They understand the concept of teamwork
- They are motivated to pay it forward

SECTION 7

HOW TO MOVE UP THE RANKS AS AN ASSISTANT AT ANY LEVEL

Force yourself out of your comfort zone.

—Coach Bob Krizancic

The number one key in facilitating this upward move is to build a great relationship with the head coach/superior and the other assistants/colleagues. It must be a relationship based on mutual respect. Networking, especially with the head coach's/superior's contacts, is essential.

CHAPTER 39

Exhibit a Strong Work Ethic

Your work ethic will determine your coaching success.

Work ethic is extremely important and will determine your coaching success. If we expect players to put in extra time, then we expect as coaches to do so also. Remember our motto, "First on the floor, last out the door." This is definitely true regarding assistant coaches. A dedicated assistant coach does more than is required. They put in time with individual players in the film room and before and after practice. They break down films and ask the head coach what needs to be done.

The importance of knowledgeable, dedicated, and dependable assistant coaches cannot be overstated. I have previously mentioned that, in addition to our regular practice session, our players came into the gym in the evening at 8:30 PM for a ninety minute to two-hour session to work on their shooting and other skills. This additional session of skill development and practice would not have been possible without our assistant coaches. Due to liability issues, no player can be in the gym without a coach present. I attribute our success as a team and a program to the work ethic and dedication of our assistant coaches.

As an assistant coach, make it a point to attend booster club meetings. Be visible at feeder-program games including seventh through ninth grades and if possible, attend their practices. This will prepare you for a head-coaching job that requires dealing on a regular basis with organizations that support your program.

It is not necessary to be a teacher in order to be a successful coach. You can network with other area high school and college coaches and observe their practices to learn from them. You develop relationships by working summer camps that other coaches organize and be a positive influence. Attend coaching clinics whenever possible. It's a great place to learn and network. Meet as many other coaches as possible and build relationships. Basically, you market yourself.

A strong work ethic can compensate for limited coaching experience. In addition, as a coach I would periodically engage in self-assessment so that you can be the best you can be. Many coaches do not realize their deficiencies, and this inevitably holds them back when being considered for certain jobs or in successfully performing their duties. It is important to recognize your weaknesses so that you can work to turn them into strengths. You can exhibit a strong work ethic by performing your duties to the best of your ability and focusing on completing assigned tasks on time.

It is also important for the assistant coach to be a model of positive energy and attitude when performing their duties. A strong work ethic will also reflect the strength of your character and present you as an overall positive person.

Have the goal of advancing in your profession. By far, the most important asset in your road to success is believing in yourself through the tough times and frustrations.

I don't do things half-heartedly because I know
if I do, I can expect half-hearted results.

—Michael Jordan
Hall of Fame NBA Player

CHAPTER 40

Display Trustworthiness

Be reliable and willing to go the extra mile.

Trustworthiness is another characteristic that you must display if you are to move up in the coaching ranks. Undertake assigned tasks and be available to the head coach to go the extra mile when needed. You must develop trust between you, the head coach, and the entire staff.

As an assistant coach, you will be involved in many staff meetings and conversations in the locker room as well. Confidential information about the program, situations that arise, and players' conditions and performance will be discussed. What is said in the locker room stays in the locker room.

Trustworthiness as an assistant coach also encompasses respecting and protecting the privacy of personal information and knowing that what is discussed with your student-athletes or parents in conferences or meetings, and even in written documents, must remain confidential.

You must be careful about what you say in the surrounding community. Additionally, you must be careful about making any comments about your program on social media. Many young coaches have lost their jobs by posting something inappropriate on social media. You must realize that once you publish something on social media, there is no taking it back. Unless it is a positive post, your comment may be misinterpreted or the wrong spin may be put on it.

Always talk positively about your program and the head coach. Always be supportive as the last thing you want to do is divulge information to the public that should stay within the program. Your attitude is either the lock or the key to the door of your success.

> *Leadership is really a form of temporary authority that others grant you, and they only follow you if they find you consistently credible. It's all about perception—and if teammates find you the least bit inconsistent, moody, unpredictable, indecisive, or emotionally unreliable, then they balk and the whole team is destabilized.*

> —Pat Summitt
> Hall of Fame NCAA Coach, Author

Don't be the one to get in the way of your success. The vast majority of the time you will need your head coach's recommendation for another job. Assets, such as trust and loyalty, are qualities every program is looking for in an assistant coach.

Choose integrity over image. Choose truth over convenience. Choose virtue over personal gain. My favorite is, "Choose hard work over the easy way out." It's your choice.

> *In leadership, there are no words more important than trust. In any organization, trust must be developed among every member of the team if success is going to be achieved.*

> —Mike Krzyzewski
> Hall of Fame NCAA Basketball Coach

GBC

As an assistant coach,
be loyal and committed to the system.
Be involved in every aspect.

CHAPTER 41

Be Loyal and Committed to the System

**Understand that you represent the
program in all that you do and say.**

Due to the competitive nature of sports, loyalty is an essential quality. As an assistant, you must be knowledgeable regarding the system of your team and committed to the philosophy that is the foundation of the program. Have a complete knowledge of your system and program from top to bottom. As a new assistant coach, it is important to know the history of your system, its ups and downs, some of the marquee players of the past, and possibly some of the former coaches. You should ingrain yourself in your team's system as quickly as possible. Always be positive about your program.

If you are an assistant coach in the system, there should be an identity and a philosophy of how you want to win. As an assistant coach, you must embrace the identity and philosophy of winning for your program. Going against this philosophy will cause major problems for yourself. The reason why your system should be synchronous is so your players progress each year and understand what they need to do to play at the varsity level. Running your own offense and defense that is inconsistent with the varsity definitely does a disservice to the players you are coaching. It should be explicitly understood that winning is not the goal with the feeder system teams. The goal is to develop players so they can be successful at the varsity level. Therefore, it is of utmost importance that you and the head coach are on the same page. There should be no questions or gray areas. When you talk about your program, never talk wins and losses. Talk about the fact that your program is competitive and fundamentally sound.

You may have an opportunity to mentor or tutor a newly-hired coach coming into your system. Take this opportunity to familiarize the newcomer with the program and its intricacies and the things you feel are important for them to know right off the bat. Do whatever you can to help this new coach adjust. Personally, this is a great thing to do for a colleague and you will also gain favor with the head coach.

Understand that change is inevitable, but the great programs are the ones that adjust rapidly and seamlessly through the change from one coach to the other. It is so important for the new coach to know that they have the support of their colleagues.

Energy level is really important. Be passionate about your program and your position as a coach in it. Without passion, you have no energy; without energy, you will not have a successful program. High energy level is not a part-time option. It is who you are or who you will become. When you walk into a gym of athletes, you can tell who is giving energy and who is taking energy. You can tell the best coaches are the ones who walk onto the court, and players play with more intensity.

To get this response from your team, to be a successful assistant coach, you must also foster an attitude of respect. The quality of coach-player interaction can determine if the coach respects the players and the players respect the coach. In this regard, respect is earned; respect is not given. Respect is earned on and off the court. by doing the right thing all of the time, not some of the time.

There are only two options regarding commitment. You are either IN or OUT. There's no such thing in life as in-between.

—Pat Riley
Hall of Fame NBA Coach

CHAPTER 42

Communicate and Prepare

Communication is essential if you are to contribute to your program and also grow professionally so that you are prepared for future opportunities.

To be an effective coach, you must be able to communicate. It is the job of the coach to educate and teach your system and be adept at dealing with parents, the media, and booster groups. As an assistant coach, you must participate as much as you can in interacting with these three groups. Experience in this area will give you the confidence to deal with these groups in many different situations.

Communication with the different levels of the organization will put you in a position to give valuable input into what the team needs and will form a foundation for a good relationship with the head coach. Develop rapport with your administration, athletic director, administrative assistants, secretaries, and custodians.

It is important for you to give your honest input to the head coach. Do not worry about being politically correct. Let the head coach know you have the goal of moving up. Communication is a two-way street, and requires cooperation from the head coach and the assistants. There has to be transparency regarding family and health issues, such as occurred with the COVID-19 pandemic. The head coach has to make it clear that family and health come first. The assistant coach must speak up if there is any issue with their family regarding health concerns or requirements, such as were caused by the pandemic. Do not be afraid to meet with your head coach and ask the head coach to be extremely honest with you regarding your strengths and deficiencies as an assistant coach. An open, honest, transparent relationship is the best situation you can have.

Unless you try to do something beyond what you have already mastered, you will never grow.

—Ralph Waldo Emerson
Essayist, Poet, Philosopher

Force yourself out of your comfort zone. Do not be reluctant to share ideas with the head coach. The decision to use or discard your suggestions is up to them as the head coach. All ideas are not going to be great, but you never know which one will make a difference.

When approaching the head coach with a perceived problem or deficiency within your program, it is highly advisable to also bring with you a solution to that problem. Also be mindful of the time and place you offer your suggestions to the head coach.

I have learned that as a head coach you just do not want to hear problems; you would rather be informed of the problem along with a possible solution. By taking this extra step as an assistant, you will demonstrate initiative. The head coach will appreciate your honesty and innovative thinking. This will enhance the quality of your relationship with the head coach.

Throughout your career, it is advisable that you approach the person who is in a position to effect a change about any situation you are not happy with. When you do this, such a conversation is not whining or complaining. Your approach should always be respectful and express your genuine concern.

Your input is often more important than you realize. The communication at halftime between the head coach and the assistant coaches is vital. The staff and their recommendations help set the tone and strategy for the second half of the game. In my career, our use of information provided at halftime resulted in our dominating the second half, time and time again.

Make sure as an assistant coach you establish rapport with the team captains and other assistant coaches. This rapport will make it easier to avoid or correct small problems before they become large.

The more you communicate with others and network, the better you will be able to learn and improve your coaching skills. This will create opportunities to move up the ranks. Networking is really important. Make it a point to attend state basketball tournaments. There you will meet other assistant coaches, head coaches, and college coaches. Make sure you attend off-season coaching clinics. Carry a business card containing your contact information and exchange phone numbers and emails with other coaches. Meet and interact with as many coaches as you can.

The will to succeed is important, but what's more important is the will to prepare.

—Bobby Knight
NCAA Basketball Coach

Life is all about timing. You must prepare for the change from assistant coach to head coach. If you are applying for head-coaching jobs, realize that you could be hired on short notice. I suggest if you have a dream of being a head coach and you have a family, explain to your partner and children that if you do get a head-coaching job, your lifestyle is going to change. As a head coach, you naturally are going to put in more time. You have to interact with support groups such as the booster club and attend radio commitments and numerous events within the community. Your time sometimes will not be your own. Prepare your family little by little so that it is not a total surprise once you do get that head-coaching job. As an assistant, take the time to learn as much as you can from the head coach. Find out what their daily schedule is like during the week, both in season and off-season.

You must be prepared for an interview. If possible, have a mock interview with your head coach and an administrator so you can be totally prepared for any questions your potential employer may propose. Know the program you are applying for from top to bottom, including the high school, junior high/middle school, and feeder programs. Stress during the interview that you are trying to build character in the student-athletes with whom you are working. Have a clear idea of your goal and what you would like to do with the program at that respective school. Be ready to talk about your job and responsibilities, as well as achievements as an assistant coach.

You will need letters of recommendation once you get an interview. Make the letter specific for the job requirements. Also have three people who are willing to give you solid references once you have the interview.

Approach every interview as an opportunity to learn. I remember one interview that will remain etched in my memory. In 1985, I was being interviewed for a head-coaching job at a prestigious Ohio school. The interview was conducted by a twelve-member panel consisting of the athletic director, principal, superintendent, four members of the booster club and a few former basketball players. It was one of the most in-depth interviews I have ever experienced.

One of the questions I was asked was to prioritize seven topics. I recall five of the seven categories. They included hobbies, basketball, family, faith, and education. The panel wanted to know the top three. I had never considered this before and so I was amazed when I ranked faith first, family second, and education third.

I was one of two finalists for the position. The panel chose the assistant coach at St. Louis University.

While I was not selected, the interview process provided a great learning experience. It confirmed that character and honesty are highly desirable qualities in a coach. Furthermore, I realized I was among the most highly qualified applicants in the state and country and was now confident I would be offered other quality opportunities in the future.

The most important thing in coaching is communication.
It is not what you say as much as what they absorb.

—Red Auerbach
Hall of Fame NBA Coach

CHAPTER 43

Motivate Others and Be Responsible

Be committed to the players you coach and bring energy and passion to everything you do.

You must be able to motivate others and this is why your energy level as an assistant coach is so important. A dynamic personality is an asset. Work with professionals on the development of needed skills. Energy and motivation are an important part of coaching. Having energy as well as motivation will allow you to pursue the goals of your program with enthusiasm. There will be times when your student-athletes will be extremely motivated and there will be other times when they appear tired and want to do nothing.

When you walk through the gym, you know who is giving energy and who is motivated. The most successful coaches are those who are able to energize and motivate their players when they walk on the court. Due to their presence, the players automatically play with more intensity. With this energy and motivation there is a mutual respect between the coaches and players.

The ones who win get inside their player and motivate.

—Vince Lombardi
Hall of Fame NFL Coach

Be honest. If any issues arise due to mistakes you might make, admit your mistakes and fix them. Responsibility is part of being a leader. For you to be a strong assistant coach, honesty and accountability are essential and must be evident. Just like the head coach, you want the captains of your team to exhibit these qualities so you must be a role model for them. Make no excuses when things do not go as planned. It is better to face reality. Then you can change reality!

An excuse is an alteration of reality; nothing about
it will move you to a better situation.

—Grant Cardone
Entrepreneur, Author, and Speaker

To rise in the coaching ranks, dedicate yourself to working with the student-athletes entrusted to you. Support and push them to develop to their full potential as athletes. Their success becomes your success. My assistant coaches serve extremely important roles. I entrust responsibility for the development of our high school program, grades 9 through 12, to my assistants. I trust that they will teach and continually improve the fundamentals of our players on an everyday basis. This includes improving speed, execution, and every facet of their game that is essential to being the most fundamentally strong team we can be. The result of the dedicated efforts of assistant coaches in these areas is a high basketball IQ in the players in our program enabling them to seamlessly move up to the varsity level.

Study people who can teach you how to deal with people.

—Don Meyer
Hall of Fame NCAA Basketball Coach

Problems in the program are usually the responsibility of the head coach. So be aware that when you move up to the position of head coach, there is a dramatic change in the scope of your responsibility. Situations involving middle school teams and coaches, possibly even cheerleaders, as well as commitments in the community, are now going to be associated with you. As the head coach of the program, you will now be responsible for every assistant coach and every player. I have been called numerous times to principals' offices at the middle school/junior high level to intervene when an athlete is not behaving or is having problems passing a class. Be aware that problems multiply ten times when you advance from assistant coach to head coach.

A good coach will make his players see what
they can be rather than what they are.

—Ara Parseghian
Hall of Fame NCAA Football Coach

SECTION 7:
HOW TO MOVE UP THE RANKS AS AN ASSISTANT AT ANY LEVEL

Overview

Display mental toughness.

- Exhibit a strong work ethic
- Display trustworthiness
- Be loyal and committed to the system
- Be passionate
- Earn respect
- Gain knowledge of the system
- Communicate
- Motivate others
- Believe in yourself
- Prepare for advancement

Neosportsinsiders.com

In basketball and in life, you will compete against some people with the same mentality as you. You will have to be a little stronger and tougher to come out on top against great competition.

SECTION 8

HOW TO HELP YOUR CHILD SUCCEED IN A HIGH SCHOOL BASKETBALL/ ATHLETIC PROGRAM

Think positive thoughts daily. Believe in yourself.

—Pat Summitt
Hall of Fame NCAA Women's Basketball Coach

It is difficult for a coach to accomplish the goal of developing an elite student-athlete if the child in their program is not self-confident and motivated to begin with. This process starts long before the child enters high school. Having a student-athlete that is coachable, respectful, a great teammate, mentally tough, resilient, and tries their best *is* a direct reflection of parenting and your choice of coaching. Your child's success as a high school player depends in large part on their attitude and motivation.

CHAPTER 44

Build Skills Through Quality Experience

Involvement in a quality program will produce measurable results.

The role of a parent is the most important gift you will ever have. Being a parent is the toughest task I have ever had and yet it is the most rewarding. You are the one who spends the most time with your child in their developmental stages of life. You are the first to hold, the first smile, the first voice, and the first caregiver your child will experience. As a young child, they can do virtually nothing without you. When you interact with your child, they are open and eager to experience the world. You are also your child's first coach. You have a lifetime of experience. You can let your child make their own decisions, but not without hearing your opinion and "gut" feelings, at any age.

I strongly suggest introducing your child to sports as soon as possible. As they progress, make sure whatever sport they are in, they are progressing to become a better athlete. Also, make certain any program in which they are involved stresses skills and training regarding such areas as running and agility. As a parent, you offer good advice to your child as far as why they are in sports. Stress to them they are working toward goals such as to compete, to deal with frustration, and to become a better student-athlete. Involvement in sports builds character. As a coach and watching my own sons play sports throughout their youth, I saw firsthand the phenomenal relationships they developed. In addition, they gained confidence in social situations.

Playing two or even three sports in high school is highly doable. However, to be successful, learning to prioritize or budget time is the key. In addition, make sure your child gets the skills needed for each respective sport. Increasing their strength and explosiveness is essential to compete and even excel in their chosen sports. As parents of a child interested in more than one sport, I suggest you talk to all head coaches in the sports your child is interested in playing to get a thorough understanding of time commitments and goals in each sport. By the time your child is a sophomore in high school, it would be advantageous that they play more than one sport because of the skill work and strength and conditioning required to be an elite player. Playing more than one sport at the high school level ensures that your child will be involved in strength and conditioning year-round and that they develop the stamina needed to be competitive and an impactful player. Playing only one sport also has its advantages. One sport players build strong relationships with their teammates who share the same passion for that sport.

Be sure as a parent your child is being taught at every level. Educate yourself about the sport and programs available to them in your area. You can pick and choose for them what programs they are involved with. The best programs will build their character as well as their athletic abilities. Be open to asking your high school coach about resources available to you and your child. In fact if you want to be a youth coach and you have knowledge in the sport, you can help teach a child how to be a good person and good athlete.

The choice of a program should be a joint parent-child decision. When being introduced to the sport, "fun" must be considered to foster the passion for the sport. However, as the child progresses, the choice should shift from being the "fun" choice to being the right choice for the child's further development. If you give the choice to the child, they will most likely want to play with their friends. If their friends are not serious about the sport, then your child may not improve. Also, by playing with their current friends they eliminate the possibility of forming new friendships. It also deters them from improvement because they will remain in their comfort zone.

Comfort is the enemy of progress.

—P.T. Barnum
Circus Entrepreneur

You cannot always pick your child's friends, but you can guide them in their choices. As I said before, "Show me your friends, and I will show you your future." One way to improve your child's skills is to find reputable organizations that will provide guidance and support. This will help them on the journey to developing and achieving a high skill set and knowledge of the game. Coaches can break the game down, explain game strategy, and offer a young person constructive criticism of their skill set so that they can turn their weaknesses into strengths early in their athletic endeavors. Your child will "see the floor" more clearly and understand the plays unfolding before them. The game will slow down as they mentally anticipate moves of their teammates and opponents, rather than merely reacting to what is going on. They will have mental control over their physical response in game situations.

The importance of engaging your child in a quality program cannot be overstated. With time, guidance, and commitment on your child's part, they can achieve an enhanced IQ in the sport which will make all the difference and prepare them to be a valued contributing player on an elite high school team. Five of our top seven players in the 2020-21 season played together on the same travel team throughout their youth. Our record that year was 25-1.

It would be advantageous for your child to play the game at an early age and potentially be a game-changing presence by junior high or middle school. To improve your child's athletic performance have them play bigger, better, and stronger athletes.

The value of building basketball skills from an early age is exhibited in the following excerpt from a news article about one of our Mentor High School elite basketball players. Luke progressed in his skills to become an All-Ohio basketball player and accepted a Division I basketball scholarship to Youngstown State University.

Luke Chicone is a 7th grader from Ohio, who was unstoppable at the 2016 NEO Youth Elite Camp. The Class of 2021 guard dazzled spectators throughout the weekend in Garfield Heights, Ohio with his **ball handling skills, outside shooting, and passing ability.** Relatively unknown before the camp, Chicone is soon to be a household name because of his on-court flair. ("Luke Chicone Shows Out at NEO Youth Elite Camp," MSHTV, March 11, 2016, 1:30 a.m. EST; emphasis added)(https://www.middleschoolhoops.com/news_article/show/624052)

You, as a parent, need to know there are three basic basketball skills your child must develop: discipline, man-to-man defense, and ball handling. These are the three fundamentals that, in priority order, help middle school/junior high players ultimately be successful at the varsity level. We do not "label" an individual in a certain position such as "guard" or "center". All players need the same skills. In junior high, student-athletes are preparing for the future. They should not be playing to win games. Student-athletes are playing to move to the next level with a goal to becoming an elite varsity player. They should concentrate on skill development and discipline. If they are disciplined, their chances of succeeding in sports and life are so much greater.

Love that kids are building confidence on and off the court and unlocking their potential through sports.

—Kobe Bryant
NBA Hall of Fame Player

The way to improve your child's skills is to find
reputable organizations that will provide the guidance,
skills, and support in the journey to achieving a
high skill set and knowledge of the game.

CHAPTER 45

The Value of Trial and Error in Developing Emotional Maturity

There are no mistakes, only lessons. Growth is a process of trial and error.

Only by being given the opportunity to try something new can a child grow and develop basic skills. As a young adult and student-athlete, the same is true. One must leave their comfort zone to grow and continue to develop. A parent can help a child in this area by setting up new experiences in which the child can participate.

Life is about forming good habits. It takes at least three weeks of consistent action after the first experience to form it into a new habit. Therefore, it is important for you as a parent to not give up or be discouraged.

When you are guiding your child into forming habits, the quality of their experience is particularly important. When a child is involved in a quality sports program, they can develop a great work ethic and make positive strides in a multitude of ways. Children, even those of preschool age, may benefit from involvement on a sports team. They learn about fitness, the importance of listening to a coach, the benefits of hard work and determination, and the challenge of acquiring a new skill. As a parent, you celebrate your child's successes. However, it is also important for you to encourage your child to review their performance and evaluate where they need to make improvement. Then you can support them while they develop skills in their deficient areas.

In an earlier chapter we discussed resilience as an element of mental toughness. Learning how to recognize one's faults and turning weaknesses into strengths is a valuable life lesson that involvement in a quality sports program provides. Another important quality that can arise from trial and error is the ability to handle disappointment and recover when things do not go your way. This is a key element of emotional maturity.

The advantage of playing on a quality team is that the coach and the other players will exude mental toughness. They will push your child so that they become aware of their limits and also their skill level.

The following statement from one of my Mentor players highlights the benefits of your child's involvement in a quality program like Mentor's:

> Growing up in a program like Mentor was an unreal experience. My teammates and coaches, especially my head coach, were more like family to me. My head coach was my biggest critic, but also my biggest supporter and changed my life in so many ways. Although I may be leaving for college, I won't be leaving behind the memories and family bond I've been fortunate enough to have.
>
> —Luke A. Chicone
> (currently at Youngstown State University)

The sooner your child is pushed out of their comfort zone, exposed to adversity and learns to handle difficult situations on their own, the more equipped they will be to meet challenges throughout their lives and careers. That is why the quality of the team and program they are engaged with is so important.

Quit? Quit? We keep score in life because it matters.
It counts. Too many people opt out and never discover
their own abilities, because they fear failure. They
don't understand commitment. When you learn to
keep fighting in the face of potential failure, it gives
you a larger skill set to do what you want to do.

—Pat Summitt
Hall of Fame NCAA Women's Basketball Coach

To find quality basketball programs use resources available in your community and network with other parents. Ask other parents about their experiences and results and determine what is best for your child. By becoming involved in your basketball booster organization you will gain a source of information regarding your high school's basketball program. It will also enable you to inquire of other involved parents as to where to find the best and highest quality of support for your child's athletic development.

Also note there are important differences between a recreational sports program and travel team opportunities. While recreational programs have their place and are more easily accessible, travel programs provide a higher level of competitive play. The Amateur Athletic Union (AAU) is one such program that has a reputation as a great way to provide a child with quality competitive experience and exposure to different sports.

If your child is to develop to their highest level of skill, it is important for your child to learn at an early age that they must devote extra time and effort to becoming an elite player. The majority of my better players understood at an early age that they had to put in extra time to be competitive. When they reached high school, these players would practice one hour before school started and also stayed in the gym after our two-hour practice ended to get in extra time.

Ultimately, it will be your child's choice to strive to be elite or accept being average. However, as a parent you can guide them in choosing to develop the discipline and dedication that will provide a firm foundation for their future success. They must be exposed to consistent quality practices and competitive games. As I said before, to become an elite player, a child must play bigger, better, and stronger athletes. That said, involvement of parents also increases when their child plays for a travel team. This is also a big commitment on the part of the parent because of time, travel, and expenses. If your child has a passion for the sport, your investment will be well worth it.

Striving to be elite applies to basketball as well as life. One of my ex-players, Colin Barth, recently included in his wedding vows a lesson he had taken away from his years on my team at Mentor High School. Colin stated: "I learned from Coach K that when you have a choice of being average or elite, why would you choose average? I promise you I will always choose elite when it comes to being your husband, a father, and a provider."

It is so gratifying to coach a student-athlete who gives maximum effort, listens, and is a great team player. Those are phenomenal qualities that you as a parent can help your child develop.

You have to be able to accept failure to get better.

—LeBron James
Hall of Fame NBA Player

It is so gratifying to coach a young person who gives
maximum effort, listens, and is a great team player.
Those are phenomenal qualities that you as
a parent can instill in your child.

CHAPTER 46

Foster Motivation through Encouragement and Support

Positivity, repetition, and reinforcement are your tools.

Your young athlete is greatly influenced by what you say to them. They become what you tell them they are and can be. If you fill your child's world with opportunity and encouragement, then they will reflect a self-confident attitude and develop to their full potential. If you fill their world with limitations and criticism, then fear will stifle their growth. I believe that the only limitations that a student-athlete has are the limitations they put on themselves. Young adults need a strong adult parental figure in their lives.

- Do not let your child make a decision without your input even though you want them to be independent.
- Do not be afraid to give your input as they need the benefit of your experience.

Young people need a net for when they fall. Therefore, stepping-stones have merit. There is no need for them to jump off a cliff! I am a huge proponent of the advantage that an adult can give inexperienced, young individuals. Share with them the pitfalls of their actions, and if they tune you out, it is their choice. But do not stop communicating your message. If they hear it often enough from you it may eventually sink in.

Positivity is important athletically. Your positive attitude keeps the child open to growing athletically. It is also important to help your child stay focused on their goal. Encourage them to keep on improving their skill level. Help them develop a "can do" attitude, which leads to determination and self-confidence, as well as the right attitude toward setbacks. These are three characteristics of mental toughness. Focus on staying positive, getting stronger, developing skills, and having a great work ethic. Those are the things that are most important at a young age. In the end, it is not the push from behind or the pull from the front, but the drive from within them that matters. Help your child develop passion and the will to succeed.

With that being said, while you want your child to be self-confident, this is a tough situation for a parent. In the last fifteen to twenty years, AAU and summer programs at community centers have been established. These programs often include offering the services where you are paying a coach, athletic trainer, or other third party to work with your child on strength, conditioning, and basketball skill development. Be cognizant of the fact that many of these individual organizations are created for the purpose of generating revenue and therefore their evaluations may be inflated on the positive end to ensure your continued business. They may inform you how skilled your child is and how successful they could be in high school or college. You may be getting the wrong impression. With these overinflated assessments, expectations will also be overinflated to give you the wrong impression. This is why involvement with a quality program that accurately measures progress in various areas over time is so vital. When in doubt as to where to find a quality program, seek referrals from the varsity coaching staff.

Athletes can only be as good as their physical capabilities allow them to be. Therefore, you must be realistic. As a parent you can set your dreams high, but to conclude that your child is going to be a Division I athlete or superstar in high school when they are still very young is not realistic. Only two to three percent of athletes that start in high school play at the Division I level. A few years back, a local AAU coach had ten players entering eighth grade. He informed all the players and their parents that every one of them were scholarship players. This was the wrong message, especially at this early age, and gave the parents a false idea of their child's skill level. You and your child should be told they have a great work ethic and how hard they have to work and that with hard work they can attain amazing results. Do not, however, give your child false hope in regard to athletic aspirations.

All kids need is a little help, a little hope,
and somebody who believes in them.

—Magic Johnson
Hall of Fame NBA Player

Participation in sports at an early age can provide opportunity
for your child to form strong, supportive friendships
with other young people who share their interests.
These two best friends went to the state finals in
2010—the first time in Mentor's history.

CHAPTER 47

Teach the Value of Teamwork

Nothing can compare in the life of a child to the experience of being part of something greater than themselves.

I feel compelled to share with you what I have witnessed as both a coach and a parent. When it comes to the development of young individuals, nothing can replace the experience of being a part of something greater than themselves. The sense of accomplishment is magnified and the sense of loss is decreased when young people are engaged in a group effort. Human beings are built to be in a relationship with other human beings. Inclusion in a positive and supportive team environment will fulfill those needs.

Furthermore, successful relationships are based on communication, compromise, support, and a willingness to work together for a common goal. In fact, learning to prioritize the goal of the group over a personal goal is another important life lesson from involvement in a sport. It is an unfortunate fact, but:

Some parents would rather have their son get all-state recognition than have his team win the state championship.

—Don Meyer
Hall of Fame College Basketball Coach

As a parent you can support your child in this area by counseling them when they become frustrated if things don't go their way. It is important for you to help your child develop the perspective that it is not about them but rather what is for the good of the team.

When you come to practice, you cease to exist as an individual. You are part of a team.

—John Wooden
Hall of Fame NCAA Coach

Through the process of engaging with team members, your child can develop patience, self-discipline, and the ability to compromise. In addition, conflict resolution is another skill that can be acquired when disagreements arise among team members. Your child must also learn that they have a role to play and that the success of the group depends on each one performing to their highest potential. When a child is given a role to play on a team, they can develop self-confidence, a sense of responsibility, and trust in other individuals. Team members socialize and can offer support away from the basketball court.

As a parent, you can impress upon your child the importance of team over self and you are setting your child on a path to a successful athletic career and life. Even though this chapter is written for parents, it applies to coaches as well. Numerous players have said, "Coach, you are like a second father figure to me." As a head coach, I have used our varsity players as coaches for our elementary summer camps. From this experience, these varsity players have taken away a deeper appreciation for the importance of teamwork and the negative impact individuals with their own agenda will have on team play.

Individual commitment to a group effort--that is what makes a team work, a company work, a society work, a civilization work.

—Vince Lombardi
Hall of Fame NFL Coach

CL

**Coaches and teams are recognized during halftime on
Mentor Basketball Association Appreciation Night.**

CL

**When it comes to the development of young people,
nothing can replace the experience of being
a part of something greater than
themselves.**

SECTION 8:
HOW TO HELP YOUR CHILD SUCCEED IN A HIGH SCHOOL BASKETBALL/ ATHLETIC PROGRAM

Overview

Encourage mental toughness.

- Build skills through quality experience
- Promote emotional maturity through trial and error
- Foster motivation through encouragement and support
- Teach the value of teamwork
- Push your child out of their comfort zone

See appendices B through K at the back of the book for further information and relevant documents.

SECTION 9

HOW TO HANDLE PRINT, BROADCAST, AND SOCIAL MEDIA

Maintain positive relationships with the media.
Always be positive and ready for questions.

—Coach Bob Krizancic

Players and coaching staff alike must understand how to effectively interact with members of media and, in particular, the perils and pitfalls of social media. This must be addressed both preseason and during the season. In your approach to the media, always be humble and complimentary, giving credit to your assistants, your staff, and the players. As a player, give credit to your teammates and your opponents as well.

Always complement your opponents.
Express gratitude and humility and you can't go wrong.

CHAPTER 48

How to Interact with the Media

You want the media to be your ally.

Public relations are important for a coach and your program. Maintain positive relationships with the media. Take a chance and reach out to the media. Don't stay in a cocoon. However, regarding interaction with the media you should be ready for questions and always be positive. Individuals want to read positive comments and stories. Take ownership of what you say and how you say it.

Be professional and careful when using social media. Inevitably you will have bad practices and bad games which is probably the worst time to use social media. Make sure you reread your social post and make sure it is a positive message before you send it.

You can also use social media as a motivational tool. Social media allows you to send a message to individual players or the entire team. Players will respect you for what you say. Again be sure to reread what you have written before you post it.

When doing a live interview, do not assume the reporter will ask for your input before it is printed or sent. The story is entered onto their computer while the interview is being conducted, and within thirty to forty-five minutes after the interview, the story is already done and published. It is really quick, almost instantaneous. We live in a no-wait society. The readers are conditioned to want to know right now.

You will have a rather good idea of what a reporter will ask you about a game—it could be after a win, but it is pretty perilous after a loss. You can prepare yourself, but if there is a question thrown at you that you didn't expect, make sure to give it some thought before you answer. There will be times when you have a choice of telling the truth or putting a positive spin on the truth, and my strong recommendation is that you put a positive spin on the truth.

As the head coach, you must take ownership to remove any controversy from the subject. Again, prepare. Coaches are on pins and needles today regarding social media. This includes Facebook, Instagram, Twitter, and all social media outlets. Players need to be cognizant of what they say and how they say it. They need to be ultra-positive. The use of social media is so devastating and sensitive that many coaches currently prohibit any use of social media by their players during the season. You may also consider implementing rules and regulations on the use of social media by your players. For instance, you may want to recommend your players stay off social media during the basketball season unless approved by a coach. Do not use Twitter, Instagram, or other forms of social media to comment about an opposing player or team.

Remind your players every time they post a picture to Facebook or send a tweet, they should think about what effect it has on their reputation. The post will not go away and can be interpreted in a negative way. One bad tweet or inappropriate Facebook picture could mean the difference in being offered a college scholarship or job. Many college coaches say they check out potential players' Facebook and Twitter accounts before offering them a scholarship because they want to be sure that the player whom they are signing will represent the institution in a positive manner. As a coach, you will be protecting your players from the negative fallout of social commentary that may come back to adversely impact either themselves, the team, the school, or their future employment.

In fact, as a head coach, I have personally received calls from colleges, professional organizations, and major companies regarding comments made by my former players five, eight, or even ten years before. These organizations hire people to investigate the social media activity of prospective athletes and employees to ensure their statements are not going to adversely impact the teams, college, and companies. In addition, the very nature of the statements made can raise issues about the character of these former players. These institutions are concerned about maintaining a quality reputation. In these instances, I have been instrumental in reaffirming the elite reputation of my prior players. In each case, these players were in their mid-teens when these questionable comments were made. That is why I highly recommend you instill in your players a cautious approach to social media. It will serve them well for the rest of their adult lives.

We tell our players that if you are interviewed, give credit to your teammates and your opponent. You want to look professional and never shift blame. Take ownership and responsibility and be professional at all times. If you get a question that you are not prepared to answer, do not give a quick response. Give yourself a few seconds to think about it and just be very careful what your answer is.

To prepare and assist our players with interviews we give our seven or eight players who are most likely to be interviewed after a game, a quick mock interview session with one of the local reporters that we know well. This gives them a little experience on how to answer questions off the cuff. I tell the reporter to give them one or two loaded questions. Our 2020-2021 season record was 25-1. As a result, after numerous games there were five or six reporters' microphones in our players' faces. They definitely had to be ready to be interviewed. The preparation we engaged in before the season started enhanced the quality of their responses.

Early in a coach's career if someone does make a mistake with the media and the answer is not the best, take ownership and accept the blame. This situation happened to me. We were playing St. Ignatius High School, and we were both 10 and 0. St. Ignatius had a solid six-foot-five defensive player for whom we had a lot of mutual respect. When I was interviewed for the story after we won the game, I said we really did not guard the six-foot-five player because we did not consider him an offensive threat. Unbeknownst to me the player was the principal's son. That quote was printed in the paper. It basically said we had not defended him because he was a nonfactor offensively. I probably should have rephrased it. The player's father was very upset that it reached the paper and that they identified the player by name. I had no control over the content of the article. It escalated on Monday, even though the game had been Saturday night. I should have said the other team was tough to defend because they had so many weapons and never singled out any one of their players by name.

A slight slip can be trouble, and the reporter can change what you say or put a different spin on it. Interactions with the media will not be a problem if you are totally positive in your comments. However, should there be any negative reaction to what you have said, by taking the blame and ownership of it, any speculation or second-guessing about that comment will end.

Try to be general in your comments. Reporters and interviewers will ask about specific situations and about some of your players. Negative-type questions may be brought up about specific players on your team. You can respond by stating that the person in question is a great shooter (or whatever their position is) and that you told him to keep on doing what he was doing. Come out positive and supportive of the player. Remember that relatives and parents will read your comments.

There will be no time usually between the interview and the publication of your comments. Any statement you make will be read quickly after the game because of the way media works. You must be positive. Say you are looking to improve. You are playing for the tournament. If it is a win, make sure you are humble and note you still have room to grow. If you lost, then say it is great loss if we can improve on the weaknesses in this game.

Be prepared. Do your homework, especially as a young head coach, and establish great relationships if you can with members of the media because they will be a little kinder to you than if you come off being pretentious.

It's the one thing you can control. You are responsible for how people remember you or don't. So, don't take it lightly.

—Kobe Bryant
Hall of Fame NBA Player

SECTION 9:
HOW TO HANDLE PRINT, BROADCAST, AND SOCIAL MEDIA

Overview

*Acknowledge the mental toughness of
your team and your opponents.*

- Maintain positive relationships with the media
- Always be positive and ready for questions
- Use social media as a motivational tool
- Give credit to your teammates and your opponent
- Be professional
- Never shift blame
- Take ownership and responsibility
- Thoughtfully prepare and review your answers

See appendix K at the back of the book for further information and relevant documents.

SECTION 10

HOW TO EFFECTIVELY ENGAGE WITH GAME OFFICIALS

Officiating is the only job in America that everybody knows how to do better than the guy who is doing it.

—Larry Goetz
Professional Baseball Umpire

Basketball is a fast and physical game and requires the focus of officials, players, and coaches. Both coaches and players do not have time to complain. Coaches and players must have mental toughness to concentrate on their respective roles in winning the game at hand.

Coaches, players, and spectators appreciate it when game officials discuss how to handle specific situations during their pre-game meeting before they even come on to the court. This ensures that when the situations present themselves, the officials' response is fluid, consistent, and keeps the game flowing. However, there are times when calls by officials create confusion and the need for clarification. Any interaction with game officials should be respectful.

CHAPTER 49

Strategic Communication with Game Officials

Tact is essential when communicating with game officials.

During games, relationships with the game officials are important and should not be overlooked. As a coach, you must walk a fine line in dealing with game officials. You must back your players yet develop a relationship with the officials based on respect.

The relationship that you as a coach and your players have with the officials assigned to your game has the potential to impact the course of that game as well as future games and even your season. A technical foul can occur when a player or coach shows up an official (verbally or by a derogatory gesture).

If a coach is assessed a technical foul, the opposing team gets two free throws and depending on who has possession, the opposing team either keeps the ball or gets possession. In Ohio and in most states, if a coach gets a second technical foul in a game, five penalties are imposed: 1) the coach is disqualified for that game, 2) the opposing team gets two free throws and depending on who has possession, the opposing team either keeps the ball or gets possession; 3) the coach is suspended for the next two games; 4) a monetary fine is imposed (in Ohio it is $100); and 5) the coach has to take a class on etiquette to improve their behavior.

If a player is assessed a technical foul, penalties are also assessed. If it is the first technical foul: 1) it is also considered a personal foul, and 2) the other team shoots two shots for every technical. The fact that a technical foul on a player results in a personal foul being assessed against that player is significant: once a player receives 5 personal fouls, they are out of the game. One personal foul added to a technical foul can change the course of a game. The second technical foul called against a player results in: 1) two shots for the other team; 2) the offending player is disqualified for that game; and 3) the offending player is also suspended for the next two games. So, a second technical foul against a player can not only affect the outcome of a game, but it can also change the course of a season. This is why I believe that this chapter is such an important part of the book and is in a section all by itself.

It is also essential for the coach to impress upon their players that many times in games, players are assessed the technical foul as the result of their retaliating from an opponent's hard foul or cheap shot. Once the game official's attention is drawn to a certain area of the floor by an opponent's hard foul or cheap shot, the game official naturally will see the player who acts last in retaliation.

When communicating with game officials regarding issues that may arise on the court, your objective should be to call attention to a situation. By communicating with the game officials, they can be alerted to a similar situation that may occur later in the game to ensure consistency. As a coach, you want calls in the game to be consistent. Especially early in the game, impress upon the officials your expectation that they call fouls in a consistent manner and also that they only make calls in the area of the court assigned to them. Use specific examples when you address this action with game officials so they can see your point. Taking action is especially important in Ohio during tournament time as you have the same group of officials working the rest of the state tournament together. It will focus their attention and awareness on issues that are significant to you.

Misunderstandings can arise no matter what the level of the official's experience assigned to your game. Keeping your composure at all times will make a huge difference. The majority of times when I react to an official it is regarding a call that may come up later in the game. As in business or life, I believe you can have an influence on how people and officials perceive a situation. One game official stated he will react differently depending on whether the coach approaches him with an accusatory statement as opposed to a question seeking the official's perspective.

In the event you do happen "to let off some steam" in the direction of the official, always soften it with an explanatory statement. I often tell the official I was not upset with their call but rather I was frustrated with the poor performance of my team. I believe this will help diffuse the negative affect of any contentious interaction. As you gain experience as a coach, you will learn to address a situation but not allow it to affect your coaching.

Until you walk in the shoes of an official you have no idea of the level of concentration and knowledge it takes to officiate at a game. I had an opportunity to experience officiating while coaching a prestigious summer camp. The coaches on teams that were not playing at the time, served as the officials. That experience taught me first-hand that officiating is a difficult undertaking. In certain contests, from the perspective of the official, the speed of the game can influence their officiating.

Officials are trained to see what is occurring in their primary areas of coverage on the floor. As noted above, depending on the level of competition and the speed of the game, this may be seen by officials, coaches, and fans as a jumble of arms and legs.

Too often a coach will argue a point with an official and use up a valuable time-out only to have the players return to the game with no positive direction. In attempting to interact with an official, the coach has used a valuable time-out which could have been put to better use coaching players on game strategy. Make your point to the officials and return to coaching.

In addition, as a coach you must instruct your players in the proper demeanor when interacting with an official. Players should be reminded of this before every game and during every practice. Impress upon your players they should not expect every foul to be called. They need to understand basketball is played as a fast and physical game.

In the event a player is frustrated by a call, they should respectfully address the official for an explanation. After respectfully addressing a concern, the player should then show mental toughness and immediately refocus on their main objective: playing to win. By spending time interacting with the officials, players may change the tempo of the game.

If a player's interaction escalates, and the issue becomes more egregious, a technical foul may be assessed which will negatively affect the team. As a coach, let your players know if there is an issue with an official it is your domain, and you will be responsible to address the official. Players should be taught that no matter what is called or is not called by the official, debating or arguing will not change the outcome of the circumstance and shows a lack of mental toughness. My players totally understand that it is my job, not theirs, to debate officials and that as head coach, I have their backs.

In my personal opinion one of the greatest high school basketball officials to ever work our games has a saying that resonates the truth about players:

Good players play; bad players complain.

—Anonymous official

The take home point of this very short prophetic and thought-provoking statement basically is good players do not have time to complain. They have mental toughness to continue to play hard. Good players know they cannot change the outcome of a call, but they can change the outcome of a game. Never in the history of basketball has a player scored a point or played good defense when preoccupied with both playing and officiating.

I instruct our players that it is appropriate to say "Thank You" when a ball is handed back to them by a game official. I am always thrilled to let our players know when officials report to me how polite our players are. In addition, the way in which a ball is returned to an official can make a big difference in the official's attitude towards individual players and your team as a whole.

Having our players show respect for game officials is also a sign of an elite program. As I said before, game officials are human.

Having my players treat them with respect goes a long way towards officials respecting our players and our program. I also tell my players if an official interacts with you with a question or comment, listen attentively but do not allow it to be a distraction.

To give your players a better insight to the officiating world, invite officials to speak to your team and enlighten them from an official's perspective. Allow your team to ask the officials questions regarding rule changes and how they officiate a game. Have them ask the official what they, the players, can do to make their interaction with officials reach a higher level.

Also, when having officials work your preseason scrimmages, allow time for interaction between the team and officials. Inform the officials that, when possible, they explain to the players what they are doing right and what they are doing wrong. This helps players get used to the correct way to ask an official for an explanation.

Finally, let your players serve as officials for scrimmages or games in your feeder system. This will give them valuable personal insight into the perspective of a game official.

Never complain about the officiating. It does no good. During the game I don't want to be fighting two opponents

—John Wooden
Hall of Fame NCAA Coach

Coaches are politicians. You are not going to change the call, but you can remind officials to be consistent in their calls.

SECTION 10:
HOW TO EFFECTIVELY ENGAGE
WITH GAME OFFICIALS

Overview

Employ mental toughness to focus on winning.

- Always keep the relationship respectful
- Your objective should be to demand consistency
- Stress that the officials only make calls in their area
- Constantly remind officials of certain situations occurring on the floor
- Make your point and return to coaching
- Diffuse any negative effect by explaining you were frustrated with the poor performance of your team
- Make sure your players are always respectful in communications with game officials
- As a player, do not debate or argue about calls
- Explain to your players how difficult it is to officiate
- Basketball is a fast physical game so do not expect every foul to be called
- Make sure your players understand the ramifications of getting two technical fouls in a game

SECTION 11

COVID-19: THE TRUE TEST OF MENTAL TOUGHNESS

*If you're trying to achieve, there will be road
blocks. I've had them; everybody has had them. But
obstacles don't have to stop you. If you run into a
wall, don't turn around and give up. Figure out
how to climb it, go through it, or work around it.*

—Michael Jordan
Hall of Fame NBA Player

Mentally tough individuals never give up. They embrace obstacles, are committed to their goals, focus on what they can control, transform negative emotions into useful energy, and thrive on adversity.

The fear and uncertainty that the COVID-19 pandemic created in the populace at large and the chaotic impact it has had on the world of sports challenged everyone to creatively approach their lives and maintain some sense of normalcy when nothing was "normal."

This chapter serves as a first-hand witness to the mental toughness of my staff and teams in the 2019-2020 and 2020-2021 seasons as we weathered the storm of the COVID-19 pandemic.

CCC

Neosportinsiders.com

The 2019–2020 and 2020–2021 Mentor teams
prepared intensely and focused on execution all year,
and as a result, both teams' mentality and basketball
IQ were really sky-high at tournament time.

CHAPTER 50

Mental Toughness—How We Conquered COVID-19

Developing the power of the mind is essential to succeeding when confronted with unforeseen challenges, such as those posed by the COVID-19 pandemic. Expect the unexpected throughout your career.

The world as we knew it seemed to be in suspended animation. In the flood of mass hysteria and the emotion of battling a never-before-encountered "enemy" of miniscule proportions, the modern world could not offer definitive answers…and as a result, no sure plan of action.

The federal and local governments stepped in to ensure the well-being and health of the public. Schools were ordered closed. Restaurants, museums, athletic facilities, theatres, and any place where the public would congregate were closed. Until when? No one knew for certain.

As a result, sports venues and the teams that played there were also suspended or even worse, canceled. As a result, the OHSAA and other states issued directives regarding competition.

When the directives were issued, the preceding seventy-two hours were the strangest and most bizarre I have ever experienced in forty-two years of being a head coach. It was unsettling, not just for me and my basketball team and not just in basketball, but in the entire sports world.

On Tuesday, March 10, the directive started being formulated. At the time we were playing the regional semifinals on Wednesday, March 11, at Cleveland State University. Usually for regional games, there are seven to nine thousand fans in attendance which is a great crowd. Our players earned that opportunity to play and were looking forward to it. On Tuesday, with the coronavirus hitting the country in collegiate and professional sports, we were informed that each player and coach would have a guest list of four attendees admitted into the game. Attendance at the regional matchup went from seven to nine thousand in attendance to five or six hundred maximum. The situation became even more bizarre due to the fact each player was only allowed four people, and this would exclude many relatives. One player had six people, including grandparents, and due to the limitation on tickets, not all family members could attend. Another family had five siblings, four parents, and four grandparents. Therefore, with only four family members being granted admission, the family had to decide which family members would attend. This became a nightmare regarding attendance.

On the positive side of COVID-19, since the fan base was limited, media outlets were now being given approval to live stream the game. We persevered and played the regional game on Wednesday, March 11. We attempted to make the best possible atmosphere for our players. We discussed with the players that, with live streaming, their fans, family, and the public still had the opportunity to see them play. All the accolades and all the respect were still there.

The games went on with the limited number of people in attendance. You either needed a wristband or a lanyard, depending on whether you were on the guest list or you were associated with the team. If you had neither, you were denied admission to the game.

The games were played under abnormal conditions. We played into a double overtime game and secured a great, great victory. We were anticipating facing our interleague rival in the regional final on Saturday at 2:00 p.m. at Cleveland State University and began our pre-game preparations. We were looking forward to the opportunity to represent our state region as one of the Final Four in the state. That Wednesday night, our game ended late, about 10:30 p.m.

We attended the post-game press conference. Our players met with representatives of the media and we boarded the bus back to the high school. On the way back we started to get information through social media that Rudy Gobert of the NBA Utah Jazz had tested positive for COVID-19. Due to this unfortunate circumstance the NBA was on the verge of pausing league games for a month. Other professional teams soon followed suit and then NCAA games were canceled. Teams were being pulled off the court. The Ohio high school girls' basketball finals were being played in Columbus that weekend. As these teams were warming up and getting ready to play, they were being pulled off the court and the weekend tournament was canceled.

It was a Twilight Zone type of atmosphere. It seemed as if every half hour or hour, the college conference tournaments were canceled. In the Big East Conference tournament, two teams were pulled from the court at half-time. The NCAA by midafternoon had canceled all winter and spring sports championships. Schools were closed or shut down, and the new norm was online classes only. The Governor of the state of Ohio held a press conference closing all schools for a minimum of three weeks. Our basketball tournament was "postponed" indefinitely.

Everybody and everything was in a state of chaos. No one knew what was happening or why it had happened because we did not know that the pandemic had reached Ohio. We were just beginning to receive reports regarding the problems in the rest of the country. All we knew was that there was a new, never-before-encountered enemy, known as the coronavirus or COVID-19. Even with the national news media outlets and ESPN, the country and the sports world were suspended in limbo and in a total state of confusion.

On Thursday, the day after the regional semifinal, I met with my players at 2:45 p.m. With the social media exploding, they had an idea of what was happening. Telling them in person was difficult, especially after two great wins. The first win was at the district final coming back from six points down with three minutes to go in front of a standing room only crowd. The second was winning the regional semifinal again in double overtime coming back from being down by five points in the first overtime. As you can imagine, our players were sky high. Their confidence level was at its highest and they were looking forward to getting a chance to play in the regional finals. We also were at the healthiest we had been all year. It was the best kind of atmosphere and mental state you could be in. Therefore, it was difficult to look them in the face and tell the team, especially the nine seniors, that there was a good chance that their season and their careers were over. It was a stunning-type atmosphere.

Our players, and in particular our seniors, sat in disbelief in the locker room. The news media was waiting outside to interview our team regarding the situation. Our athletic director and administrators also came over and addressed the team. They were as devastated as the players. It certainly was difficult for your season to be over, not because of a loss but because of something you could not control. It was deflating.

When the season had been placed on pause, that became a totally different scenario. I imagine for the high school teams and the NCAA teams in the country, whose season was cut short, this is something that no coach would ever think that they would have to address. To tell athletes from ages fifteen to twenty-two or twenty-three that you will not get that chance to realize your dreams is a devastating message. We still tried to make the best of the situation. We continued to approach the season as if there was still the possibility to resume play.

We told our players, "What you have accomplished is amazing. As a result of your comeback and level of play in the last two games, people have so much respect for you."

With the OHSAA directive that the games were postponed and with the governor's mandate that the schools were shut down, no one was able to get into the gym to practice. Many questions remained unanswered: Can we use a health club, gym, athletic facility to practice? If the tournament could have been rescheduled, we wanted to keep our players in basketball shape. This time of the year, every game is the biggest game because the state tournament is imminent. Therefore, every game is the biggest game. Every game you play, you have to be at your peak physically and mentally. We attempted to find legal venues where we could practice.

The state was in the process of finding venues where they could continue tournament play. So where could we play a regional/state tournament? Could it be at a Division III college? Could it be at a Division II? Since The Ohio State University was no longer available as a venue, could it be at another Division I or did it have to be at a high school? Did the venue have to be sanitized? Who could get in? So many questions.

Hopefully, we thought, we would get answers. Things seemed to change by the hour. Every state was deciding on whether to play, postpone, or cancel their games. No one knew how long schools would be closed. Decisions were still being made about spring high school sports and professional sports. This certainly was a first for the country. The entire country was a question mark and in a state of chaos.

Our commissioner of the OHSAA informed us they were working with state authorities and health experts to determine the next steps. If you looked at the country, not every state had taken Ohio's approach. The majority of states had postponed or canceled their tournaments, but Nebraska, Colorado, and New Mexico were playing the following weekend under limited regulation fan base. I was certain the OHSAA was trying to coordinate and contact the schools, and if they got the okay, then the people in position to make decisions would be more positive.

We received an update week by week while we waited for a decision by the OHSAA and the other states as to when the postponed tournaments could be played. However, all school buildings in the state of Ohio remained closed indefinitely. As the OHSAA Commissioner had noted in his earlier news conference, the OHSAA is inextricably intertwined with the educational institutions and school system. In addition, the governor ordered all social venues to be closed indefinitely.

Unfortunately, on March 26, 2020, the OHSAA informed us that all winter tournaments in the state of Ohio were canceled. Our season was permanently over. The dream of playing in the state championship could never become reality even though we had gotten so close and worked so hard to earn that right. And so, once again, I had the challenge of addressing my players and keeping them informed on this latest development. Again, my nine seniors' careers ended in a very bizarre fashion. Personal social contact with the team as a group was forbidden. Everyone was self-quarantined in their homes to avoid the spread of the coronavirus.

Here is what I told the captains of the team:

> Not getting our chance to prove we were the best team in the state is so hard for me to accept. Hopefully, the OHSAA will declare us co-regional champs and possibly, something like co-state champs but I am not sure. We have to accept that it is the final decision.
>
> We finished unbelievably strong. Our motto is "We never rebuild; we always reload." Next year begins today. Someway, somehow, we have to start building today for the future. I do not have answers just yet because of current guidelines and lack of facilities. But you, as leaders, have to communicate with next year's players and do what we can now. Then it is all about "busting" as soon as we get cleared to be in the gym. Let me know what you need. Most importantly, our only goal and expectation is to be state champs in 2021, and you four captains must be "elite" in every way possible. Have a great day.

The following is the message I posted on social media to address my players:

> We never rebuild. We always reload with players and coaches who know the work it will take to get to the state final in Columbus. I am not sure when we will get back in the gym, but when the time comes, be ready to kick it in high gear. Have a great night.

The effect of the COVID-19 pandemic continues to impact our Mentor high school boys' basketball program. The 2020-2021 Mentor boys' basketball season was characterized by uncertainty, occasional chaos, and the need to be flexible.

Our normal summer routine of preparing for the upcoming season could not be followed. COVID-19 concerns prohibited any basketball camps or other group activities in June and negated normal summer programs. As a result, the Mentor basketball program fell behind schedule. Restrictions seemed to be easing up as of October 20. On Friday October 30, we started but twelve days later on November 11, we went in a 'pause' mode for 25 days due to the high number of COVID-19 cases in Lake County.

It was not until December 7 that we were able to have the full team, including football players, practice together on the court. The season did not commence until Wednesday, January 6, 2021 which was five to six weeks later than the normal scheduled date of early December. That following Sunday we were placed on an eleven-day quarantine as one player tested positive for COVID-19. Every time we had a game postponed, we stressed the positive and told our players that they now had time to improve their skills.

The normal schedule of social activities that promote team bonding also required revision. As a group we brought in food to the practices for the players to share together and stressed teamwork when practicing together in the gym. Our players have learned to value socializing with their teammates while honoring a strict curfew.

The erratic season continued with games being canceled every week and being rescheduled. The atmosphere during the games was also surreal in that where the game would normally be played before a packed house, now there were virtually no fans in attendance. This affected the energy level upon which the teams could draw throughout the game to fuel their momentum. Wearing a mask made communicating as a coach with game officials more difficult. No longer did game officials have a pregame meeting with team captains and coaches.

One of the positive outcomes of the COVID-19 crisis was that the restriction on live-streaming games was lifted and so many more fans and even the general public could support the team, enjoy the competition, and watch from home.

Playoffs were affected. Because of COVID-19, the district tournament games were all home court for us as the number one seed. However, regional tournaments were played at neutral high school sites. The OHSAA Final Four was played at the University of Dayton in lieu of The Ohio State University. Dayton proved to be an exceptional venue due to its size and a seventy-six million dollar renovation that had just recently been completed. We played in front of a sizeable crowd of two thousand fans and media entities increased their coverage because of limitations on the number of attendees imposed by the State and County Health Departments.

In 2019, we started writing this book with the central theme of mental toughness, unaware of the pandemic looming on the horizon. In spite of the challenges COVID-19 created at the end of the 2019-2020 season, it must be noted that ultimately Mentor's 2019-2020 team was recognized by the OHSAA as co-regional champions for the 2019-2020 season. The 2020-2021 season presented more uncertainty than ever before in the sports world, yet my team rose to the challenge. I was never so impressed by a group of young men who overcame adversity through their mental toughness as I was with that 2020-2021 team.

Players on the 2020-2021 team shared the following insights regarding COVID-19 and their season:

> Being a part of the Mentor Cardinals and being blessed to play for someone like Coach K is truly a life changing ordeal, but in the best way possible. It was more than just basketball; it was about creating a certain mentality. That mentality was one of always holding yourself accountable and striving to be the best, but first making sure you believe you are/can be the best and that nothing can stop you but you. With everyone having this mentality drilling in, it created a unit that was tight like a family and that had ONE GOAL,

and that was to be the best and have fun while doing it...AND WE HAD A BLAST!

Unfortunately, playing through COVID-19 was a pain and it made it difficult at times, especially for those of us wanting to be recruited at the level we knew we could/should play at, but in the end, we just had to deal with it and, as painful as it was, Coach K told us we could either bi*ch about it, or work even harder and use it to our advantage. You know which one we chose.

—Steven Key (currently at Alabama A&M)

Being a Mentor basketball player didn't just prepare me to be a basketball player; it prepared me for anything that is thrown at me for the rest of my life. You learn to be the hardest worker in the room and to always push yourself to the max. Playing through COVID-19 was extremely difficult for everyone because of the pauses. Everyone had to find ways to stay in shape and work out on their own. At the end of the day, the work ethic and lessons taught me from Coach K are things I will carry with me for the rest of my life.

—Kyle Culler (currently at Ohio University)

Being a part of the Mentor basketball program is something that will always hold a special place in my heart. Not only does it develop you physically for the sport; it develops you to become a man and learn life-long lessons along the way. The mental aspect of the game is by far the most important part because you need to be ready for anything that is throw your way and in the Mentor program, mental toughness is the main reason the program is successful. Playing through the COVID-19 year taught me to never take anything for granted and to know that it was grind day in and day out to adjust to all the different rules thrown at us.

—Cael Gray (currently at Ohio University)

The 2020-2021 team accomplished so much. These young men were undefeated in the regular season, the first regular season undefeated team in the history of Mentor basketball, ranked number one in the state of Ohio in the final AP poll, GCC Champs, District Champs, Regional Champs, and they secured a berth in the Final Four. In addition, this 2020-2021 team was ranked #40 in the country.

To put the 2020-2021 season in perspective, all nineteen regular season and all twenty-six games were played in the year 2021. It is the first time we never played any games prior to the first of the year. Usually, we play five to nine games before January 1. And, after the pause and quarantine, we played sixteen games in thirty-one days, which is more than the NBA teams play. That is why, when I reflect on both seasons and the accomplishments of both those teams, I firmly believe that we conquered COVID-19 with mental toughness.

Life is 10 percent what happens to you and
90 percent how you react to it.

—Charles Swindoll
Pastor, Author, and Educator

NH

Obstacles to success won't stop us.
Armed with mental toughness, we will find a way to climb them,
go through them, or work around them.

SECTION 11:
COVID-19: THE TRUE TEST OF
MENTAL TOUGHNESS

Overview

Overcome obstacles with mental toughness.

- Maintain focus on your goals
- Find the positive in the negative
- Be realistic in your assessment of the situation
- Be creative in your response to unexpected challenges
- Seize the opportunity to leave your comfort zone and chart a new course
- Celebrate each successful step on the journey to realizing your goals
- Believe in yourself

APPENDICES

APPENDIX A—Holiday Mailing to Colleges, Ex-Players, Media, and Friends of the Program

APPENDIX B—Player Information Sheet for College Recruiting Purposes

APPENDIX C—Mentor Summer Camp Handout, Awards, and Nutrition Information Sheet

APPENDIX D—Invitation to Junior High Night and Junior High Program Outline

APPENDIX E—Players' Handouts: Player's Personal Goal Sheets and Basketball Skill Progress Charts, Individual Player Personal Evaluation Forms, Shooting Chart, Rules on Playing Time, and End-of-Game Situation Instructions

APPENDIX F—Player Rating Sheet for Coaches to Evaluate Player's Skills

APPENDIX G—Coach's Drill Practice List and Game Planning Sheets

APPENDIX H—Mentor's Defensive Numbering System for Play Calling

APPENDIX I—Mentor Basketball Skills and Philosophy Handouts

APPENDIX J—Booster Club Communication Regarding the Team, Membership, and Fundraisers

APPENDIX K—2019-2020 Press and Information Guide

APPENDIX A

Holiday Mailing to Colleges, Ex-Players, Media, and Friends of the Program

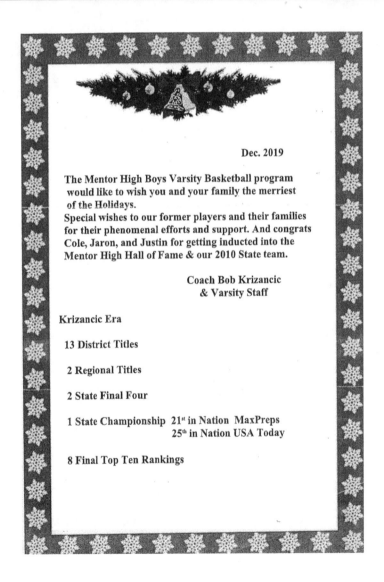

Dec. 2019

The Mentor High Boys Varsity Basketball program would like to wish you and your family the merriest of the Holidays.

Special wishes to our former players and their families for their phenomenal efforts and support. And congrats Cole, Jaron, and Justin for getting inducted into the Mentor High Hall of Fame & our 2010 State team.

Coach Bob Krizancic
& Varsity Staff

Krizancic Era

13 District Titles

2 Regional Titles

2 State Final Four

1 State Championship 21st in Nation MaxPreps
                      25th in Nation USA Today

8 Final Top Ten Rankings

APPENDIX B

Player Information Sheet for College Recruiting Purposes

Name_____MENTOR_
                                              CARDINALS

Address_____Mentor, Oh 44060

Home #_____ Cell_____

E-Mail_____

Parents:_____

GPA_____ SAT_____ ACT_____

Retake date or Test Date_____

Projected Major_____ _Class rank _____

Ht._____ Wt._____Year of grad:_____
Head Coach: Bob Krizancic
Mentor High School   Pts./game_____
6477 Center St.   Reb./game_____
Mentor, Oh 44060   Assists/game_____
                2 pt %_____3 pt %_____FT%_____

2007-08 Season   2008-09 Season
20-5   18-7
Lake Erie League Champs   Sectional Champs
Sectional Champs   District Champs
District Champs   Rankings: 1st in News Herald
Rankings: 12th in State of Ohio   7th in Plain Dealer
1st in News Herald/ 3rd in Plain Dealer

Basketball Honors:_____

_____

_____

MENTOR CARDINALS   Coach K ▬▬▬▬▬▬

334

APPENDIX C

Mentor Summer Camp Handout, Awards, and Nutrition Information Sheet

MENTOR HIGH SCHOOL

BOYS BASKETBALL PROGRAM

I. COACHING PHILOSOPHIES

    A. Discipline/Attitude
    B. Fundamentally – Sound
    C. Best Conditioned Team
    D. Smart Role Players
    E Tremendous Defensive Pressure
    F. High Percentage Shot (Shot Selection)

II. STRATEGIES FOR DEVELOPING A PROGRAM

    A. Cohesiveness Throughout Entire Program
    B. Junior High Program
        1. Discipline
        2. Defensive Fundamentals Man-to-Man
        3. Ball-Handling
        4. Shooting
    C. Off-Season
        1. Weight Training Program
        2. Play Against Best Possible Competition
        3. Shooting
    D. Get as Many People Involved as Possible

III. GAME STRATEGIES

    A. Play Our Game – Control Tempo
    B. Total Organization
    C. Take Advantage of Other Team Weaknesses
        1. Mismatches
        2. Speed
    D Intimidate by Our Style of Play

IV. COMMUNITY & SCHOOL INVOLVEMENT

    A. Open Pep Rally
    B. Senior Citizens
    C. Fan Involvement

V. PUBLIC RELATIONS

    A. Meet the Team Night
    B. Tip-off Dinner or Breakfast
    C. Posters / Press Guides
    D. Excellent Rapport with Media – TV / Newspapers / Radio

VI. GOALS

    A. League Championship
    B State Championship
    C. Most Respected Program in State

MENTOR
BASKETBALL

You can win and still not succeed, still not achieve what you should, and you can lose without really failing at all. Bob Knight

Winning isn't everything - but making the effort to win is. Vince Lombardi

I play not my 5 best, but my best 5. unknown

THE MAN IN THE GLASS
"When you get what you want in your struggle for self
and the world makes you king for a day,
Just go to the mirror and look at yourself
and see what that man has to say.

"For it isn't your father or mother or wife
whose judgement upon you must pass,
The fellow whose verdict counts most in your life
is the one staring back in the glass.

"You may be Jack Horner and chisel a plum
and think you're a wonderful guy.
But the man in the glass says you're only a bum
if you can't look him straight in the eye

"He's the fellow to please --never mind all the rest
for he's with you clear to the end;
And you've passed your most dangerous, difficult test
if the man in the glass is you're friend.

"You may fool the whole world down the pathway of years
and get pats on the back as you pass,
But your final reward will be heartache and tears
if you've cheated the man in the glass."

—Dale Wimbrow
American composer, radio artist, and writer

THE COMPLETE TEAM

THE GAME OF BASKETBALL - NO MATTER WHAT THE LEVEL, THE RULES, THE STRATEGY OF THE PERSONNEL, IS SIMPLY A MATTER OF EXECUTING FUNDAMENTALS.

--- Lewis Cole A Loose Game

WHAT ONE DOES IS NOT AS IMPORTANT AS HOW WELL ONE DOES IT.

1. Chemistry - people accepting their roles with pride.
- players who like the style.
- players who are extremely competitive.
- players who put forth hard work.
- mixture of talent, character, role-play, and sacrifice.
- is a fragile, elusive thing.

2. Know thy teammates - weaknesses and strengths.
- sound guard play, strong inside game.

3. The team that comes closest to maximizing its potential.

4. Flexibility - read opponents defense and take advantage of what the defense gives.

5. Plays both ends of the floor.

6. Players do not criticize each other, are unselfish, are enthusiastic, and have positive relationships on and off the court.

7. Balanced Team - all five players scoring
- a fine guard defender
- a front line defender
- a good ballhandler
- a good rebounder
- everyone running the floor
- being unselfish
- sharing the ball
- not caring who gets credit
- driven players with killer instincts

THE COMPLETE PLAYER

Are you a complete player?

1. There are three factors that are vital to success in basketball; fundamentals, conditioning, and teamwork.

2. A player must:
   A) maintain academic requirements.
   B) be sound fundamentally - stance offensively and defensively, balance, control, etc.
   C) have a feel for winning (not afraid of failure) - a determination to win.
   D) show leadership on and off the court.
   E) maximize potential - a player does not have to start to maximize potential.
   F) have the ability to play defense, pass, shoot, and play within the team concept.
   G) not care about individual stats.
   H) understand the mental part of the game - have knowledge of the game (life-long).
   I) be under control at all times.
   J) have an attitude that generates team play among teammates.
   L) be unselfish and enthusiastic.
   M) have a positive towards hard work and setbacks.
   N) accept his role.
   O) discover strengths and how to use them.
   P) confront weaknesses and dedicate yourself to eliminating them.
   Q) want imptovement and perfection of the game - A COMMITMENT TO EXCELLENCE.
   R) have self-understanding (How do you fit into this team? What can you bring to the
      team that will help it to be successful?) - set your own goals for improvement.

: Success awaits only those athletes who are not lulled into false security by their egoes.
                                                                        - Mike Krzyzewski

: Above all, don't forget that your team must come first.
                                                        - Roland Lazenby

338

Hustle Award

This award presented to _____
for outstanding hustle displayed during camp.

Dribble Races

This award presented to _____ for displaying superior ballhandling skills.

Congratulations on your Outstanding Effort!

This Award Presented to

_____

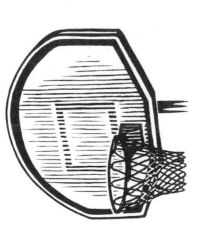

Mentor Camp 2010 Team Champions

341

Moneyball Champions

BASKETBALL

This award presented to _____

NUTRITION FOR ATHLETES

-Eat 6 times/day: 3 meals and 3 snacks
  **Low Glycemic Foods are best- see list provided

-Game Day: eat 3 hours prior to game time.
  -Drink a sports drink or two – prior to game
    **Gatorade is recommended- it has carbohydrates-7%
    electrolytes and proteins

  -Continually drink during game: especially halftime and
    during time-outs

Post game: within 45 minutes of end of game- replenish
  what you lost- low-fat chocolate milk is recommended
  by NCAA and OHSAA- has proteins, carbs, nutrients,
  and vitamins.

**When you are thirsty- you have lost 1-2 liters of body
fluid- do not get to that point.

Recommended for meals:
40% grains
40% fruits and vegetables
20% dairy products/ meats- chicken, fish, lean meat

*Always eat something before you work-out
**Breakfast is extremely important- do not skip this meal.

***Eliminate pop and fast foods when possible.

+++Do your own research but note that recently
we have discovered that *Pedialyte for Athletes*
has really helped eliminate hydration
problems and so it works for us.

APPENDIX D

Invitation to Junior High Night and Junior High Program Outline

Junior High Night
Friday
Jan. 16, 2009
At MHS Gym
MENTOR VS. EUCLID

-All 7th, 8th, 9th Boys Basketball & Cheerleaders

MHS Boys Basketball is Teaching Values and Sharing Dreams!

PROGRAM GOALS

Teaching Values
1. Discipline
2. Learning
3. Understanding
4. Decision making

Sharing Dreams
1. LEL championship
2. State championship
3. State ranked

The Final Product
The "final product" is polished, classy All American type student athlete who brings pride and recognition to his school, his family and himself. The "Final product" is a young man who is sound academically and strong athletically with the competitive edge and ability to be productive socially.

*YOU WILL BE INTRODUCED RIGHT AFTER JV GAME (APPROX> 7:15)

Be at the gym at 7:oo p.m, wear Khakis & polo shirt

CHAPTER 11

JUNIOR HIGH PROGRAM OBJECTIVES

I.   DISCIPLINE
II. MAN-TO-MAN DEFENSE
III. BALL-HANDLING

Although we all strive to be winners, winning or losing is a minor aspect of a junior high program. The major part of this program will be the development of the ballplayer, both physically and mentally, and the reaching of individual goals. If this is accomplished, it will greatly enhance the success of their varsity careers. Players must be coachable and must listen to all of the coaching staff. Therefore, seventh, eighth, and ninth graders must be disciplined ballplayers by the time they reach the varsity level. Good coaches will not put up with a non-coachable ballplayer.

Discipline is a very important cog in the next step of the program. I believe the best defense in basketball is the Man-to-Man defense. If you, as a team, can play Man-to-Man you can play any defense. If a player is fundamentally-sound defensively by the time he reaches the varsity level, more time can be spent on the more intricate aspects of the game. The fundamentals and the basics become a natural movement.

Many times players reach the sophomore year and cannot handle the basketball. Dribbling is a very essential part of the game. If a player is adept at ball-handling (both hands) by the time he reaches varsity competition, he will be a valuable asset on any team.

I used this outline in my first three or four years when I was head coach when I went in to interviews and I wouldn't change a thing... These are the three fundamentals that in priority order help Junior High players ultimately be successful at the varsity level and even in life. We don't differentiate between big man or guard, etc. All players need the same skills. In Junior High you are preparing for the future. You are not playing to win games; you are playing to move up to the next level. The goal is to be an elite varsity player. If you are disciplined the chances of you succeeding in life are so much greater.

APPENDIX E

**Players' Handouts:
Player's Personal Goal Sheets
and Basketball Skill Progress
Charts, Individual Player Personal
Evaluation Forms, Shooting Chart,
Rules on Playing Time, and End-
of-Game Situation Instructions**

*The Personal Goal handouts included in this Appendix are from a publication entitled "Goal Book" which was purchased for our use 25 to 30 years ago.

PERSONAL GOAL PAGE

PERSONAL BASKETBALL GOALS- Short term

_____
_____

PERSONAL BASKETBALL GOALS- Long term

_____
_____

TEAM BASKETBALL GOALS- Short term

_____
_____

TEAM BASKETBALL GOALS- Long term

_____
_____

ACADEMIC GOALS- Short term

_____
_____

ACADEMIC GOALS- Long term

_____
_____

FAMILY-SPIRITUAL-CITIZENSHIP GOALS- Short term

_____
_____

FAMILY-SPIRITUAL-CITIZENSHIP GOALS- Long term

_____
_____

OTHER GOALS-

_____
_____
_____
_____

PERSONAL GOAL BOOK

This Goal Book is designed to help you keep track of your basketball goals, workouts, progress and results. Each day you simply fill in what you have accomplished during the day to improve yourself as a basketball player. Below is an explanation of the abbreviations written in your calendar and some possible ways to use them. ALWAYS check with your coach to get input into your workout program. Use this Goal Book to develop into the player your coach (and you) want to be!

FREE THROWS- FT: Record how may free throws you shot and how many you made. Remember to shoot with the correct form. Shoot between 10 and 25 in a set. Shoot as many sets as you like.

SHOOTING- SHG: Shoot from one spot, or shoot from a certain range (4-12ft) or (10-20ft) depending on age and your coaches preference. Shoot a specific number of shots (100), or until you make a certain number (50). Which ever way you choose to shoot, MAKE IT A GAME LIKE SHOT! Record how many shots you took, or both how many shots you took and how many you made. Remember to shoot with the correct form. Use any drills that your coach has shown you.

Also, work on your offensive moves: Slice, Jab step, Crossover, and Shot fakes. Record 3 point shooting separately.

BALL HANDLING- BH: There are two kinds of ball handling to work on during this time.
1. Stationary ball handling skills: These include dribbling the ball with each finger, moving the ball around your head, waist and feet, figure 8 dribbling, etc. Your coach should have a large list to choose from. Start out spending 5 -10 minutes mastering several of these and as time goes on, increase the time and the number of drills you practice.
2. Moving ball handling skills: These include working on crossover dribbles, pull back dribbles, power dribbles, speed dribbles, etc.. Work on your right and left hand. Work on the areas your coach wants you to improve on.

CONDITIONING- COND: Conditioning is a very important part of being a good basketball player. After stretching out, there are a number of things you can do to better condition your body. Push-ups, sit-ups, weight lifting, sprints, vertical jumps and jumping rope are some examples. Do a number of different things during the course of a week and record your results. Increase your conditioning efforts each month. Again, consult with your coach and incorporate his/her ideas too.

GOALS: Each month you should make a list of goals you want to accomplish by the end of the month. Make realistic goals, but also challenging goals. Evaluate your goals at the end of each month and see the improvement you have made! For longer term goals check out the last page of this book. These goals are equally important!

The following 2 pages have a "sample" month with some ideas of how an individual may fill out the Goal Book. This is simply a guide to help you get started.

GOOD LUCK!

GOALS FOR THE MONTH:_____

FT:_____ SHG:_____ BH:_____ COND:_____

SUNDAY	MONDAY	TUESDAY	WEDNESDAY
FT: SHG: BH: COND:	FT: SHG: BH: COND:	FT: SHG: BH: COND:	FT: SHG: BH: COND:
FT: SHG: BH: COND:	FT: SHG: BH: COND:	FT: SHG: BH: COND:	FT: SHG: BH: COND:
FT: SHG: BH: COND:	FT: SHG: BH: COND:	FT: SHG: BH: COND:	FT: SHG: BH: COND:
FT: SHG: BH: COND:	FT: SHG: BH: COND:	FT: SHG: BH: COND:	FT: SHG: BH: COND:
FT: SHG: BH: COND:	FT: SHG: BH: COND:	FT: SHG: BH: COND:	FT: SHG: BH: COND:

"It's what you learn after you know it all that counts." - **John Wooden**

"If you train hard, you'll not only be hard, you'll be hard to beat." - **Herschel Walker**

THURSDAY	FRIDAY	SATURDAY	TOTALS FOR WEEK
FT: SHG: BH: . COND:	FT: SHG: BH: COND:	FT: SHG: BH: COND:	FT: SHG: BH: COND:
FT: SHG: BH: COND:	FT: SHG: BH: COND:	FT: SHG: BH: COND:	FT: SHG: BH: COND:
FT: SHG: BH: COND:	FT: SHG: BH: COND:	FT: SHG: BH: COND:	FT: SHG: BH: COND:
FT: SHG: BH: COND:	FT: SHG: BH: COND:	FT: SHG: BH: COND:	FT: SHG: BH: COND:
FT: SHG: BH: COND:	FT: SHG: BH: COND:	FT: SHG: BH: COND:	FT: SHG: BH: COND:

GOAL RESULTS:

FT:_____   SHG:_____   BH:_____   COND:_____

_____   _____   _____   _____
_____   _____   _____   _____

NAME: _____

YEAR IN SCHOOL: _____

STRENGTHS: _____

_____

WEAKNESSES: _____

_____

Where do you see yourself on the team (your role)? _____

_____

What do you need to do to improve? _____

_____

What team do you think you will make this year (1st team, 6th man, etc.)?

_____

What do you think will be the strengths and weaknesses of the team next year?

_____

How hard have you worked since last March? _____

_____

How does your decorum come across to everyone who watches you play?

_____

Are you fun to play with? _____

_____

If we voted for one caption or leader today, how many votes would you get? (out of 12 varsity players)

_____

Coaches can use this form to learn what the player thinks of their own skill level and how they see themselves as a basketball player in every aspect, especially the younger players who may have been given various feedback from a number of coaches: junior high coach, AAU coach, and personal trainer.

INDIVIDUAL GOALS

NAME_____

OFFENSIVELY;
   1._____
   2._____
   3._____

DEFENSIVELY;
   1._____
   2._____

One Split for each goal not reached.

Examples:
- 4 to 5 rebounds/ every 10 minutes
- At least 4 FT's- 75 % min.
- 4 Hustle baskets – off Reb, Break, Press
- At least 5 3's- 40 % min.
- At least 2 offensive put-backs
- 1 or less Turnovers
- Create great shots for other players
  -Box every shot- contact
-Get at least 3 tips on presses
-Not let my man get 1 offensive board
-

BE A GREAT LEADER- BY EXAMPLE AND
COMMUNICATION/ DOMINATE EVERY
FACET

It has been proven that if you put your goals in writing there is a greater success rate in reaching them. So, I use this form with my team to self-identify where they need to focus their efforts to improve their skill level. Usually two days before a game, I will ask the players to complete this form. Then, one day before the game, **I will read out loud to the team the ones that stand out**. Then, two days after the game, **I will once again read out loud to the team the sheets of the players who reach their goals**. It has been proven to make the players concentrate more and bust more to succeed in what they have identified and improve their skills.

Date	Shot # 1	Shot #1 Location	Time	Shot #2	Shot #2 Location	Time	Shot #3	Shot #3 Location	Time	FT	Ballhandling
	100/			100/			100/			/100	
	100/			100/			100/			/100	
	100/			100/			100/			/100	
	100/			100/			100/			/100	
	100/			100/			100/			/100	
	100/			100/			100/			/100	
	100/			100/			100/			/100	
	100/			100/			100/			/100	
	100/			100/			100/			/100	
	100/			100/			100/			/100	
	100/			100/			100/			/100	
	100/			100/			100/			/100	
	100/			100/			100/			/100	
	100/			100/			100/			/100	
	100/			100/			100/			/100	
	100/			100/			100/			/100	
	100/			100/			100/			/100	
	100/			100/			100/			/100	
	100/			100/			100/			/100	
	100/			100/			100/			/100	
	100/			100/			100/			./100	
	100/			100/			100/			/100	
	100/			100/			100/			/100	
	100/			100/			100/			/100	
	100/			100/			100/			/100	
	100/			100/			100/			/100	
	100/			100/			100/			/100	
	100/			100/			100/			/100	
	100/			100/			100/			/100	
	100/			100/			100/			/100	

NAME _____

Player shooting chart

By the time you are through with the chart
you are really tired. Do it in this order.

PLAYING TIME

-Every possession—Bust/Sprint/All-out Effort

-Take care of the ball—(3 guards- less than 4 TO's)
  1.0/1.4/1.5 TO's/game
  Ave/min/game-26.9

-Intelligent Decisions—throwing up "crap" is like a
  wasted possession/turnover.

-Ability to press/Athleticism—Traps/Rotations/
  Splitting 2 players

-Communication/Listening Skills

  Shooting- %- 3's /2's/ FT's
  Ability to Finish - 55-60%
  Hitting/Finding open man- knowing who our
    shooters are!
  Playing Big
  Being in Great Physical Shape

HOW MUCH "PLAYING TIME" WILL YOU GET???

1.) Do you "Hustle" all the time?

2.) Are you aggressive?

3.) Do you play tough, solid man-to-man defense?

on the ball

off the ball

4.) Do you box out and rebound? > *READ: B. HUGGINS ARTICLE*

5.) Do you get loose balls? dive on the floor?

6.) Do you react, or are your feet stuck to the floor? > *AGILITIES / QUICK FEET*

7.) Do you pout, swear, or jog when things don't go your way?

8.) Can you handle the ball-do you turn it over? > *VS. SHAKER / IGNATIUS / ED'S*

9.) Are you an inside-outside threat? > *20 FT. "J" / STRONG POWER MOVE*

10.) Do you run the floor? break? > *EVERY POSSESSION*

11.) Do you understand your responsibilities-Presses, Pressbreaker, Offense, Defense, OB's? > *NO MENTAL BREAKDOWNS*

12.) How much time do you put in to improve your skill-level- FT, shooting, ball-handling, 1 on 1 moves?

LAST SUMMER > WE PLAYED A LOT, BUT, OUR SKILL LEVEL DID. NOT IMPROVE A LOT BECAUSE WE DID NOT PUT IN A LOT OF TIME ON SKILLS- SHOOTING

FT'S
1 ON 1
DEFENSE
"HANDLE"

EVERYONE- DEVELOP "POINT GUARD SKILLS"
REBOUNDING- GUTS / WANTING THE BALL
✳ LEADERSHIP / COMMUNICATION

TEAM MTG- JUNE 10

Coach's notes on what to focus on in evaluating playing time.

355

HOW MUCH "PLAYING TIME" WILL YOU GET???

1.) Do you "Hustle" <u>all the time?</u>

2.) Are you aggressive?

3.) Do you play tough, solid man-to-man defense?

                on the ball

                off the ball

4.) Do you box out and rebound?

5.) Do you get loose balls? dive on the floor?

6.) Do you react, or are your feet stuck to the floor?

7.) Do you pout, swear, or jog when things don't go your way?

8.) Can you handle the ball-do you turn it over?

9.) Are you an inside-outside threat?

10.) Do you run the floor? break?

11.) Do you understand your responsibilities-Presses, Pressbreaker, Offense, Defense, OB's?

12.) How much time do you put in to improve your skill-level- FT, shooting, ball-handling, 1 on 1 moves?

"WINNING TIME"
END OF GAME SITUATION COMPETITION
COURT ASSIGNMENTS

*The 4 teams in the main gym will rotate after every two situations until the designated time concludes.
*Each team will play the situation. (i.e. both teams will have the ball down 4 in situation #1)
*The 4 teams in the Aux gym will do the same.
*We will play a round robin format each day. You will play two situations against each team in your gym
*Each team has a full and a 30 second time out for situations 1,3, and 5.
**Team listed first is home team & wears light jerseys/each pair of situations will last 14 minutes

SATURDAY   4:15-5:00
Court 1   1-8
       2   2-7

       3   3-6
       4   4-5

Situations:

1. Full-Court: Down 4 with the ball (1:00 to go, each team has six team fouls)

2. Shooting a 1+1 free throw, up 1, with :08 to go

3. Full-Court: Up 2 with the ball (1:00 to go, trailing team has 5 team fouls, leading team has 10 fouls)

4. Half-Court, Down 1 with ball, :08 to go, each team has 10 team fouls, side OB

5. Half-Court: Tied Score, 1:00 to go, each team has 8 team fouls

6. Full-Court, down 1, :03 to go, each team has 6 team fouls

SUNDAY   1:45-2:30
Court 1   4-7
       2   1-6

       3   2-3
       4   8-5

Situations:

1. Half-Court: Tied Score, 2:00 to go, both teams have 5 team fouls.

2. Half-Court: Down 2, then down 3 with the ball, :03 to go, side OB and baseline OB

3. Full-Court: Down 3 with the ball, 1:00 to go, both teams with 5 team fouls.

4. Half-Court: Down 3 with the ball, :08 seconds to go, both teams with 10 team fouls.

5. Full-Court: Up 6 with the ball, 1:30 to go, both teams have 7 team fouls.

6. Shooting 1 free throw, down 2, :03 to go, both teams with 8 team fouls.
   Shooting 1 free throw, down 3, :05 to go, both teams with 8 team fouls.

APPENDIX F

Player Rating Sheet for Coaches to Evaluate Player's Skills

Ratings for Boys Basketball-
Priority – Who we need on the floor to win.

1) _____15 pts

2)_____14 pts_

3)_____13_pts

4)_____12 pts

5)_____11 pts

6)_____10 pts

7)_____9_pts

8)_____8_pts

9)_____7 pts
10)_____6_pts
11)_____5_pts
12)_____4_pt
13)_____3 pts
14)_____2 pts.
15)_____1 pt.

<u>PLAYER EVALUATION</u>

<u>NAME OF PLAYER</u>_____

<u>COACH</u>_____ TOTAL.
GAME
_____

WHEN YOU ARE RATING / EVALUATING:

1) <u>INTENSITY</u> — SPRINTING EVERY POSSESSION
FILLING LANES / CRASHING BOARDS
SPRINTING IN PRESSES / CUTS ON OFF.

2) <u>INTANGIBLES</u>— TIPS / LOOSE BALLS / CHARGES

3) OFFENSIVELY— SHOT SELECTION / SEEING THE FLOOR /
HARD, SOLID PASSES / MOVING ALL THE TIM

4) POWER GAME— ATTACKING HOOP / GETTING TO THE GLASS,
USING BODY & GETTING BALL ON GLASS / # OF.

5) <u>INTELLIGENCE</u>— NO MENTAL LAPSES / COMMUNICATION

	(1-LOW) RATING (10-HIGH) 1—10	EXPLANATION / SUGGESTIO.
<u>I</u>NTENSITY		
<u>I</u>NTANGIBLES		
OFFENSIVELY		
POWER GAME		
<u>I</u>NTELLIGENCE		
DEFENSIVELY — OVERALL FUNDAMENTALS		

<u>COMMENTS / RECOMMENDATIONS</u>

A form to be used by each coach in the system to rate a player for the head coach.

APPENDIX G

Coach's Drill Practice List and Game Planning Sheets

CONCEPT	DRILL	1	2	3	4	5	6	7	8	9	10	11	12	13	14	15	16	17	18	19	20	21	22	23	24	25	26	27	28	29	30	31
Box																																
Shell	drive by guard																															
	drive by wing																															
	with post																															
	5 on 4																															
	5 on 3																															
	6 on 4																															
	Open Post																															
Transition	5 on 5 -Call the #'s																															
	3 on 3 -Call the #'s																															
	3 on 2/2 on 1																															
	Advantage/Villanova																															
Continuous	1on1-4on4																															
100 Center	1on1 Full																															
	2 on 2 Full																															
	3 on 3 Full																															
Aggression	1 on 1/4 on 4																															
Closeout	Closeout																															
	Diamond Drill																															
	Single Man Shell																															
Stance	Zig-zag																															
	Lane slides																															
Wing Denial	1 on 1																															
	2 off, to 1 def.																															
	2 on 2																															
Screens	Hedge Drill																															
	Get Over The Pick																															
	2 On 2 Cross-screen																															
	2 on 2 down/back screen																															
Help and recover	Shell variations																															
	1/2 court advantage																															
Post	Front the Post Drill																															
25 Press																																

OPPONENT: _____

DATE: _____

AT: _____

TEAM
RECORDS: _____
_____

DEFENSIVE MATCH-UPS

G - (1) _____ - ___

G - (2) _____ - ___

F - (3) _____ - ___

F - (4) _____ - ___

C - (5) _____ - ___

PRIDE DEFENSE	PRIDE OFFENSE	OPP. DEFENSE	ROTATION PATTERN
M - M	M - M	M - M	1. _____ 2.___
1.	1.	1.	3. _____ 4.___
2.	2.	2.	5. _____
3.	3.	3.	

ZONE	ZONE	ZONE	NOTES:
1.	1.	1.	
2.	2.	2.	
3.	3.	3.	

COMBO	COMBO	COMBO	
1.	1.	1.	
2.	2.	2.	
3.	3.	3.	

PRESSES	PRESS OFFENSE	PRESSES	
1.	1.	1.	
2.	2.	2.	
3.	3.	3.	

OB PLAYS	OB PLAYS	BASELINE DEF.	GAME EMPHASIS
1.	1.		TEAM DEFENSE
2.	2.	SIDELINE DEF.	1.
3.	3.		2.

GAME EMPHASIS

TEAM DEFENSE
1.
2.
3.
4.
TEAM OFFENSE
1.
2.
3.
4.

**I still use this form which I used in my days with the
Youngstown Pride/World Basketball League.**

GAME PLAN

_____ (-) VS. _____ (-) DATE _____ AT _____

OFFICIALS _____ ᐟ COMMENTS _____

MATCHUPS

US	POS	OPPONENT	#	COMMENTS
_____	G	_____	___	_____
_____	G	_____	___	_____
_____	F	_____	___	_____
_____	F	_____	___	_____
_____	C	_____	___	_____
		_____	___	_____
		_____	___	_____
		_____	___	_____

SCOREBOARD

OPPONENT

NAME	NUM	1ST Q	2ND Q	REB	3RD Q	4TH Q	FOULS

✓ = MISSED SHOT, **2** = 2 PT SHOT, **3** = 3 PT SHOT, **0** = MISSED FREE THROW, **X** = MADE FREE THROW

TIMEOUTS	US	1	2	3	4	5
	THEM	1	2	3	4	5

PRE-GAME TALK

1) _____
2) _____
3) _____
4) _____
5) _____
6) _____
7) _____

HALF-TIME REMINDERS

1) _____
2) _____
3) _____
4) _____
5) _____
6) _____
7) _____

POST-GAME NOTES

1) _____
2) _____
3) _____
4) _____
5) _____
6) _____
7) _____

Alternative Game Planning Sheet

APPENDIX H

Mentor's Defensive Numbering System for Play Calling

Used for everyone at every level in the program.
Review with the coaches at the beginning of every
season and then go over with the team.
We don't teach plays; we teach how to play—reading
defense and developing basketball IQ (high-low-medium).

MENTOR
DEFENSIVE
NUMBERING SYSTEM

100 Center -	Full Court Man-to-Man
	Total denial
	Centerfielder
100 Contain -	Full Court pressure M-M
	No denial
75 -	3/4 Court pressure M-M
	Pick up foul line extended
50 -	1/2 Court M-M
25 -	1-2-1-1 into Man-to-Man
45 -	2-2-1 into Man-to-Man

Note: At the half court level, we are playing man-to-man 100 percent of the time. The last three above (25, 45 and 1) are zone defense.

APPENDIX I

Mentor Basketball Skills and Philosophy Handouts

OFFENSE

Teach them how to play rather than teaching plays. Players must be able to read the defense. Get away from patterns, patterns are easy to defend.

Our basic offense is the motion, but we use a lot of specials trying to look for as many mismatches as possible. This also allows us to keep the ball in the hands of our scorer. The motion-open post is an excellent offense to put in, especially if you want to your players toleam offensive and defensive fundamentals.

Things to emphasize on offense:
 1) good foot movements - v cuts
                        - constant picks and movement
 2) read defense - back cut
               - flare
               - c cut
 3) picks and screens - shoulder to shoulder
                       - downscreen
                       - crosspick
                       - backpick
 4) no set shots during practice - do everything at game speed

BALL HANDLING - development of the weak hand
 1) full court speed dribble - get from one end of the court to the other in as few
    dribbles as possible.
 2) full court - crossover dribble
                   - behind the back dribble
                   - through legs dribble
                   - spin dribble
 3) use two balls - 2 ball dribbling (full court)
                   - crossovers
                   - behind the back
                   - through legs
                   - speed dribble
***emphasize - low dribble
                   - head up to see the floor
                   - push ball out in front
                   - use fingertips

GETTING OPEN:
 1) v cut - 3 steps and then toward the ball.
    - a v cut can be made toward or away from the basket depending on the
    defense.
    - if the defense is even or below cut high.
    - if the defense is above the man cut toward the baseline.

 2) downscreen - set the screen so that the screeners back is in direct line with
    the ball.
    - the person coming off the screen should make contact with the screener.
    - read the defense instead of looking at the ball.

    FOUR OPTIONS FOR THE CUTTER:
    1. straight cut to the ball looking for the shot, drive, etc.
    2. tight cut (c cut) over the top of the screen.
    3. pop straight back (flare cut)
    4. back door to the hoop
    *****read the defense not the basketball.

3) backscreen - screener back should be to the basket.
   - screen 5 to 6 feet from the defensive man.
   - if the defense is low go high.
   - if the defense is high go low
   - the backscreen can be set up anywhere on the court.
   *** never set a screen in a position in which the offensive player will get the
      ball in a position where he can not shoot.

4) cross screen - screener must read the defense
   - cutter moves off the lane to allow room
   - if defense is high cutter goes low
   - if defense is low cutter goes high

   Counter the switch - the screener becomes the primary scorer not the cutter.
                     - the screener should roll back towards the ball.

SHOOTING

1) good technique and position
2) ball on the fingertips
3) elbow in
4) follow through
5) get into the air on the jumper
   ***emphasize - shoulders square to the basket
                  - follow your shot
                  - triple threat position
                  - head and ball fakes

I. MECHANICS OF SHOOTING
   1. Finger pad control
   2. Hand directly behind the ball
   3. Keep elbow straight
   4. Left hand supports ball
   5. Wrist flex
   6. Gun barrel approach
   7. Follow thru freeze - 1 second
   8. Target is front of rim
   9. Develop proper arc
   10. Hang ball close to rim

II. PSYCHOLOGY OF SHOOTING
   1. Conceptualization or Image Shooting
   2. Concentration
   3. Confidence

III. COMMON MISTAKES OF SHOOTING
   1. Right or left arm crossing in front of face
   2. Elbows sticking out
   3. Head moving to much
   4. Do not move fingers once the grip on the ball is established
   5. Not having enough arc on the ball
   6. Releasing the ball to slowly
   7. Being to jerky
   8. Releasing the ball as you are coming down

POWER MOVES:
1) 1 foot layup
2) player should not end up under the basket (body control). He should be able to
   get the rebound if the shot is missed.
3) shoulders square to the backboard
4) lean in to draw contact, but stay balanced

DEFENSE

Teams with less than average offensive talent can be successful by playing hard, intelligent, team defense. _A teams success depends on its defense._

Three basic thoughts have determined the type of defense that we play.
1. We want the individual responsibility for man-to-man and the aggressiveness that is a part of accepting the challenge in this type of defense.
2. We feel it is also important that we are able to get the weakside help on the ball and sagging into the middle that are such an integral part of zone defense.
3. While we believe that certain aspects of both man-to-man and zone defense are necessary for us to have an effective defense, we do not feel that we can do a good job teaching a variety of defenses nor do we think that it is necessary.

To combine what we feel are the best parts of man-to-man and zone, we have put our primary emphasis on the ball rather than a man or an area. We tell our players that it is the responsibility of each defensive man to STOP THE BALL. To do this, we divide the team into a ballside and helpside. The ball side simply refers to that side of the court where the offense is attempting to penetrate with the ball. Helpside simply refers to the side opposite the ball.

Our ballside defense is responsible for putting immediate pressure on the man with the ball. It must also prevent or contest the penetrating pass to the corner or post. At the same time, those players on our helpside must be in position to aid in preventing penetration of the ball. Their primary responsibility and the focal point of their attention is the ball and not the man. We spend seventy percent of our time the first four weeks of practice on defense. A minimum of fifty percent of each practice session from the fifth week until the end of the season will be devoted to defensive work.

1. **Defensive goals:**
    a) limit uncontested shots - reduces scoring opportunities by the offense.
                                  -opens scoring opportunities for the defense.
    b) pressure defense - leads to steals, interceptions, and rushed shots.
                          - allows the defense high percentage shots in transition.
    c) limit second shots

2. **Factors that determine defensive success:**
    a) EMOTIONAL - desire (wanting to play great defense). Desire is limited by physical condition. As fatigue sets in, you lose the ability to execute skills accompanied by a more harmful loss in the desire to compete.
                1. heart - giving maximum effort every second on the court.
                2. contesting shots.
                3. not letting your man score.
                4. not letting your man rebound.
                5. playing in a balanced stance.
                6. transition from offense to defense.
                7. drawing the charge.
                8. diving for loose balls.
                9. communicating with teammates

    b) DISCIPLINE - developing superior physical condition.
                2. practicing defensive skills.
                3. must be full-time not part-time.
                4. mental toughness; overcoming the physical discomfort and
                    pain. (Bounce up from the floor when you get knocked
                    down.)

c) AGGRESSIVENESS - do not react to the offense; force the offensive player to react to the defense. Manipulate what the offense does.

2. DOMINATE OPPONENT IN ALL WAYS.
3. pressure dribbler.
4. fight over screens.
5. pressure shooter.
6. deny passes.
7. take the charge.
8. dive for loose balls.
9. box out and rebound shots.

Webster's defines aggressiveness as "the disposition to dominate." In order for us to win, we feel that our defense must dominate the offense. We want the offense doing what we want, not what they want. Therefore, just as some defenses are built in quickness, size, or strength, our defense is built on aggressiveness. This ideas permeates all of our defensive thinking and the players are well aware of this. We feel, that while not everyone can be quick, big, or strong, there is no reason why each of our players can not be extremely aggressive.

d) MENTAL - knowledge of your opponent. Observe during the early part of the game. Judge quickness and strength. Know what your opponent does and try to take it away tendencies.

1. anticipation - know your opponents next move.
2. concentration - focus completely and do not be distracted by trash talk, the action of fans, an officials call, your own negative thoughts.
3. alertness - being ready at all times.
   - able to react instantly.
   - see ball, man, screens, etc...
4. judgement - ability to size up the game situation and decide on appropriate action (making good decisions).

e) PHYSICAL - the desire to compete is proportional to physical condition.
   - domination requires strength, muscular endurance, quick movements, and circulatory respiratory endurance.
   - quickness without balance is useless. This involves the ability to start, stop, and change direction under control.

Defense is one of the unglamorous, pain stakingand non recognized aspects of basketball, but it is directly responsible for success in all championship teams.

DEFENSIVE PRINCIPLES:
VISION (Always be able to see the ball by taking an open stance to the ball.)
COMMUNICATION
CONSTANT BALL PRESSURE (Force the loss of vision.)
FORCE OUTSIDE (Every offensive man should receive a pass going away from the basket.)
FORCE LOSS OF DRIBBLE
HELPSIDE AT THE BALL LEVEL (React to any movement of the ball.)
UP THE LINE, ON THE LINE

DEFENSIVE RULES:
NO LAY-UPS (Nothing in the paint.)
NO SECOND SHOTS
NO PENETRATION
NO BALL REVERSAL (Keep the ball to one side.)
DON'T GET BEAT
BE IN PROPER POSITION
POSITIVE DEFENSIVE ATTITUDE
NO REST

MENTOR VARSITY MAN-TO-MAN DEFENSE (KEEPING IT SIMPLE)

The primary emphasis is on the position of the ball.

1. Big three: anticipate, convert, pressure the ball
2. Protect the paint.
3. On the ball
   A) Head below, hands in the passing lane.
   B) Push to the outside.
   C) Pressure <u>with</u> containment.
4. Off the ball
   A) One pass
      1) up line, on line
      2) early help and recover
      3) deny reversal
      4) dead front post
      5) screens -- help plus fight though
   B) Two passes
      1) helpside
      2) ball, you, man, principle
      3) good spot -- take away the weak side flash cut
      4) screens -- help plus fight through
      5) protect the paint from penetration
      6) rotation

Heaven/Hell Theory - We want to keep the ball out of the middle(heaven). Force the ball to the outside and down to the corner.

FUNDAMENTALS: *We can not be afraid of getting beat.*   *Repetition is the key.*

I. ON THE BALL

Good pressure means that there is: no dribble penetration, no uncontested shots, the dribbler never faces the basket, the dribbler is forced to the outside, hand pressure on the ball, hand in the vision.

    A. Points of emphasis - mirror the ball
        the offensive player should not be able to face the open court
        active hands, do not reach.
        good balance, do not cross feet.
        pressure with <u>containment</u>
        force sideline -limits pass to one direction

II. ONE PASS AWAY
    A. Points of emphasis- jump to the ball
        stop the penetrating pass.
        play the passing lanes aggressively.
        have confidence in the help.

III. HELPSIDE (Ball-You-Man principle)
    Defending a man on the weakside.
    -ball above the foul line - 1 foot in the paint.
    -ball below the foul line - middle of the lane (both feet in the lane).
    - flat triangle (one hand in the passing lane)

    A. Points of emphasis- give help to the ball side players who have been beaten.
        stop penetrating passes and drives
        do not let your man receive a penetrating pass
        stop ball reversal pass.
        stop all dribble penetration before the ball gets to the paint

DEFENSIVE DRILLS

1. Wing denial
   - defense denies on the wing
   - as the offense goes to the block, the defensive man opens up
   - as the offense goes through the paint, the defense is cmpletely open and must feel where the man is
   - as the offense goes to the opposite wing, therdefense closes and denies the wing
   * the drill can be adapted to fit various situations (i.e. denial of the point to stop ball reversal)
   * man stays on defense for (45 seconds) 6-8 passes through the paint
   * this is a good drill for working on back door defense
   * do not trail the ball through the lane
   * must stay open to the court to see the ball

2. Close out
   - put a line under the basket and a coach on the wing or the top of the key
   - the player rolls the ball to the coach and closes out
   - when the ball is down, the defensive player retreats a step, when the ball goes above the coaches head, the player pressures the ball
   - the coach will take a couple of dribbles and pick up the ball, the player should immediately yell "pull, pull, etc."and mirror the ball
   * emphasize talking at all times
   * emphasize staying in a proper defensive stance
   * emphasize a break down during the close out

3. Zig-zag
   - one offensive and one defensive player
   - offense dribbles within a set of boundaries and the defense tries to turn the offensive player as many times as possible without getting beat
   * can be shortened to 1/2 and 1/4 court
   * emphasize good position, proper stance, quick feet, and balance

4. Full court one on one
   - put offensive man (line) under the bucket
   - the defensive man hands the ball to the offensive man and plays defense to the other basket (full court) until the ball goes through the hoop or the defense gets the rebound
   - they will then do the same thing coming back to the original hoop
   - put a new offensive player in and keep the defense the same
   - the defense stays on for 3 offensive players (6 trips)
   * emphasize ball pressure
   * keep the offense out of the middle of the court
   * the defense should turn the man as many times as possible
   * BALL PRESSURE

5. Full court one on one denial
   - defensive player fully denies offensive player
   - as the ball goes in (no lob passes), the defensive player must bust to cut off the offensive player and then play good defense down the court

6. Three man weave defense
   - run a 1/2 court weave the third guy will:
     1) close out
     2) box shooter
     3) box helpside

7. Transition Drill
   - offensive group on the baseline, defensive group at the foul line extended
   - each player of each group has a # between 1 and 5
   - the coach calls a # and rolls the ball to an offensive player on the baseline
   - the offensive team fast breaks down the floor
   - the player whose # was called runs and touches the baseline and then gets back on defense
   - the defensive team must stop the break and play solid defense
   *stop the ball early and force to the outside

8. Shell drill
   - four on four pressure defense

   Phase 1 - working on midpoint vision and position as four offensive players move the ball around the outside quickly

   Phase 2 - skip passes back and forth with the defense working on proper help positions

   Phase 3 - offense can drive baseline right or left, the defense must then force the ball back to the inside for help

   Phase 4 - penetration with the ball inside the shell, defense will help and recover, proper rotation of weakside help

9. Aggresion
   - two players start on the baseline under the basket
   - the coach rolls the ball towards the foul line (can roll the ball 1/4, 1/2, or full court)
   - on the command of go the players sprint towards the ball
   - the player who gets the ball is on offense, the other player is on defense
   - the defensive player should apply pressure to the ball forcing to the outside
   - they go until the defensive player gains possession or the offensive player scores

10. Three on three
   - Start this full-court transition game in the backcourt with the offensive players limited to passes only until they reach 1/2 court. Then go regular with pass-screen away, pass-cut, pass-screen the ball, etc. Defense can help and recover but no switching, and they should fight over screens. Both teams rebound until the defense gets the ball.

11. Full court denial (three on three or four on four)
   - defensive man on the ball is in center field position
   - defensive players in denial should be completely turned away from the ball (they should not be looking toward the ball)
   - center fielder yells "ball" when the ball is thrown in
   - center fielder must help until the defensive man can play defense

12. 3 on 2/2 on 1
   - it is essential that we give up no layups off the fast break. Designate a guard to be back to stop the layup.
   - we must force teams to take jumpshots when they have the advantage.
   - In a 2 on 1 situation, the man back on defense must get back to the hoop. He can not pick up at the foul line because he can not recover to stop the layup.
   - With a 3 on 2 situation, make sure that all defenders know to drop toward the hoop. Tandem up. The back man has the first pass.

370

POINTS OF EMPHASIS

1. communication - defense should always be talking so that everyone can hear
   If your man goes to set a pick, you should be yelling "pick, pick" and then
   communicate as to whether the player should get through or hedge.

   - Talk when your man has the ball. If he still has a dribble, the defensive man
   should be saying "ball, ball". When he picks up his dribble pressure the ball
   and yell "pull, pull". This lets the rest of the defense know that they should
   deny their man the ball so that we can get a 5 second call.

2. force outside - keep the basketball going away from the hoop.
   - do not give the baseline, force to the help.
   - keep the basketball in the corner.

3. no ball reversal - establish a ball side and a weak side.
   - once established do not let the ball cross the middle of the floor because the
   help has to adjust.
   - denial one pass away.

4. pressure the ball - there should always be tremendous pressure on the ball
   - there should be a hand in the face of anyone taking a shot

5. no penetration - we must have great closeouts
   - do not let penetration down the gut, force to the corner
   - must have a balanced defensive stance (head behind the knees)
   - stay low (never stand)
   - use feet, not the hands (do not reach)

6. beat the ball up the floor - no defender should ever be farther than the ball to
   the basket.
   -do not let the ball beat you up the court.

IN ORDER TO PLAY AT THE VARSITY LEVEL, YOU MUST BE ABLE TO DO THE FOLOWING:

POINT GUARDS
1) handle the ball - break pressure, no turnovers, penetrate and create high % shots, get the ball to our scorers
2) see the floor - read the defense
3) play great man-to-man defense - 90 feet and half court
4) shoot the "3" - jump shot (not a set shot)
5) be able to score in the paint
6) be a leader - communicate and control the tempo
7) get stronger - play against the best competition / weights / flex bands

*** ATTITUDE ***

WING MEN (#2and #3)
1) score - run the floor / break
            - box out and rebound
            - score in the paint / draw contact
            - be able to shoot the "3" / jumper not a set shot
            - INSIDE OUTSIDE THREAT
2) handle the ball - break pressure
                    - penetrate - no strips or weak shots
3) rebound - crash and box out
4) play great defense - 90 feet and half court
5) get stronger - plyometrics / weights / agility
6) ***develop weak hand***

ATTITUDE

BIG MEN:
1) play solid defense - 90 feet and half court
2) rebound both ends - crash and box out
3) run both ends of the floor - offensive and defensive transition
4) handle the ball - passing / pressbreaker / open court
5) score in the paint - no bricks, no strips, no traveling, no excuses
6) get stronger - develop inside moves (power) / agility / weights / dots / sprints / foot speed

ATTITUDE

Note that the Big Man has evolved and changed… Big Men are now shooting threes, handling the basketball, and running the floor…the Big Men have actually gotten smaller…6'9"-6'10" in college and the NBA. So, even if you are a Big Man, you need the skills of a guard—you need to be a complete player no matter what position you play. That is why we never label anyone in the earlier years…because of height, etc. You need to develop the skills for every single young man on the team.

APPENDIX J

Booster Club Communication Regarding the Team, Membership, and Fund-raisers

Mentor Boys' Basketball

To Mentor High School Boys' Basketball Fan:

It is that time again for the Mentor Boys Basketball team to begin their quest for the state championship in Division I. After making its first ever trip to the Final Four in 2010, the Cardinals lost in the Regional Finals to Garfield Hts., the #1 ranked team in the state of Ohio. It was another great year for the Cards: ranked #10 in the state, LEL Champs, #1 in the News-Herald for the fourth consecutive year and #3 in the Plain Dealer. The team was 21-5, their third 20 win season in the past four years. Cole Krizancic and Justin Fritts were named 2nd team All-Ohio. Cole will be playing collegiate ball at Ashland, Collin Barth at Wheeling Jesuit and Matt Solden at Baldwin-Wallace. Derek Bryner will be attending Lakeland, majoring in nursing. Cody Kern and Brad Kukula will be attending Bowling Green University. The players, coaches and parents are committed to working hard all Fall and then into the season to bring home the state title. The tremendous support of the past players and their families is what makes Mentor Basketball one of the elite programs in the country. Our success has enabled us to be invited to some of the most prestigious Holiday tournaments in the country. The team will play in the exclusive Arby's Classic Tournament in Bristol, Tennessee over the Christmas holidays for the second consecutive year. Last year the Cardinals finished 3rd, losing to Columbia, GA, the 23rd ranked team in USA Today. Cole Krizancic was named MVP of the tournament.

The Cardinal Cage Club would like to invite you to join our organization. The Cage Club is a non-profit organization made up of parents, friends, alumni and other supporters of the Mentor High School Boys' Basketball Program. Our goal is to promote and continue the quality of the basketball program by providing funding for team camps and athletic training and the purchase of training equipment and team apparel. We hope you will consider becoming a member of the Cardinal Cage Club. Enclosed you will find a membership enrollment form.

The Cardinal Cage Club is also pleased to announce our **12th Annual Reverse Raffle** scheduled for Friday, November 11, 2011 at the Croation Lodge Party Center in Eastlake. Good food, dancing and a Chinese Auction are some of the evening's festivities in addition to the Raffle! If you would like to attend, a ticket order form is enclosed.

On behalf of our players and our coach, Bob Krizancic, thank you for your consideration in supporting the Mentor High School Boys' Basketball Program. If you have any questions or would like additional information, please feel free to contact any officer.

Sincerely,

Cardinal Cage Club Officers

Mentor Boys Basketball

Cardinal Cage Club Sponsorship

Mentor Boys' Basketball

Thank you for your interest in our membership in Cardinal Cage Club. The Cardinal Cage Club is a non-profit organization made up of parents, friends, alumni and other supporters of the Mentor High School Boys' Basketball Program. Our goal is to promote and continue the quality of the basketball program by providing funding for **team camps, athletic training, the purchase of training equipment and team apparel.** Your contribution is greatly appreciated. Please review the sponsorship/membership options below. To be included in promotional material, we will need your commitment by **September 1, 2019.**

$500 SLAM DUNK SPONSOR/MEMBERSHIP:
Direct support of the team
Social media recognition
Name and logo on game flier each week (logo must be provided from donor to Heather Kiggins or Tonya Ferritto by no later than September 1, 2019
Name recognition at each home game
10 FREE tickets valid at any home game
Your name on the team poster distributed throughout the city

$300 THREE POINTER SPONSOR/MEMBERSHIP:
Direct support of the team
Social media recognition
Name and logo on game flier each week (logo must be provided from donor to Heather Kiggins or Tonya Ferritto by no later than September 1, 2019)
Name recognition at each home game
6 FREE tickets valid at any home game

$100 JUMP SHOT SPONSOR/MEMBERSHIP:
Direct support of the team
Social media recognition
2 FREE tickets valid at any home game

$25 ASSIST SPONSOR/ MEMBERSHIP:

Direct support of the team

To Benefit the Mentor High School
Boys' Basketball Program

Cardinal Cage Club

12th Annual Reverse Raffle

Friday, November 11, 2011 from 6:30 pm -11:30 pm
~~Lodge~~
~~Blvd.,~~

Order your Reverse Raffle Tickets Now!

Name: _____

Address: _____

_____

Phone: _____

_____Yes, I would like to reserve a ticket for the Reverse Raffle
Couple - $120   Single - $80

Please make checks payable to Cardinal Cage Club and return to:
Cardinal Cage Club
P.O. Box ~~~~
Mentor, OH 44061

Questions? Contact ~~~~ (~~~~, ~~~~@aol.com)

APPENDIX K

2019-2020 Press and Information Guide

The Press and Information Guide was originally printed in the High School Print Shop, but now is produced at a local printing company. We mail it out the first week of December at the beginning of the season and also at the Holidays to businesses, alumni, parents, former players, sponsors, media, press, colleges, and those who support our program. It also highlights our senior players.

YEARS AS MENTOR HEAD COACH	26
MENTOR RECORD VS LEL/NOC/GCC	189-95
MENTOR RECORD VS INDEPENDENTS	223-93
OVERALL COACHING RECORD	634-290
OHSAA TOURNAMENT RECORD	101-33

MENTOR BASKETBALL HEAD COACH - BOB KRIZANCIC

In 26 years as Mentor boys basketball coach, Bob Krizancic has helped shape the Cardinals into one of the premier Division I programs in the state. In March 2013, that elite status was further elevated as Krizancic led the team to the pinnacle of the sport in Ohio. Mentor defeated Toledo Rogers 76-67, at Value City Arena on the Ohio State University campus to claim the program's first boys basketball state championship. The Cardinals knocked off previously unbeaten Columbus Northland in State Semifinals. The triumph over Toledo Rogers gave Krizancic 2 State Championships at 2 different schools - only 4 coaches in the history of Ohio basketball have achieved that feat.

In 1993, Krizancic led his alma mater, Girard, to the Division II State Championship, beating Columbus Whitehall with future NBA player, Samaki Walker on the roster. On the way to the title, Girard defeated Villa Angela-St. Joseph, who had won state titles in 1991 and 1992 and went on to win state championships in 1994 and 1995. He did not get to defend his title at Girard as he left for Mentor following the 1993 title. At Girard, Krizancic's teams won 11 sectional titles in a row and played for the district title six times, winning four.

Since arriving at Mentor with his up-tempo, full-court aggressive style of play 26 seasons ago, the Cardinals have won over 400 games and won the Division I Euclid District Championship 12 of the last 17 seasons. From 2010-2013, the Cardinals had won 21 games or more four consecutive seasons, advanced to the program's first state final four in 2010 by defeating St. Edward in a memorable regional final at Cleveland State, and in 2013, Mentor rolled to the State Championship by winning 8 postseason games all by 9 points or more. The Cardinals that year finished ranked #1 in MaxPreps in Ohio, #25 MaxPreps in the US, and #25 in the country in USA Today.

Now in his 27th season with the Cardinals, Krizancic is attempting to again earn titles as he continues to mark win after win in his overall career. In January of the 2017-18 season, Krizancic earned his 600th career win for boys basketball in the state of Ohio. Only 13 other coaches have ever surpassed such distinction in the Buckeye State. Krizancic has a career record of 634-290, placing him 9th on the all-time list of career wins by a boys basketball coach in Ohio. In 2019, he was named the Division I All-Ohio and Northeast Lakes District Coach of the Year. The Cardinals' regular-season record also marked a personal-best in Krizancic's 38-year coaching career. Mentor won the Greater Cleveland Conference outright and earned the No. 1 seed at the Euclid District. Additionally, Coach K was recognized in 2019 by the Associated Press/Sportswriters of America as the Ohio HS Coach of the Year, an honor he held in 2008 & 2010, as well.

In the fall of 2013, he was offered a job with Nike that would have taken Krizancic across the globe to work in video production for basketball camps in China, Europe, South Africa and Australia. He has been invited to speak at numerous Nike Clinics with such storied coaches as Bob Knight, Roy Williams of North Carolina, Billy Donovan of Florida and Jamie Dixon of Pitt. His most popular topic at the clinics is "How to win with an undersized team." In 2011 he was invited to coach in the prestigious Nike Camp in San Diego attended by LeBron James. During previous summers he has coached all-star teams in Florida, Hawaii, Australia, New Zealand, Germany, Italy, The Netherlands, and Greece. In 2005, he coached in Vienna, Prague, and Budapest.

Both of Krizancic's sons played basketball for him at Mentor. Cole Krizancic, a two-time News-Herald player of the year and 1st Team All-Ohio, graduated with a Bachelors Degree from Ashland University & a Masters Degree from Tulane University. Connor Krizancic, who, in 2013, was named the News-Herald's Tony Fisher Award winner for top high school football player as well as the Division I AP Offensive Player of the Year and 2nd Team All News-Herald basketball team, was a key member of the Cardinals run to the state title in basketball. Connor attended the University of Minnesota on a football scholarship & graduated from Ohio University in 2018.

Bob Krizancic graduated from Youngstown State University with a major in Psychology & a minor in Math/Science, and has a graduate degree in Secondary Administration. He retired from teaching in 2015.

Coaching Record By Season: 1993-94(14-7), 1994-95(15-8), 1995-96(9-13), 1996-97(16-8), 1997-98(8-14), 1998-99(13-9), 1999-00 (17-5), 2000-01(21-4), 2001-02(14-12), 2002-03(18-7), 2003-04(13-9), 2004-05(17-6), 2005-06(19-6), 2006-07(11-11), 2007-08(20-5), 2008-09(18-7), 2009-10(23-4), 2010-11(21-5), 2011-12(22-3), 2012-13(25-5), 2013-14(15-11), 2014-15(15-10), 2015-16(15-11), 2016-17 (21-6), 2017-18(17-8), 2018-19(23-3)

🐦 2013 OHIO DIVISION 1 STATE CHAMPIONS

NEIL GRANTZ - VARSITY ASSISTANT COACH

Coach Grantz is in his 27th year with the Mentor basketball program. His style of hustling, aggressive play has been incorporated into his coaching style & philosophy. He is responsible for coaching team and individual defense. Coach Grantz is a former player for the Girard High School Indians who were coached by Coach Krizancic. He played on the 20-6 Girard team of 1987-88 that was a Regional Finalist and he was Co-Captain of the 1988-89 team that finished 15-9 & District runner-up. Neil graduated *cum laude* from Youngstown State University with a major in Secondary Education and a Ceritification in Comprehensive Sciences. He earned his Masters in Administration from Cleveland State University. He is married to Stephanie, who is employed as a speech pathologist for the Willoughby-Eastlake School System. They have a son, Jaron and daughter, Kiersten.

AARON MAY - VARSITY ASSISTANT COACH

This is Coach May's 14th season as an assistant coach. For two seasons he was the Freshman Coach at Ridge Middle School. Along with his in-season duties on the offensive side of the ball, Coach May coaches the Mentor Varsity & JV teams in the summer leagues and shoot-outs with a focus on offense and skill development. He hopes to help the Mentor Basketball Program continue as one of the top programs in the state of Ohio and beyond. Aaron graduated from Mercyhurst college in 2005 with a B.A. in History and in 2006 earned a Certification of Social Studies Education. In 2012, Aaron completed his Gifted Education Certification from the University of Cincinnati. Aaron is a 2001 Mentor High School graduate and currently a teacher in the Willoughby-Eastlake School District. Aaron is married to Jennifer, and their family includes twin 12-year-old girls, Annabelle and Lillian.

DAVID KRYZ - JUNIOR VARSITY HEAD COACH

Coach Kryz is in his 6th year coaching at Mentor. He spent 13 years as the Boys Varsity Basketball Coach at Wickliffe High School, where he was selected GCBCA Division III Coach of the Year twice. Prior to Wickliffe, he was first the Assistant Girls Coach and then Assistant Boys Coach for his alma mater, Strongsville High School. He played basketball at Adrian College (MI), graduating with a degree in Criminal Justice, and later he earned his Masters of Education from John Carroll University. Coach Kryz teaches 8th grade math at Wickliffe Middle School. David is married to Christine who works for the Mentor Public Schools as a Special Education Supervisor. They have two children, Alexa, a 2016 graduate of Mentor, and Caden, a 2018 graduate of Mentor and former basketball player for the Cardinals.

TONY WILSON - ASSISTANT COACH

Coach Wilson has been involved in the Mentor Basketball Program for the past 20 years. He coached at Memorial Middle School for four years. He also was the JV Basketball Coach at Lake Catholic High School for four years. He has worked as an instructor for Dick Baumgartner's Shooting Camp. He lives in Mentor with his wife Cookie, who is a manager at Ladies and Gentlemen Hair Salon. They have raised three children, Anthony, Talia and Adam who graduated from Mentor High School. Coach Wilson is employed by Honda of Mentor as a Sales and Leasing Associate.

CHRIS PARSONS - FRESHMAN COACH

Coach Parsons enters his 30th season of coaching this year. He coached for two years at Riverside and 15 years at Ridge Middle School. He is responsible for coaching the freshman team and assisting with scouting. Chris grew up in Northwest Ohio, attending Hardin Northern High School where he lettered in basketball, football and track. He earned his B.S. in Education from Bowling Green State University and his Masters in Curriculum and Instruction from Ashland University. He currently teaches World History at Mentor. Chris is married to Laura who is an elementary teacher in the Willoughby-Eastlake School System. They have four children, Alexis, Olivia, Eliza, and Ian.

JIM FUNK - FRESHMAN COACH

Coach Funk is in his 27th season of coaching this year. He coached for one year at Madison, two years at East Liverpool and 15 years at Shore Middle School. He is responsible for coaching the freshman team and assisting with scouting. Jim grew up in Mentor-on-the-Lake, attending Mentor High School where he lettered in football. He earned his B.S. in Education from Kent State University and his Masters in Sports Education from Cleveland State University. He currently teaches World History at Mentor.

#14 SEAN COLLINS - SOPHOMORE
SPORTS/HONORS/ACTIVITIES:
Mentor Basketball, Honor Roll

FORWARD
6'3" 170LBS

MIDDLE SCHOOL:
Memorial
TWITTER:

#15 CAEL GRAY - JUNIOR
SPORTS/HONORS/ACTIVITIES:
1 Year Letterman-Basketball, 2019 OHSAA Basketball District
Champions; Baseball-2019 OHSAA D1 State Runners Up
Honor Roll

GUARD
5'10" 165LBS

MIDDLE SCHOOL:
Memorial
TWITTER:

#21 ANDREW WITTE - SENIOR
SPORTS/HONORS/ACTIVITIES:
Mentor Basketball
3 Year Letterman - Baseball, 2019 OHSAA Baseball
D1 State Runners Up
Honor Roll

GUARD
5'10" 185LBS

MIDDLE SCHOOL:
Memorial
TWITTER:

#22 LEE FARKAS - SENIOR
SPORTS/HONORS/ACTIVITIES:
Mentor Basketball, Honor Roll

GUARD
6'1" 180LBS

MIDDLE SCHOOL:
Attea
TWITTER:

#23 TIMMY SHEA - SENIOR
SPORTS/HONORS/ACTIVITIES:
2019 OHSAA D1 District Champions

GUARD
6'1" 162LBS

MIDDLE SCHOOL:
Memorial
TWITTER:

#25 CALEB PIKS - SENIOR (CAPTAIN)
SPORTS/HONORS/ACTIVITIES:
3 Year Letterman - Basketball, 2019 All District
Honorable Mention, 2019 OHSAA Basketball D1
District Champions

FORWARD
6'4" 185LBS

MIDDLE SCHOOL:
Memorial
TWITTER:

#31 JAKE FERRITTO - SOPHOMORE
SPORTS/HONORS/ACTIVITIES:
Mentor Basketball, Honor Roll

6'1" 175LBS

MIDDLE SCHOOL:
Ridge
TWITTER:

#34 ANTONIO DIFRANCO - JUNIOR
SPORTS/HONORS/ACTIVITIES:
Mentor Basketball, Honor Roll

GUARD
6'2" 165LBS

MIDDLE SCHOOL:
Shore

#40 ANDREW SMITH - JUNIOR
SPORTS/HONORS/ACTIVITIES:
Mentor Basketball, Mentor Football

FORWARD/
CENTER
6'5" 190LBS

MIDDLE SCHOOL:
Memorial
TWITTER:

#1 JOHN SIERPUTOWSKI - JUNIOR
SPORTS/HONORS/ACTIVITIES:
Mentor Basketball, Mentor Football

GUARD/
FORWARD
6'2" 165LBS

MIDDLE SCHOOL:

TWITTER:

#2 LUKE CHICONE - JUNIOR (CAPTAIN)
SPORTS/HONORS/ACTIVITIES:
3 Year Letterman-Basketball, 3rd Team All-District,
3rd Team News-Herald All Star, 2019 OHSAA Basketball
D1 District Champions, Honor Roll

GUARD
5'10" 160LBS

MIDDLE SCHOOL:
Ridge
TWITTER:

#3 KYLE CULLER - JUNIOR
SPORTS/HONORS/ACTIVITIES:
Mentor Basketball

GUARD
6'1" 155LBS

MIDDLE SCHOOL:
Ridge
TWITTER:

#4 JARON GRANTZ - SENIOR
SPORTS/HONORS/ACTIVITIES:
2019 OHSAA Basketball District Champions
AP Capstone, CCP, Honor Roll

GUARD
5'10" 155LBS

MIDDLE SCHOOL:
Memorial
TWITTER:

#5 LUKE FLORIEA - SENIOR (CAPTAIN)
SPORTS/HONORS/ACTIVITIES:
3 Year Letterman-Basketball, 2nd Team All Ohio, 1st Team
All-District, 2019 OHSAA Basketball District Champions, Clark Kellogg Finalist,
1st Team News-Herald All Star; 3 Year Letterman-Football, 1st Team All-Ohio,
1st Team All-District

GUARD
5'10" 170LBS

MIDDLE SCHOOL:
Shore
TWITTER:

#10 NOAH CORWIN - SENIOR
SPORTS/HONORS/ACTIVITIES:
2019 OHSAA Basketball District 1 Champions,
Honor Roll

CENTER
6'4" 175LBS

MIDDLE SCHOOL:
Memorial
TWITTER:

#11 CHAD ROGERS - SENIOR (CAPTAIN)
SPORTS/HONORS/ACTIVITIES:
2 Year Letterman-Basketball, 2nd Team All-District, All-Ohio
Honorable Mention, 3rd Team News-Herald All Star, 2019 OHSAA D1 District
Champions; 4 Year Letterman-Baseball, 2018 OHSAA D1 District Champions,
2019 OHSAA D1 State Runners Up

FORWARD
6'5" 215LBS

MIDDLE SCHOOL:
Memorial
TWITTER:

#12 JEFF NORWOOD - JUNIOR
SPORTS/HONORS/ACTIVITIES:
Mentor Basketball, Mentor Football

GUARD/
FORWARD
5'10" 185LBS

MIDDLE SCHOOL:
Memorial
TWITTER:

#13 CAMDEN MILLER - SENIOR
SPORTS/HONORS/ACTIVITIES:
1 Year Letterman - Basketball, 2019 OHSAA
Basketball D1 District Champions
CCP

GUARD
6'1" 165LBS

MIDDLE SCHOOL:
Memorial
TWITTER:

PHOTO CREDITS

The photograph on the front cover is from the *News-Herald* sports article by Nate Barnes entitled "Mentor Basketball: Coach Bob Krizancic Named OHSBCA 2020 Coach of the Year." Permission for use was granted on 12/15/21 by Sports Editor Mark Podolski. *See* https://www.newsbreak.com/news/2061443023471/mentor-basketball-bob-krizancic-named-2020-ohsbca-coach-of-the-year

The photograph on the back cover is from the *News-Herald* used with permission granted 12/15/21 by Sports Editor Mark Podolski.

Unless otherwise specified, the photographs included in the chapters of this book come from Coach Bob Krizancic's personal collection. Photographs not from his own personal collection are identified by a code in the lower right corner below the picture as follows:

- **"GBC"**—Photographs provided by George and Brittany Chay from their personal collection. Brittany Chay's photos appear on pages 68, 167, 176, 197, and 267. George Chay's photos appear on pages 83, 109, and 210.
- **"NH"**—Photographs associated with sports articles published in the *News-Herald* with permission granted 12/15/21 by Sports Editor Mark Podolski.
- **"CCC"**—Source of the photo is CardinalCageClub.com
- **"CL"**—Photographs provided by Cathy Lombardo
- **"WKBN.com"**—*See:* https://www.wkbn.com/news/girards -93-basketball-team-reflects-on-improbable-state-championship-win/ *by Stan Boney posted Mar 27, 2018 / 08:41PM EDT Updated Mar 27, 2018 / 08:41 p.m. EDT*
- **"Cleveland.com"**—Top picture on page 145: https://i.ytimg.com/vi/Jq5i1Zx57jw/maxresdefault.jpg

https://www.cleveland.com/highschoolsports/article/ second-quarter-burst-seizes-district-title-for-mentor-in- 77-73-win-vs-brush/ *by Matt Goul Updated: Aug. 07, 2019, 10:10 p.m. | Published: Mar. 09, 2019, 5:15 p.m*

- **"Neosportsinsiders.com"**
    1. Picture on page 276: https://www.neosportsinsiders. com/shaker-heights-mentor-win-in-cleveland- setting-up-an-all-gcc-regional-final/ by Billy Kosco March 12, 2020
    2. Bottom picture on page 318: https://www.neosports insiders.com/wp-content/uploads/2021/03/ 9893F2B0-5EAD-4561-95F0-564D5BB0727D. jpeg *See article:* https://www.neosportsinsiders.com/ boys-hs-hoops-mentor-tops-medina-66-55-to-ad vance-to-dayton-in-d1-regional-final/ *by Mark Perez March 15, 2021*
- **"CR"—Canton Repository**—Bottom picture on page 145" https://www.cantonrep.com/picture-gallery/sports/ 2021/03/14/medina-vs-mentor-boys-basketball-di-region- al-final-twinsburg-saturday-march-13-2021/4686305001/ *by Scott Heckel March 13, 2021*

*Given the public nature of sports reporting, some photos may appear in more than one source and more than one medium.

REFLECTIONS OF
THE CO-AUTHOR

To be successful in the game of basketball requires a high level of mental and physical focus. The game is extremely fast-moving and requires continual physical exertion and mental concentration. Ask any fan. Boredom in the stands is extremely rare. Turn your head away for a minute and the game can change in that instant. The transition from offensive to defensive play can occur in seconds.

Basketball is the only sport that holds my attention for four quarters and more. It keeps me on the edge of my seat at all times, engrossed in the activity on the court and challenged mentally by the speed at which the game unfolds before me. You can feel the individual focus and drive of the players and the physical energy they expend with every play. I knew that I wanted to learn more about the mental and physical aspects of playing the game.

When Coach Krizancic and I talked about writing his book, I only knew that he had much to share about his philosophy of life, his coaching style, his ability to unleash the potential in his players, and his unrelenting passion for basketball. Little did I know that he had developed an unshakable, deep-rooted faith.

In developing the contents of this book, the goal was to provide a resource for coaches to use in creating an elite public high school basketball program. But, with every proof-reading session, we realized that there was still more to share and that its contents could provide valuable guidance to almost everyone who reads it. That is why the book grew into eleven "sections of interest" and fifty chapters.

The repetition in this book is not a mistake. It is meant to be a vehicle for remembering key points. The quotes are also meant to facilitate remembering its contents. They reflect Coach Krizancic's coaching style. In writing this book, he is coaching you, the reader, to be the best you can be. In the process of writing this book, I learned the meaning of synergy. The whole is greater than the sum of the parts. This is true in basketball, in business, in families, in human relationships, and in life. It is true of this book.

I am very fortunate to be a part of the Mentor basketball family. My sons, both former players, graduated from Mentor High School in 2007 and 2009. Over the years, I have found that Coach Krizancic values people and believes that we are all here to fully develop our potential. He surrounds himself with positive and motivated individuals.

Coach Krizancic showed me that, if you have mapped out specific goals, are committed to your goals day in and day out and have a great work ethic, you will overcome all obstacles in your path and reach your 'mountaintop.' You will achieve mental toughness which will serve to propel you more surely toward the achievement of even greater goals. This strategic approach to living is the key to success.

Of course, the importance of having a supportive network around you cannot be overstated. Our publication director, James Gordon (currently the administrator of operations at Newman Springs Publishing), tirelessly worked and guided us throughout this entire process. Finally and most importantly, creating and writing this book with Coach Krizancic would not have been possible without the understanding and support of my family.

FINAL THOUGHTS

I learned so much in my first year as head coach.

I learned how much I hated to lose.

I am thoroughly convinced that the concepts in this book will make you, your team, and your program stronger.

I have one parting thought for you to take with you as you travel the path to elite status: Success is born out of faith, undying passion, and relentless drive. Few have all three, and that is what separates the average from the "elite."

LIVE IN THE PRESENT. BUILD FOR THE FUTURE. DON'T LOOK BACK.

AND REMEMBER

ARMED WITH MENTAL TOUGHNESS, SUCCESS IS IN YOUR FUTURE.